# GEOGRAPHY
# AND ECONOMICS

# GEOGRAPHY
# AND ECONOMICS

## MICHAEL CHISHOLM

FREDERICK A. PRAEGER, *Publishers*
NEW YORK · WASHINGTON

BOOKS THAT MATTER

Published in the United States of America in 1966
by Frederick A. Praeger, Inc., Publishers
111 Fourth Avenue, New York 3, N.Y.

Printed in Great Britain

# EDITH

# Contents

# Tables

# Maps and Diagrams

# Preface

Between the subjects economics and geography there has for long existed a surprising lack of communication, with the result that much work in both disciplines has been less effective than otherwise might have been the case. The present book is addressed primarily to geographers—teachers, research workers and students in the second half of their university course—in an attempt to show how concepts in economics have a fundamental bearing upon all kinds of studies in the human aspects of geography. In setting myself this task, I am very conscious of my own inadequacies in relation to the mass of material, both factual and conceptual, that is relevant to the theme. The choice of topics and the sequence of their presentation is based on a personal assessment of what the relationships between geography and economics ought to be in relation to the availabiliy of published work and I trust that the selection will commend itself to readers.

I owe a great debt to many people for help in the collection of material and for criticizing drafts of the manuscript. I am particularly indebted to the following persons for helpful comments during the writing: Professor R. W. Steel, University of Liverpool; Mr. A. A. L. Caesar, University of Cambridge; Mr. G. Manners, University College, Swansea; Mr. G. Peters, University of Oxford; and Mr. F. Livesey, University of Manchester. The complete text was read by Dr. R. H. T. Smith, University of Wisconsin and by Mr. A. M. Hay, University of Cambridge, to both of whom are due many improvements. A number of business concerns have very kindly given information about pricing policies and the library staff at Bedford College, London, assisted me greatly in obtaining works that were not easily accessible. The illustrations were drawn by Mr. T. K. S. P. Amachree and Mr. B. S. Faoye, both of the Department of Geography, University of Ibadan.

Ibadan                                                            M.C.
March, 1965

# CHAPTER 1

# Introduction

Geographers are interested in the spatial patterns of phenomena, their inter-actions within defined areas and in relation to the whole world. Geography is, therefore, a wide-ranging subject which cuts across many formal frontiers of knowledge, relating findings in geology, climatology, agriculture, technology and economics to name but a few of the cognate disciplines. To achieve worthwhile results, it is clearly necessary for the geographer to know something about the subjects that are closely related to his own. Ideally, he should be an expert in all the relevant spheres but, as this is manifestly impossible, some criteria must be selected whereby the necessary minimum qualifications in the neighbouring disciplines may be judged. The geographer should know enough about the cognate subjects to understand when and how to use:

1. The 'facts' that other disciplines study.

2. The techniques of analysis that they employ.

3. The conceptual framework upon which they are founded.

If the geographer is thus equipped, he will at the very least know when to seek advice and where to turn for it.

Traditionally, geography has had very close links with the physical sciences, especially geology, and geographers have been well-grounded in this side of their subject. Consequently, there have been some outstanding achievements by geographers in fields as diverse as glaciology, climatology and the geomorphologic evolution of the landscape, achievements that have been widely noted outside the ranks of geographers as well as within. While it is usual for a geographer to receive some training in geology whatever his particular field of special interest, no comparably close relationship has in the past developed with any of the social sciences, in particular with economics.

This is a serious lack because any study in the human aspects of geography, being concerned with the way man lives, locates his activities and is related to the natural environment, involves problems in economics to a greater or lesser extent. Unless economics is incorporated into such studies, their value is impaired. Even between economic geography and economics there has been much less commerce of ideas than would reasonably have been expected, as was pointed out in 1931[1] and again in 1936.[2] Although the situation has changed since then, and is now changing fairly quickly, M. J. Wise in 1956 felt that it was 'clear that there is still a no man's land between the respective studies of economics and economic geography'.[3] Since the last war, an increasing number of economists has become interested in spatial problems and likewise the number of geographers familiar with economics is growing; but the gap between the two disciplines remains wide.

The present book is intended to aid the process of rapprochement between economics and geography and to this end is addressed primarily to geographers in an attempt to show how economics is relevant in the study of the human aspects of geography. Although J. C. Stamp urged that a 'geographer who aims at strengthening his grasp of causality especially for expository purposes, by learning economics, would do well to cover the whole field first, in a preliminary way, and then to specialize on the particular applications . . .'[4] that are relevant to geography, there are good reasons for reversing this procedure. Not least is the fact that, although standard texts in economics have for long been readily available, and although a fair number of geography students do study economics as a subsidiary subject, few geographers have in practice been disposed to explore very far and fully to incorporate economic reasoning into their geographic studies.

The specific intention of the present book is therefore to explore the conceptual framework of economics (item number three on p. 1) and thereby to show how the ideas and logic of the subject are highly relevant to geographic studies. Fundamentally, the method employed is to expound a particular concept in general terms and to illustrate its geographic significance by means of actual examples. At no stage of the argument should the particular cases be read as affording *proof* of the validity of a concept or of the universality of its application. In effect, the examples that are cited should be treated as being *consistent with* the relevant concept, which can only be justified by *a priori* reasoning.

This book is *not* a textbook in economic geography treating the world distributions of various economic phenomena. Nor is it an introductory text in economics. It attempts to expound the spatial implications of some parts of economics, to provide an account of the spatial aspects of economic doctrine. It is hoped that by showing how economic concepts in multifarious ways are basic to human, and especially to economic, geography, that geographers will be better equipped for their own studies and, more important, that they will be prompted to further explorations in the field of economics.

The economist will not here find a single new concept, for economic doctrine has been accepted in the form that can be pursued more directly by recourse to works such as P. A. Samuelson's *Economics: an Introductory Analysis*. The economist may find applications and implications of fundamental ideas which will at least put some things in a new light and, in particular, he may find some interest in the diversity of spatial implications of quite ordinary economic concepts.

In pursuit of this theme, material published in the English language has been the main, though not the exclusive, source of reference. The literature available is ample and only in some instances is it imperative to look further afield, while the author himself is insufficiently knowledgeable of foreign languages to do full justice to work published other than in English. It is hoped and believed that the deficiency is not very serious and that it does not mar what is attempted in the following pages.

### REFERENCES

1 K. Sapper, 'Economic geography', *Encyclopaedia of the Social Sciences*, vol. 6, 1931, pp. 626–28.

2 Sir (later Lord) J. C. Stamp, 'Geography and economic theory', presidential address, Geographical Association, 1936. Published in *Geography*, 1937, pp. 1–14.

3 M. J. Wise, 'Economic geography and the location problem', review, *Geographical Journal*, 1956, p. 100.

4 J. C. Stamp, 1937, *op. cit.*, pp. 13–14.

# CHAPTER 2

# Relations Between Geography and Economics

The questions 'Where?' and 'Why there?' are of central importance to geographic studies, whether the questions relate to human or inanimate phenomena on or near the surface of the earth. The analogy has often been drawn that whereas the hall-mark of historical studies is the integration of data with respect to time, in geography the distinguishing characteristic is concern with (terrestrial) space. Indeed, an examination of the wealth of geographic literature displays an abiding concern for the reasons why one area differs from another and why particular activities are localized.

By contrast, the writings of most economists make very little reference, if any, to locational questions, so that P. A Samuelson could write in 1952 that 'Spatial problems have been so neglected in economic theory that the field is of interest for its own sake'.[1] The point is confirmed by referring to E. Roll's study of the history of economic thought,[2] wherein the only references to location are, with one exception, connected with ideas on economic rent (p. 37). The exception is a brief mention of J. H. von Thünen, whose work is in this context regarded more highly for his contribution to marginal analysis (p. 46) than for the advancement of location studies. Yet numerous economists have interested themselves in matters of location: and, since locational questions do have an important economic influence, why, one may ask, have they been so neglected in the main-stream of economic thought? Furthermore, why has the considerable geographic literature with its interest in location and regional differences failed to make much impact upon economists? An examination of these two related questions is illuminating. Such a survey enables us to look briefly at the development of thought in both economics and

4

geography bearing upon location patterns, or the spatial distribution of economic activities. This will help us to understand the achievements that have already been made and the deficiencies of the edifice that has been erected and thereby the rôle that economic analysis has to play in the study of the spatial patterns of human activities.

## Location and Economic Thought

To answer the first of the above questions, it is necessary to delve briefly into the development of economic thought.[3] The early students of political economy—as economics used to be called—were interested in some aspects of location. Adam Smith, for example, was concerned to know why some countries were richer than others and what could be done to increase the wealth of a country: the title of his great work testifies to this preoccupation—*Inquiry into the Nature and Causes of the Wealth of Nations*.[4] Like other early economists, Smith was also interested in spatial variations within a nation in that he desired to know the factors determining the value of land, something that varies markedly from place to place. Unfortunately for geographic studies, the incipient interest in the spatial distribution of economic activities was swamped by concern with different aspects of the subject.[5] The central problems were for long the nature of wealth and value, the manner in which prices are determined and hence the forces that determine the rewards obtained by the factors of production. Since many of the early economists were trained in philosophy or mathematics, an interest in these quasi-philosophic problems was natural: it was also necessary to establish the fundamental principles upon which the whole edifice of economic thought depends.

In attempting to solve problems such as the nature of value, economic doctrine early evolved the trichotomy of land, labour and capital as the three factors of production which, in varying proportions, enter into all productive enterprise. To examine the way in which these are combined and remunerated, a theoretical framework was developed in which man was supposed to behave in a consistently and completely rational manner. These basic ideas, now known as 'perfect competition', which we owe largely to Smith[6] and D. Ricardo,[7] were published during and immediately after the Napoleonic wars and achieved rapid recognition and acceptance. They were subsequently refined and elaborated by J. S. Mill in 1848, whose major work[8] represents the quintessence of the doctrine of *laisser faire* and free trade, based upon the concepts of perfect competition. Nevertheless, even in the hey-day of free trade in the 1840s, the doctrines of Smith, Ricardo, Mill and others were already under attack. However severely their works have been criticized and their conclusions contested by subsequent generations, they remain an inspiration to economists to this day and many of their assumptions, implicit and explicit, have been carried into modern thought.

For there to be a state of perfect competition, certain conditions must be fulfilled. There must be a large number of both buyers and sellers who do not collude and who, individually, have no appreciable effect upon the state of the market. A single price will then rule for each commodity determined by the balance of supply and demand. For such an equilibrium to be possible, all buyers and all sellers must have perfect knowledge of the state of the market and furthermore, there must be an instantaneous adjustment throughout the whole economy to any change which occurs. This implies that production can be expanded and contracted at will to meet any changes in demand. Such a situation requires that resources are fully mobile as between occupations and also as between places. The last point—of instantaneous mobility between places—was met by assuming that all transactions took place at the same spot, which amounts to assuming a dimensionless economy. During the nineteenth and twentieth centuries, the inadequacy of this basic scheme has become more and more evident. But although the element of time, imperfections of knowledge, elements of monopoly, etc., have been recognized and incorporated, the influence of distance has received little notice, partly because other problems have been more obviously pressing and until they were solved it would not have been possible adequately to account for spatial matters. For example, A. Marshall wrote:

> markets vary with regard to the period of time which is allowed to the forces of demand and supply to bring themselves into equilibrium with one another, as well as

with regard to the area over which they extend. And this element of Time requires more careful attention just now than does that of Space. For the nature of the equilibrium itself, and that of the causes by which it is determined, depend on the length of the period over which the market is taken to extend.[9]

Another reason is that economic thought has adopted the convention that transport costs are an element of production costs. This convention does *allow* the analysis of spatial patterns arising from differences in transport costs due to varying location patterns but the device does not *require* such attention to be given. Furthermore, there was no problem while perfect or near-perfect competition was assumed to exist, for each firm, in seeking to maximize its returns, would search out the optimum location and an optimum spatial allocation of resources would automatically occur. No explicit problem is raised unless one enquires why one location should be preferred to another, and this question has not seemed to be a pressing one.

Nevertheless, quite a large body of literature on location problems has accumulated, especially since the turn of this century, though this literature seems to have developed parallel to, rather than as a part of, the general body of economic doctrine. It is not necessary to make an exhaustive survey of the location literature to discover why this has been so, since the history of ideas on location has been ably documented elsewhere.[10] The salient point to be made here is that the pioneering work of von Thünen,[11] Weber[12] and Hoover[13] was primarily, though not exclusively, concerned with principles by which costs could be minimized in the choice of location. In this manner, the spatial pattern of supply was analyzed and therewith some contribution was made to the study of total supply. Very little attention was paid to the complementary question of how location patterns affect demand, though one must notice the attempt of W. Launhardt[14] and H. Hotelling[15] to show how firms locate themselves to maximize their sales. Without fully considering the related questions of supply and demand, location studies have until recently contributed very little to a solution of the price-supply-demand relationships. For this reason, while analyzing the spatial *patterns* of output and/or consumption, location studies

B

have contributed little to our understanding of the *quantities* involved. Since the problem of price, and the related question of the quantities demanded and supplied, has been central to economic thinking, location studies have tended to be of peripheral interest to economists.

A. Lösch[16] recognized this defect and tried to incorporate the demand factor by introducing an analysis of the size of market areas. However, he went too far, virtually ignoring the question of supply. Other workers have tackled this question, notably C. Ponsard and M. L. Greenhut, but their studies, as with the English translation of Lösch, only appeared in the mid-1950s. Much of the groundwork has now been laid but the problems are so complex that in practice location theory still tends to fasten on the problem of *where* activities occur and to give little weight to the question of *how much* takes place at each locality.

Only in the last few decades has the theoretical analysis of location by economists begun to approach what remains one of the central problems in economics: the determination of supply, demand and price and the aggregate level of production. This is one reason why 'The theory of industrial location has remained largely outside the general scope of economics'.[17] But there is another reason. Even in terms of equilibrium location analysis based primarily on transfer costs, there have been some important defects of reasoning. The following passage shows that transfer costs are central to Isard's work:[18]

> only the transport factor and other transfer factors whose costs are functionally related to distance impart regularity to the spatial setting of activities. ... we are concerned with the development of equilibrium analysis for the firm as an integral part of a general theory of space-economy which is independent of any particular cultural, institutional, or geographic frame of reference.

Nevertheless, transport is regarded as an input but is never included as an output. This is pointed out by L. Lefeber[19] and it implies that transport is readily available (nevertheless, at a cost) without any call upon the resources of the economy, which is not a tenable position, for in fact the transport sector competes with other sectors to command productive resources.

Any essay in general equilibrium analysis must logically take account of this situation and the matter cannot be ignored by assuming that transport is a very small sector of the economy. This would be logically untenable if transport is given the central position in the analysis and is in any case disproved by estimates of the economic importance of transport. For example, it has been calculated that in 1953, internal transport accounted for 26·7 per cent. of the Canadian Gross National Product, while for Australia in 1956–57 the equivalent proportion was 25·4 per cent.[20]

Formal location theories attempt to provide a spatial equilibrium of activities, which implies that the economy as a whole is in equilibrium. Even in the absence of spatial considerations, and ignoring dynamic factors such as population growth and technical innovation, it is a delicate question whether an equilibrium situation can be obtained, and whether, if attained, it will necessarily be at a level that requires the full use of resources, especially labour. J. M. Keynes, in 1936,[21] set out arguments to show how conditions of unemployment could arise and persist and since that date economists have been greatly exercised by the nature of the economic mechanisms governing the level of activity in an economy. For any given level of activity, there will naturally be an optimum spatial pattern of the economy but as a priority for analysis these spatial optima are probably less important than the question of what controls the general level of activity in an economy.

Especially since the last war, economists have become increasingly interested in questions of economic development, in the factors that encourage growth in some countries (regions) and impede it elsewhere and how adjustments can be facilitated. As economic development progresses, some regions gain in prosperity and importance while others lose, either in relative or absolute terms. Real and pressing problems are involved in these matters of economic development but formal location theory has contributed very little to their solution, primarily because these are questions which involve time—a sequence of events—and are not amenable to treatment as a series of inter-related decisions with a single solution by means of a system of simultaneous equations. More generally, each location decision affects the probabilities attending those taken subsequently (p. 96) and, therefore, location patterns are closely affected by the element of time. If the main-stream of economics has largely ignored spatial matters, location theory has neglected time.[22]

The economic recession of the 1930s was much more acute in some regions than in others and the attention of both governments and economists became directed to the reasons for this and the discovery of cures for the trouble. For example, the British parliament passed legislation designed to attract industries into the Special Areas (primarily coastal coalfield areas) where unemployment was especially severe; in the United States, the New Deal programme of public works swept F. D. Roosevelt to power. Economists in both countries and elsewhere have maintained an active interest in the problems of regional economic disparities, as may be illustrated by work done in the United Kingdom.[23] These problems are closely akin to those involved in economic development generally, and the former interest has grown into something much greater. At the present time, study of the differing national rates of economic growth and of regions within states has become highly fashionable, giving rise to a rich and rapidly growing literature[24] of great interest to the geographer.

While this interest in national and regional economic growth is important for geographers, there are two subsidiary aspects of the matter that are also tending to bring economic and geographic studies together. Economists are realizing that to explain existing disparities in economic development and differing potentials for growth, proper account must be taken of the conditions of the natural environment. For example, P. T. Bauer and B. S. Yamey[25] in their handbook on under-developed countries devote a whole section to natural resources. This is a field of study where in the future the two disciplines should be able to co-operate in seeking solutions to the question: Why are certain activities and stages of economic development localized where they are?[26]

The second aspect is less evident but potentially no less important. Until the revolution in economic thinking wrought by Keynes, there had been developed a set of concepts relevant to the study of the actions of individuals. With the growing awareness of problems of aggregate output and employment and changes therein, economists have perforce been driven to examine the factors that influence corporate or social behaviour. A simple example will illustrate the changing emphasis. In Western society, it used to be assumed that individuals seek to maximize their income. It has, therefore, been disconcerting to find that in fact leisure also has a value and the concept of economic man has been modified to the assumption that individuals seek the maximization of personal welfare. This takes account of the fact that after the last war wages for coalmining in Britain were very high and absenteeism was also rife; that when the price of cash-crops was high, the 'lazy' African worked less hard. In both cases, people adjusted their work at what they regarded as unpleasant occupations to the level that afforded them an income to which they were accustomed. In the short run, they did not know how to use more cash. Such patterns of behaviour are largely determined by the social environment and economists have had to interest themselves in these phenomena of group mores.[27] This kind of enquiry impinges upon the interests of the geographer. The spatial distribution of societies, the means by which they live and their general characteristics have for long formed an important subject of geographic enquiry.[28]

Another element of modern economic thinking conducive to a geographic interest is the development of ideas about the gains to be had from foreign trade. Economists have in the past visualized the following curious situation. If there are two or more countries possessing different endowments of soil, labour, minerals, etc., trade between them will be of mutual benefit. This will arise because the productive factors of land, labour and capital are unable to pass from one country to another (are immobile) whereas goods may (are mobile). Each country will then export those goods for which it has the greatest comparative advantage (p. 40) and import those for which it is relatively least well endowed. But for this to be possible, productive resources within each country must be mobile, otherwise it would not be possible for each nation to concentrate its activities on the kinds of production where its comparative advantage lies. There was thus erected the logically absurd situation in which certain resources were supposed to lose all mobility at political frontiers. Further-more, although at the frontier the 'cost' of movement became absolutely prohibitive for the productive factors, the costs incurred in moving goods between countries were ignored. For example, in 1927 F. W. Taussig wrote that 'the cost of transportation is so small an item that it may be neglected'.[29] B. Ohlin[30] qualified this notion in 1933 by pointing out that trade is merely a manifestation of the fact that activities are localized: trade and location are interdependent. Further-more, there is no essential difference between inter- and intra-national trade, although national frontiers present special obstacles to transfer and the cost thereof therefore rises irregu-larly with distance. There is thus a graduation of the spatial extent over which differing types of transactions can take place: diamonds can readily be flown from one end of the earth to another; bricks, on the other hand, usually are carried only a few tens of kilometres by road, rail or canal.

One element of Ohlin's work is particularly relevant to the next and last strand of economic thought to be discussed here. In the situation he described, it is evident that some manu-facturers (or retailers, if one wishes) will be protected owing to the distance that separates them from potential competitors; they will enjoy a degree of local monopoly. This idea was independently elaborated by E. H. Chamberlin in his study of monopolistic competition published in 1933.[31] Although in the main body of this work Chamberlin regarded transport as a part of the productive process, he included two appendices which clearly show that a degree of monopoly is conferred by location. In fact, the monopoly element that arises from location and the cost of overcoming distance is more important than Chamberlin seems to have realized. Isard is right to insist that it is the theory of monopolistic competition that provides the discipline with which to analyze spatial problems adequately. In previous thinking, absolutely 'pure' or 'perfect' competition had been distinguished from the monopoly situa-tion as being two quite different circumstances. Chamber-lin's contention was that in *all* circumstances there is *some* degree of monopoly. Clearly, this notion is very relevant to locational matters. Until the ideas of monopolistic competition were published in 1933 and subsequently refined, economic doctrine did not possess the conceptual tools adequately to deal with locational matters.

There is one field in particular in which these ideas have been readily taken up, namely the selection of sites for retail shops. As a branch of applied economics, this is now producing a considerable volume of literature,[32] much of which is American. This is closely linked with the work done by urban geographers on the form and structure of urban societies[33] and spheres of urban influence.[34]

Thus two important developments are taking place within the field of economics relevant to location matters. The first is the refinement of conceptual analysis so that progressively in the future it may be possible explicitly to incorporate spatial considerations in the analysis of problems. Second, at the level where economic thought is applied to practical problems, there is a growing awareness of areal differences of economic development and the significance of transfer costs. There is thus a growing interest among economists in the field of study that geographers have long claimed as their own, justifying the view that mutual understanding will grow in the future. But given the growing awareness of location problems and spatial variations in the distribution of economic activities, why has the work of geographers hitherto made so little impression on economists? To this question we now turn.

*Location and Geographic Thought*

Just as the history of economic thinking illuminates the nature of economic doctrine, so also with geography. The long and honourable tradition of modern geography began with the early cartographers and the accounts of foreign places brought back by explorers, traders and later missionaries. As the descriptive material accumulated, curiosity was aroused as to why there were such marked differences of climate, terrain, society and economy between one part of the world and another.

The great period of European discovery and exploration began in the fifteenth century with the Portuguese voyages along the African coast and in effect continued until the middle of the nineteenth century, when the mysteries of the African interior were finally resolved. The greater part of this period of five centuries preceded the industrial revolution and the great expansion of commerce that has been a feature of the last one hundred years but which even now does not equally embrace all parts of the world. The geographic tradition, therefore, developed in the context of societies that had evolved with comparatively few external contacts, whose mode of life was therefore strongly conditioned by the nature of the local physical environment. There naturally grew up a close affinity between geography and anthropology: what geographer has not, at some stage in his career, read the work of D. Forde?[35] Close links were also forged with the biological sciences, since exploration and an interest in the natural sciences are easy bedfellows: the outstanding name in this context is A. von Humbolt, whose explorations in South America are too well known to need recounting here.

An important effect of this association between geography and the exploration of the world has been the abiding interest of geographers in the effect of the physical environment upon man. In its extreme form, this interest degenerated into the notion that human activities are completely conditioned by the physical environment; geographic determinism, associated in particular with E. C. Semple and E. Huntington,[36] became acceptable doctrine early in the twentieth century. The inadequacy of this view is so patent that 'There can be no doubt that most human geographers in the last twenty-five years have claimed to reject determinism as a fundamental hypothesis. . . .' But the rejection of determinism has raised baffling problems and, as A. F. Martin proceeded to remark, 'unconsciously and almost inevitably, [we] shift our ground to a determinist footing.'[37]

The quasi-determinist stance is manifest in the preoccupation of many geographers with the influence of the natural environment on patterns of human activity even though other considerations are accepted as relevant. For example, the authors of some recent texts in economic geography have based their explanation of the geographic distribution of activities on factors such as climate and geology very largely to the exclusion of other considerations.[38] The comment of J. O. M. Broek, made in a 1941 review of the then recent books in economic geography, is still relevant:

In several cases I had the impression that, although the authors have publicly disavowed environmentalism, they have been unable to rid themselves of the mental habit.[39]

The mental habit affects the form of reasoning adopted and therefore the value of the findings. To seek to know the effects of the natural environment on human affairs is legitimate but this knowledge can only be achieved if all the other relevant influences are taken into account. Unless this is done, no true assessment can be made of the rôle of the physical environment, neither the nature of the effects nor their strength. An important reason for the lack of recognition accorded to geographic work is therefore the partial nature of the solutions that are offered, in which the dominating influence of the natural environment is implicitly assumed:

> Hitherto many geographers have been far too conscious of possessing a vested interest in environment, and this has caused serious defects to much otherwise excellent economic geography. . . . Of course, the assessment of the part played by the factors of [the] physical environment is supremely important, alike as a practical and as a philosophical problem, but a balanced answer will never be obtained until we are willing to give appropriate weight in our considerations to all relevant factors. Either we must stop pretending to be 'causal geographers' or else we must honestly seek the right causes.[40]

In the passage above, C. A. Fisher makes a cogent plea for the honest search for causes, whithersoever this quest may lead us. One might imagine that the search for causes would be an axiom of geographic study and that the only question is where and how to seek; in fact, there is not unanimity on this score:

> Difficulties which have arisen in connection with the search for causes of the locations of individual economic activities are associated with the complexity of locational processes . . . a partial solution to this procedural problem has come from shifting the emphasis from cause to association. By this procedure (which is as old as field observation) the analyst's major goal is to discover types of phenomena whose patterns of areal distribution resemble those of the economic phenomenon he is investigating. . . .

Its proponents take the pragmatic view that if one knew that two phenomena always appear together in space and never appear independently, the needs of geographic science would be satisfied, and there would be scant additional virtue in knowing that the location of one phenomenon caused the location of another. Beyond these considerations, however, lies the very practical fact that in accepting the significance of these relationships the analyst is freed from the obligation to track down every element that might have a bearing on his problem and to relate that element to the processes that are presumed to have brought about the locational pattern he is trying to explain. Therein lies the main reason for concluding that principles composing a body of theory would be stated mainly in terms of areal association rather than cause and effect.[41]

A more subtle attack on the search for causal relations has been made by R. Hartshorne,[42] in the form of an attempt to limit the range of causal relationships to be investigated. The argument adduced is that the geographer is interested in the *inter-relationships* of phenomena in space and that therefore 'it is not the function of the geographer to explain the distribution of any phenomenon, [although] it is at the same time clear that he may be concerned with such an explanation in order to interpret the relations of that phenomenon to other geographic phenomena'. In other words, the world distribution of wheat production is the province of the wheat agronomist while that of dairy cattle falls to the student of livestock, and the geographer will be concerned with the inter-relationships of the two distributions. This is logically untenable:

1. The world distribution of both phenomena is partly conditioned by their local inter-relationships, either as competing or complementary uses of the land.

2. The nature of the local inter-relationships (or the lack thereof because one phenomenon is absent) is affected by the wider relationship each phenomenon has with the rest of the world, in particular in comparison with the costs of production and marketing of the same commodity elsewhere, *i.e.*, the reasons governing the world distribution materially affect the local inter-relationships of one phenomenon with others in a particular locality and *vice versa*.

The implicit but untenable assumption is that the distribution of one phenomenon occurs for reasons that are essentially unrelated to the reasons for the distribution of any other phenomenon. 'The systematic geography of any particular phenomenon depends ..., for the principles governing its distribution, on the systematic science concerned with that phenomenon.' In this we may recognize one of the more important legacies to which geography is heir: the common assumption that geographic values have an absolute validity, whereas in practice everything is relative. An easily recognized form of this assumption is the supposition that the production of any commodity ought to be carried on where the natural conditions are most favourable for it. This view was explicitly propounded by G. G. Chisholm, whose major contribution to economic geography has been revised since his death and still occupies an important place in the literature:

> The full advantage [from the growth of commerce] is not reaped until every kind of production is carried on in the place that has the greatest *natural advantages* for the supply of a particular market. By natural advantages are meant such as these—a favourable soil and climate, the existence of facilities for communication external and internal so far as these lie in the nature of the surface and physical features, the existence of valuable minerals in favourable situations ... All these advantages are more or less permanent, or at least such as are exhaustible are for the most part liable to exhaustion by slow degrees.
>
> With natural advantages may be contrasted *historical advantages*, which are in their nature more temporary, though they are often in fact of long continuance.... We may refer in illustration of this to the losses that fell upon Italian commerce after the discovery of the sea-way to the East, the prosperity of that commerce being based in a large measure on the central position of Italy—a position which was permanent only so long as the geography of the world was imperfectly known. ...
>
> The advantages that may be expected to be reaped when the development of commerce has reached its goal are the enjoyment of the greatest possible variety of commodities at all the habitable parts of the earth (that is, the greatest variety possible for each place), and the utmost

attainable stability of prices. When the network of commerce is complete in its main lines, when it has only to be gradually and regularly extended or made more intricate with the development of population, the deficiencies in the natural products of one region will be supplied with the least possible delay and at the least possible cost from any surplus that may accrue in other regions. It is true that this will take place only on condition that the region so supplied has something to give in exchange . . . [his italics].[43]

The same place may provide optimum conditions for more than one product which cannot all be produced there and, therefore, the somewhat absolutist approach of many geographers does not conduce to a full understanding of the reasons for localization and the nature of inter-relationships between phenomena in a particular place. In making this point at some length, it would not be either fair or true to imply that all geographers have adopted the same bent of mind, but those with a different disposition have been comparatively few and only in recent years have they begun to make a considerable impact in the literature. Among the writings that show a full realization of the relative, causally inter-related nature of the mechanisms affecting distributions, one must note the 1921 article by O. E. Baker in which he bagan his analysis with an exposition of economic rent to demonstrate the changing rôle of the physical environment in affecting location patterns in agriculture and forestry.[44] Four years later, he analyzed the potential world supply of wheat in terms that took account of competition from other crops for the use of the land.[45] Ten years after that, R. O. Buchanan published his work on the pastoral industries of New Zealand, in which he expounded his idea of economic geography in the following terms:

> Put briefly, it is that, in industries organized on a commercial, as distinct from a purely subsistence basis, geographical conditions express themselves, if at all, in economic, mainly monetary, terms; and that the nature and extent of the influence of the geographical conditions are themselves dependent on the precise nature of the economic conditions. That will be recognized as merely specifying one type of instance of the generally accepted

view that geographical values depend on the cultural stage achieved by the human actors. If that argument be accepted, it will follow that the geography of production must be a study of the *interaction* of geographical and economic conditions in the area and for the products concerned, and it is such a study of material cause and effect that is here attempted.[46]

A curiously neglected but nevertheless extremely well-founded general text in economic geography was published by W. H. Carter and R. E. Dodge in 1939.[47] After the war, W. Smith published his study of the economic geography of Great Britain, in which the search for causal relations treated in an historical sense was pressed to good effect.[48] As an example of a regional monograph with a strong economic flavour, W. R. Mead's work on Scandinavia should be noted,[49] while B. H. Farmer's researches in colonization in Ceylon provide an example of the tackling by a geographer of a particular problem in its geographic, economic and social context.[50] The Hutchinson University Library has published several geography books since 1960 that are strongly oriented toward economics and the general idea that geographic values are relative.[51] Finally, R. S. Thoman has published a general text in economic geography which, albeit at an elementary level, incorporates much sound economic reasoning.[52]

Reference in the preceding paragraph to a selection of works in the field of economic geography that seem to the present writer to conform, even though imperfectly, to the principles of economic thinking should not be taken to imply that none other exists. As a generalization, it is only since the mid-1950s that the quantity of material published by geographers in this vein has begun to be significant.

## The Practical Approach to the Problem of Location

Two quotations will illustrate the way in which economists approach the problem of the localization of a particular industry:

> The value of an economic resource depends upon the terms on which the requisite complementary factors of production are available and on the strength of the market demand for its products. Thus its value depends in part

on the market for the goods which can be produced with or from it; it also depends in part on the market for other goods which can be produced with the necessary co-operant factors of production. Thus the market, in the widest sense of the term, is crucial. An example may be useful. The value of land suitable for rubber cultivation in Sumatra depends not only on the price of rubber, but also on the remuneration in the alternative employments open to the labour which is required to develop the holdings and to tap the trees, as well as on the cost to labour of moving from one district or island to another. The value of the land therefore is contingent on the price of rubber itself, as well as on the prices of rice, pepper and coconuts both in Sumatra and in other parts of Indonesia, and on the cost of internal migration. . . . In short, the value of a resource does not depend upon its physical qualities or technical efficiency alone; a complex network of present and future market influences forms part of the environment in which value is conferred upon resources.[53]

The same basic point was made by A. Cairncross in 1944:[54]

Suppose, for example, that we ask why some industry— say shipbuilding—has become localized on the Clyde. We have really two questions to answer, not one. First, why the Clyde rather than some other *place*—the Thames or the Severn? Second, why shipbuilding rather than some other *industry*—steel or textiles? We have to show, not only that there is a pull on shipbuilding to the Clyde, but that the pull is *relatively* greater than the pull on other industries.

We do not find this concept of relative values clearly and fully grasped in a great deal of geographic literature, as may be seen by considering the localization of cotton textile manufacture in Great Britain. This is one of the finest examples that there is of the regional concentration of an industry but the standard texts on the geography of Britain do not give a satisfactory explanation of the pre-eminence of Lancashire and adjacent areas.[55]

If we accept that after the initial phase of experiment, when the industry was widely distributed, a process of regional concentration was advantageous owing to the technical organization of the business,[56] there is the interesting problem why this concentration should have occurred in Lancashire and not elsewhere. It is not sufficient to reply that 'The secret of the expansion of the industry in Lancashire lies in the fact that as each new development arose, so the natural environment of the region was found capable of being utilized in the desired manner'.[57] As W. S. Thatcher[58] has pointed out, the same would be true of South Wales (which never had a cotton industry) and Scotland (where it once flourished), while on the Continent the cotton industry exists in areas that appear to be quite unsuited on grounds of physical geography.

The matter has been taken one stage further by remarking the competition that Scotland gave Lancashire until about the time of the American Civil War. The demise of Scottish cotton manufacturing has been ascribed to two principal factors:

1. Scotland specialized in high quality goods whereas Lancashire concentrated on the cheaper range of products for which the market was growing much more rapidly.

2. The cotton famine of the 1860s, due to the American Civil War,[59] caused industrialists in Scotland to turn to the more lucrative metal trades.

From the juxtaposition of these two propositions, we must infer that the Scottish entrepreneurs found it easier to change from textiles to metals than from high-class to lower quality textiles, a proposition that seems inherently unlikely. But much more important, if the Scottish industrialists were induced by the cotton famine to quit cotton textile manufacturing, why did the same not happen in Lancashire?

The reason must be sought in the alternative employments that were locally available. Scotland possessed good coking coal and Coal Measure iron ores and therefore had the basic requirements for the expansion of her metal trades. The Clyde also provided excellent opportunities for ship construction, for which iron was being increasingly used in the second half of the last century. By contrast, Lancashire possessed no very ready alternatives. Although there were Coal Measure iron ores, these were not as abundant as on other coalfields and there was a marked lack of local coals suitable for coking. She therefore was relatively poorly endowed for the basic iron and steel trades. The somewhat inaccessible inland location of the coalfield, combined with the rather poor quality of her coals and the high costs of working them (because of severe faulting, thin seams, etc.), rendered the Lancashire coalfield a poor competitor with South Wales and the north-east for the export of coal. Finally, the midland coalfields had some advantages of location for the supply of the home-market demand for small iron-ware and the like.

Most of the industries alternative to textiles were predominantly male-employing whereas women and children came to dominate the cotton mills. On the face of it, therefore, the whole of the above argument is groundless but this is not so, for the availability of male employment and the wages that could be commanded by the men would greatly affect the willingness with which women and children went to work, indeed, whether or not the head of the household would permit the practice.

During the industrial revolution, Lancashire therefore had no special natural advantages for cotton manufacture sufficient to explain the continuation of the textile industry, which had long historical connections with the area.[60] The progressive concentration of the cotton textile manufacturing in Lancashire and adjacent areas must therefore be explained in terms of industrial opportunities in Lancashire and in other parts of the country plus the man-made advantages which accrued from concentration. This permitted highly specialized working whereby the advantages of scale economies could be reaped but this benefit was not fully realized until the middle of the nineteenth century (p. 86).

A fascinating field of research is the question why South Wales never developed the manufacture of cotton. Bristol, where the physical conditions were much less suitable than in South Wales, had a small cotton industry from the eighteenth century until 1926.[61] There was a widespread woollen industry throughout Wales that might have taken up the newer fibre but which remained small-scale and in fact served very largely to clothe the local inhabitants who gained a living in coal-mining and metalworking.[62] That none of the ports in South Wales had trade connections with the Middle East, Far East and America can hardly be taken as a serious impediment, for neighbouring Bristol had just such trading links.[63] Furthermore, as late as 1789, London was the chief port of import for cotton and it was not until 1835 that nearly 90 per cent. of cotton imports came through Liverpool.[64] The advantage of having Liverpool as a local port of import cannot have been decisive, or even necessarily very important, for Lancashire in the early development of her cotton industry.

Thus, it is incorrect to assert that 'South Wales was completely isolated from any tradition other than that of metallurgy' and that lacking trans-oceanic sea connections 'It thus showed no tendency to develop a textile industry'.[65] Along with Shrewsbury and Carmarthen, Cardiff was a 'staple' town through which wool was sold to England[66] during the sixteenth and seventeenth centuries; about 1800, a wool spinning mill employing some 100 persons was established at Bridgend; and in the 1920s there were over a hundred (albeit small) woollen factories in the Teify and Towy valleys and their tributaries, west of the main industrial areas of the coalfield.[67]

The lack of success of textiles generally and of cotton in particular in South Wales appears to lie in the fact that the opportunities favoured the copper and iron trades and the export of coal. This is reflected in the almost complete absence of reference to textiles in A. H. John's study of industrial development in South Wales;[68] the single reference is to the decline that occurred in the years immediately preceding 1750, which marks the beginning of the period of his study. The probability that this is the correct interpretation is strongly reinforced by the fact, of which John makes a good deal, that most of the capital and enterprise for industrial development in South Wales was provided by Englishmen, notably from Bristol and London. The entrepreneurs and bankers, the latter including those of Bristol who would be familiar with textiles, saw that the best opportunities in South Wales lay elsewhere than in fabrics. That this should have been so is surely a reflection of the relative advantages of the various regions.

*Conclusion*

In this chapter, some of the reasons for the separation that has long existed between geography and economics have been explored. Two considerations seem to have been dominant. The first is the lack of attention given by economists to spatial

C

matters, largely because problems of spatial organization have not until recently seemed to be as important as other issues. This has been partly because of the history of the subject and partly a result of the complexity of the problems of price, value, rewards to factors of production, etc., in which economists have mainly been interested. The second important reason for the estrangement of the two subjects lies in the character of geography as a discipline. With its roots in exploration, geography has tended to emphasize the rôle of the physical environment in conditioning the geographic distribution of phenomena. With this emphasis has gone the habit of taking each phenomenon in turn and relating it to the physical environment, whereby the mutual relationships between the phenomena have been under-emphasized. The somewhat absolutist approach of the geographer does not accord with the economist's view that values are relative. There has therefore in the past been quite a fundamental difference between the approach of the economist and that of the geographer.

However, it has been noted that modern developments are bringing the two subjects together. This is especially evident in the field of economic growth, studied at the national and regional levels. The conditions of the geographic environment are important in explaining differences in the rates and patterns of growth, but these are also influenced by economic and social factors. Greater mutual understanding between geography and economics is likely in the future on account of the common interest in patterns of economic development.

Against this background, the case of cotton textiles in Lancashire was discussed at some length to illustrate the kind of economic approach that ought to be employed by geographers in examining the localization of an industry or the fortunes of a region. It was argued that the localization of the industry in Lancashire was due not so much to the suitability of the area for cotton manufacture (other regions being equally good) but rather to the lack of ready alternative occupations in competition with other coalfields. To be conclusive, the matter would have to be examined at much greater length. However, the purpose of the study was to establish the form of analysis that ought to be generally applied. In arguing the reasons for the localization of cotton textiles in one part of Britain, several fundamental concepts of economic analysis have been introduced, although they have not been named. In the pages that follow, these ideas and others are elaborated in some detail.

## REFERENCES

1   P. A. Samuelson, 'Spatial price equilibrium and linear programming', *American Economic Review*, 1952, p. 284.

2   E. Roll, *A History of Economic Thought*, 3rd edition, 1954.

3   The reader interested in this topic, viewed from the geographer's standpoint, is referred to: C. A. Fisher, 'Economic geography in a changing world', *Transactions and Papers*, Institute of British Geographers, 1948, pp. 71–85; R. B. McNee, 'The changing relationships of economics and economic geography', *Economic Geography*, 1959, pp. 189–98.

4   A. Smith, *Inquiry into the Nature and Causes of the Wealth of Nations*, 1776.

5   Nevertheless, interest in location matters did not entirely disappear. A. Marshall, in *Principles of Economics*, first published in 1890 (an annotated edition was published in 1961, edited by C. W. Guillebaud), devoted a short chapter to the reasons for industrial localization.

6   A. Smith, 1776, *op. cit.*

7   D. Ricardo, *The Principles of Political Economy and Taxation*, 1817.

8   J. S. Mill, *Principles of Political Economy*, 1848.

9   A. Marshall, 1961 edition, vol. I, *op. cit.*, p. 330. See also: M. J. Pullen, 'Transport costs and the disappearance of space in the theory of the firm', *Yorkshire Bulletin of Economic and Social Research*, May 1964, pp. 3–14.

10  W. Isard, *Location and Space-Economy*, 1956. M. L. Greenhut, *Plant Location in Theory and Practise: the Economics of Space*, 1956. C. Ponsard, *Histoire des théories économiques spatiales*, 1958. W. Warntz, *Toward a Geography of Price*, 1959.

11  J. H. von Thünen, *Der isolierte Staat in Beziehung auf Landwirtschaft und Nationalökonomie*, Pt. I, 1826, and later editions, summarized in M. Chisholm, *Rural Settlement and Land Use: an Essay in Location*, 1962 and translated into English by P. Hall (ed.), *von Thünen's Isolated State*, 1966.

12  A. Weber, *Theory of the Location of Industries*, English translation, 1929, reprinted 1957 (first published 1909).

13  E. M. Hoover, *Location Theory and the Shoe and Leather Industries*, 1937: *The Location of Economic Activity*, 1948.

14  W. Launhardt, *Mathematische Begründung der Volkswirtschaftslehre*, 1885.

15  H. Hotelling, 'Stability in competition', *Economic Journal*, 1929, pp. 41–57.

16   A. Lösch, *The Economics of Location*, English translation 1954 (first published 1940).

17   M. L. Greenhut, 1956, *op. cit.*, p. 3.

18   W. Isard, 1956, *op. cit.*, p. 140.

19   L. Lefeber, *Allocation in Space*, 1958.

20   Australian Transport Advisory Council, *Transport Costs in Australia*, 1959, Table No. 61.

21   J. M. Keynes, *General Theory of Employment, Interest and Money*, 1936.

22   However, see: R. L. Morrill, 'The development of spatial distributions of towns in Sweden: an historical–predictive approach,' *Annals*, Association of American Geographers, 1963, pp. 1–14; A. P. Hurter and L. N. Moses, 'Transportation and the spatial distribution of economic activity', *Research Report*, Transportation Center, Northwestern University, undated.

23   S. R. Dennison, *Location of Industry and the Depressed Areas*, 1939. *Royal Commission on the Distribution of the Industrial Population*, report, 1940, Cmd. 6153, with an important appendix by J. H. Jones. P. S. Florence, 'The selection of industries suitable for dispersion in rural areas', *Journal*, Royal Statistical Society, 1944, pp. 93–97: *Investment, Location and Size of Plant*, 1948: *Post-war Investment, Location and Size of Plant*, National Institute of Economic and Social Research, *Occasional Papers*, XIX, 1962. The National Institute of Economic and Social Research has sponsored several industrial studies, including F. W. Luttrell, *Factory Location and Industrial Movement*, 2 vols., 1962. Scottish Council, *Inquiry into the Scottish Economy 1960–1961*, under the chairmanship of J. N. Toothill, undated.

24   For an account of the evolution of economic thinking about development, see: B. F. Hoselitz, (ed.), *Theories of Economic Growth*, 1960 and S. Enke, *Economics for Development*, 1963, chap. 4. Useful surveys of recent literature on economic and regional development are: Y. Lacoste, 'Le sous-développement: quelques ouvrages significatifs parus depuis dix ans', *Annales de Géographie*, 1962, pp. 247–78 and 387–414 and J. R. Meyer, 'Regional economics: a survey', *American Economic Review*, 1963, pp. 19–54.

25   P. T. Bauer and B. S. Yamey, *The Economics of Under-Developed Countries*, 1957.

26   See for example: J. J. Spengler (ed.), *Natural Resources and Economic Growth* 1961; N. Ginsburg (ed.), *Essays on Geography and Economic Development*, University of Chicago, Department of Geography, Research Paper No. 62, 1960.

27   See, for example: W. W. Rostow, *The Stages of Economic Growth: a non-Communist Manifesto*, 1960, reprinted; W. A. Lewis, *The Theory of Economic Growth*, 1955; P. T. Bauer and B. S. Yamey, 1957, *op. cit.*

28   The reader will recall the writings of J. Brunhes, Vidal de la Blache, E. C. Semple and E. Huntington, to mention only a few of the workers in this general field.

29   F. W. Taussig, *International Trade*, 1927, p. 10.

30   B. Ohlin, *Interregional and International Trade*, 1933.

31  E. H. Chamberlin, *The Theory of Monopolistic Competition*, 1933. See also, J. Robinson, *Economics of Imperfect Competition*, 1933.

32  For example: R. L. Nelson, *The Selection of Retail Locations*, 1959.

33  For example: A. E. Smailes and G. Hartley, 'Shopping centres in the Greater London area', *Transactions and Papers*, Institute of British Geographers, 1961, pp. 201–14.

34  For example: R. E. Dickinson, *City, Region and Regionalism*, 1947.

35  C. D. Forde, *Habitat, Economy and Society*, 1934.

36  E. C. Semple, *Influences of Geographic Environment*, 1911. E. Huntington, *Civilization and Climate*, 1915.

37  A. F. Martin, 'The necessity for determinism,' *Transactions and Papers*, Institute of British Geographers, 1951, pp. 6 and 7.

38  C. F. Jones and G. G. Darkenwald, *Economic Geography*, revised edition, 1954. S. N. Dicken, *Economic Geography*, 1955. N. A. Bengtson and W. van Royen, *Fundamentals of Economic Geography*, 4th edition, 1960.

39  J. O. M. Broek, 'Discourse on economic geography', *Geographical Review*, 1941, pp. 663–64.

40  C. A. Fisher, 1948, *op. cit.*, p. 76.

41  H. H. McCarty, 'An approach to a theory of economic geography', *Economic Geography*, 1954, pp. 96–97.

42  R. Hartshorne, *The Nature of Geography*, 1956 printing, especially pp. 417–19.

43  G. G. Chisholm, *Handbook of Commercial Geography*, tenth revised edition, 1925, pp. 6–9. The passage is almost identical to the one in the sixteenth edition, 1960, rewritten by L. D. Stamp and S. C. Gilmour.

44  O. E. Baker, 'The increasing importance of the physical conditions in determining the utilization of land for agricultural and forest production in the United States', *Annals*, Association of American Geographers, 1921, pp. 17–46.

45  O. E. Baker, 'The potential supply of wheat', *Economic Geography*, 1925, pp. 15–52.

46  R. O. Buchanan, *The Pastoral Industries of New Zealand*, Institute of British Geography, 1935, p. xv.

47  W. H. Carter and R. E. Dodge, *Economic Geography*, 1939.

48  W. Smith, *An Economic Geography of Great Britain*, 1949, reprinted 1953.

49  W. R. Mead, *An Economic Geography of the Scandinavian States and Finland*, 1958.

50  B. H. Farmer, *Pioneer Peasant Colonization in Ceylon*, 1957.

51  R. C. Estall and R. O. Buchanan, *Industrial Activity and Economic Geography*, 1961. M. Chisholm, 1962, *op. cit.* G. Manners, *The Geography of Energy*, 1964.

52  R. S. Thoman, *The Geography of Economic Activity: an Introductory World Survey*, 1962. Cf. N. J. G. Pounds, *An Introduction to Economic Geography*, 1951.

53  P. T. Bauer and B. S. Yamey, 1957, *op. cit.*, pp. 43–44.

54  A. Cairncross, *Introduction to Economics*, 1944, p. 53; pp. 100–01 in the third edition of 1960. Note that an identical formulation was presented by W. H. Carter and R. E. Dodge, 1939, *op. cit.*, p. 4.

55  W. Smith, 1953, *op. cit.* G. H. Dury, *The British Isles*, 1961. L. D. Stamp and S. H. Beaver, *The British Isles*, fourth edition, 1962. J. B. Mitchell (ed.), *Great Britain: Geographical Essays*, 1962.

56  J. Jewkes, 'The localization of the cotton industry', *Economic History*, 1930, pp. 91–106.

57  L. D. Stamp and S. H. Beaver, 1962, *loc. cit.*, p. 494.

58  W. S. Thatcher, *Economic Geography*, 1949, pp. 140–41.

59  E. A. Brady, 'A reconsideration of the Lancashire "cotton famine" ', *Agricultural History*, 1963, pp. 156–62. The shortage may have been much less than previously thought.

60  E. W. Miller, *A Geography of Manufacturing*, 1962, pp. 440–42. J. H. Jones, Appendix 2, Royal Commission, 1940, *op. cit.*

61  S. J. Jones. 'The growth of Bristol. The regional aspect of city development,' *Transactions and Papers*, Institute of British Geographers, 1947, p. 77.

62  W. E. Minchinton, *The Place of Brecknock in the Industrialization of South Wales*, Brecknock Society in Brycheiniog, 1961, pp. 3–6. A. M. Jones, *The Rural Industries of England and Wales, IV, Wales*, 1927, p. 19.

63  S. J. Jones, 1947, *op. cit.*

64  R. Robson, 'Location and development of the cotton industry', *Journal of Industrial Economics*, 1953, pp. 111–12.

65  H. Carter, 'The growth of industry, 1750–1850', in *Wales: a Physical, Historical and Regional Geography*, edited by E. G. Bowen, 1957, p. 214.

66  A. M. Jones, 1927, *loc. cit.*, p. 18.

67  *Ibid.*, p. 19.

68  A. H. John, *The Industrial Development of South Wales, 1750–1850*, 1950.

# CHAPTER 3

# The Location Problem : Some Basic Concepts

Three inter-related questions underlie a study of the spatial pattern of production of any commodity: what is (will be or has been) produced, how much of it and where? To answer these questions, account must in principle be taken of all other patterns of production, for the existence of products competing for the same sites or productive resources or as alternatives in the same markets, has a profound influence upon the geographic distribution of any one commodity.

Consider the problem of locating an entirely new factory. For a works, the nature and scale of whose output has been decided, there is in principle an optimum location which can be found by examining:

1. The cost of assembling the necessary materials.
2. The cost of processing.
3. The cost of marketing the produce.

Following Weber[1] and Hoover,[2] one may envisage the optimum location as that which minimizes total cost, taking account of the three sets of consideration listed above. (The over-all optimum location may or may not coincide with one or more of the subsidiary optima.)

This simple formulation overlooks a number of complications of which it is necessary to be aware, even though they will be set aside for the moment. These difficulties arise in the following way. If perfect competition characterizes the economy, there will be a large number of producers, each of which is unable to influence the price of its product, and the volume of sales available to each will be identical to that which is potentially available to all other manufacturers of the same commodity. There will be no possibility of earning excess profits. Under these conditions, any deviation from the optimum location would result in profits less than 'normal' being earned. Hence, the optimum location is that which minimizes production costs. In practice, these conditions are often not met and as a consequence the location of a factory may influence both the volume of its sales and the price that can be charged. Furthermore, there are economies of scale in many kinds of manufacture, which means that variations in volume of sales will affect the costs of manufacture. Hence, in the real world the location that minimizes manufacturing costs may not be the one that maximizes profits.

For the moment, it is convenient to ignore these problems and to assume that the type of production has been decided and also the scale of output and that there is only one price for the product. To discover the location that will minimize costs, it is necessary to consider the resources that are used in manufacture—fuel, labour, materials, etc.—and the proportions in which they are employed.

## Structure of Costs

Combinations of resource-use vary greatly from one industry to another for obvious reasons that need not detain us. However, the data available to show the magnitude of these variations are not very plentiful, largely because most official censuses of industry collect information on only a limited range of topics. One of the more comprehensive surveys has been carried out recently in Northern Ireland and a selection of the results is shown in Table 1.[3]

Variation in the structure of inputs between firms making similar goods may be as great as, or greater than, the differences between industries. Table 2 shows the percentage distribution of costs for two unnamed but real motor car manufacturers in the United Kingdom, one of which is an integrated firm making as large a proportion as possible of all parts while the other sub-contracts on a much larger scale. The relative importance of components and raw materials is so different that the locational considerations for the works are likely to differ in the two cases. Similar variation is found within other industries, plastics being one for which some data have been published.[4]

TABLE 1

NORTHERN IRELAND, 1959–60: production costs as percentage of the
value of sales for selected industries

| INDUSTRY | Value of sales in the enquiry as % of sales shown by 1959 census of production | COST AS PERCENTAGE OF VALUE OF SALES | | | | | | Transport | |
|---|---|---|---|---|---|---|---|---|---|
| | | Raw materials | Wages | Salaries | Fuel, light and power | Rent and rates | Depreciation | To customers | Inward |
| Bacon curing, meat and fish products | 61·8 | 83·0 | 4·2 | 0·8 | 0·6 | 0·04 | 0·5 | 2·2 | 0·05 |
| Shirts and pyjamas | 49·5 | 62·0 | 21·4 | 2·2 | 0·5 | 0·2 | 0·7 | 1·2 | 0·0 |
| Paper, printing and publishing | 40·7 | 56·4 | 18·7 | 4·8 | 1·1 | 0·6 | 2·2 | 1·0 | 1·5 |
| Leather and footwear | 99·6 | 54·9 | 18·9 | 4·7 | 1·0 | 0·5 | 0·8 | 1·0 | 0·6 |
| Light engineering | 36·5 | 43·3 | 23·7 | 6·8 | 1·6 | 0·9 | 2·4 | 0·6 | 1·9 |
| Bleaching, dyeing and finishing | 18·6 | 24·2 | 35·9 | 6·4 | 10·6 | 0·7 | 5·3 | 2·6 | 1·0 |

*Source:* Northern Ireland Development Council, *Fifth Report 1960–61*, Appendix.
The transport items represent the costs borne by the firms replying to the
questionnaire and therefore understate the total transport costs to the extent
that the suppliers and/or purchasers pay for transport (see Chapter 7).
The difference between 100·0 and the sum of the cost items for each industry
represents profits, taxation and other expenses (*e.g.* administration).

TABLE 2[5]

UNITED KINGDOM, MID-1950s: percentage distribution of costs in
passenger car manufacture

| Item | Non-integrated Firm | Integrated Firm |
|---|---|---|
| Body (complete) | 33 | — |
| Tyres, wheels and brakes | 9 | 9 |
| Electrical equipment | 7 | 7 |
| Castings and forgings | 6 | 2 |
| Front suspension (complete) | 4 | — |
| Other proprietary components | 10 | 12 |
| Raw materials and non-proprietary parts | 6 | 25 |
| TOTAL material | 75 | 55 |
| Share of car manufacturer | 25 | 45 |
| TOTAL cost of car | 100 | 100 |

Differences in operating structure between firms making
similar goods will affect the choice of location for the individual

plants. It may be, however, that these variations reflect the efforts made by firms to adjust their operations to the best pattern that is available for the particular location that they occupy. If this is the case, then the problem of where to locate a new plant is more complicated than has been indicated above, for the production-function of a firm is not something to be taken as given but is itself variable within greater or lesser limits. The location question, as it relates to the minimization of production cost, thus becomes:

1. For each possible production-function, which is the best location?

2. Of these alternatives, which will give the lowest unit cost of production?

A large number of variables is involved in the location decision and many of these are mutually inter-related.[6] Consequently, if there is a unique solution, other answers may be only slightly inferior and may be chosen owing to imperfections in the knowledge available for making decisions. Such variations in choice of location and production-function among firms in the same industry are particularly likely where different solutions give only small differences in cost and where firms' experiences differentiate them. For example, Ford at Dagenham had until the early 1960s a somewhat eccentric location in relation to other passenger car producers in Great Britain and was the most highly integrated single plant in the country (it may be the integrated works referred to in Table 2). Ford maintains a tradition of vertical integration which in Britain did not long outlive the 1914–18 war but which before then had been a marked feature of the British industry. S. B. Saul[7] considers that the slow development of specialized component manufacture for motor vehicles before 1914 was largely due to the unwillingness of British vehicle manufacturers to standardize their parts, to allow other firms to use parts identical to those used by themselves and to concentrate production on a limited range of models. Morris led the way in buying parts extensively from specialist manufacturers but these were unable to provide an adequate supply and in 1914 Morris had to import parts from the United States.[8] Although Morris was a comparatively long-established firm, total output was only 300 vehicles in 1913, whereas Ford, starting in Manchester in 1911, made 6,139 machines in the year before the First World War.[9] Ford began by assembling engines and chassis imported from Detroit and 'bodies were at first bought from Scott Brothers; then, when this firm proved slow, their works were taken over and Ford, Ltd., began making and upholstering all its own bodies.'[10] In view of these difficulties, and those of Morris in getting components for an output one-twentieth the size of Ford's, it was hardly surprising that Ford chose to make its own parts whenever possible, especially as this accorded with the personal predilections of Henry Ford himself. Furthermore, when the Manchester site became too small and another was being sought for a comprehensive removal, a plant such as Ford that desired to be integrated could more easily consider moving to an entirely different region than could one that was more dependent upon specialist suppliers who would stay where they were: the Dagenham site, occupied in the early 1930s, was chosen partly because the tidewater facilities permitted the operation of a blast furnace and steel plant to supply the materials for the forge shops.

The early history of Ford in Britain represents a special case of the more general problem of scale, to which Chapter 4 is largely devoted. Another problem in the real world in the choice of the optimum location is the fact that technical change causes continual alteration in the structure of costs. It follows:

1. That any explanation of past or existing patterns of industry must be framed in terms of the circumstances relevant for time at which the firms were established.

2. That an existing distribution of firms may be a poor guide to the location of a new one making the same goods.

3. That the decision where to locate a new works must take account of probable changes in cost-structure during the life of the plant.

The retention of obsolete equipment, perhaps in disadvantageous locations, will occur where the fixed installations have a long life and demand for the commodity is rising sufficiently rapidly to stretch the productive resources; it is justified until the point is reached when the capital cost of replacement would be balanced by the savings in maintenance and operation expenses. An industry in which these considerations apply with particular force is that of electricity generation (Table 3), where the locational requirements of new stations are very different from those obtaining in the 1930s.[11] Obsolete equipment may also be retained during periods of economic recession, when business prospects are poor and new capital investment is unlikely to earn an adequate return. This was a common occurrence in the United Kingdom during the depression of the 1930s. Finally, new investment may mean a substantial increase in capacity and will not be undertaken if demand is rising slowly (p. 109). Thus, obsolete equipment may be retained either because business is very good or because demand is slack.

TABLE 3

GREAT BRITAIN: the percentage distribution of electricity generating costs (capital charges excluded), average of all stations

| YEAR | FUEL | | | Repairs and maintenance | Other operating costs* | Total |
|---|---|---|---|---|---|---|
| | Coal and coke | Oil | Other | | | |
| 1963 | 75·4 | 10·2 | — | 7·9 | 6·5 | 100·0 |
| 1961 | 73·1 | 13·4 | — | 6·8 | 6·7 | 100·0 |
| 1956 | 85·3 | 1·5 | — | 6·4 | 6·8 | 100·0 |
| 1951 | 83·9 | 0·8 | 0·1 | 8·0 | 7·2 | 100·0 |
| 1946 | 83·9 | 0·4 | — | 8·9 | 6·8 | 100·0 |
| 1941 | 82·0 | 0·5 | — | 9·3 | 8·2 | 100·0 |
| 1936 | 71·3 | 0·7 | 0·2 | 13·9 | 13·9 | 100·0 |
| 1931 | 61·3 | 1·1 | 0·3 | 17·9 | 19·4 | 100·0 |

Source: Ministry of Power, Statistical Digest, 1964, p. 113.

* Almost entirely wages and salaries, though excluding those incurred in handling fuel and in repairs and maintenance, which are charged to the respective heads.

We have so far treated cost structures in isolation from geographic variations in prices, a procedure that can only be justified as a first approximation to the resolution of the location problem. Geographic differences in prices have two effects. First, if one resource, say labour, is cheaper in one place than in another, greater amounts of labour are likely to be used where it is cheap than where it is dear. That is, labour would be substituted for capital and other inputs. This is very clearly seen in the case of farming in the United States and Nigeria: in the former country, agriculture is highly mechanized whereas in the latter only rudimentary tools are used and very large numbers of man-hours are applied to the land. But there is usually a limit to the amount of substitution that is possible; for example, however highly mechanized American farming may be, some labour is still required to operate the equipment. If, therefore, the first effect of differences in prices from place to place is upon the manner of production, the second effect is upon the location thereof. This arises from the limited possibilities for substitution and the consequential advantages of employing resources where they are cheapest: if a certain minimum amount of labour is needed, then, other things being equal, it is advantageous to employ that labour where wages are low rather than where they are high.

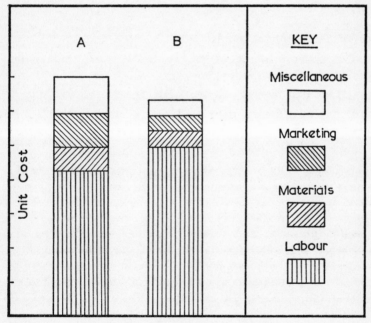

Figure 1.   Hypothetical structure of manufacturing costs in two locations

Examination of the structure of costs for a new plant might suggest that the location thereof will be largely determined by the element that dominates costs, be it wages, materials, fuel, etc. However, if the price of the major item of cost does not vary with location, it will have no effect upon the decision where to build the new works. Conversely, a small item in the total cost may vary greatly in price from place to place. The optimum location is therefore a function of neither cost-structure alone nor geographic price variation alone but the combination of these two considerations determines the share of each element in the geographic *variation* in unit cost of production. The items of cost that will dominate the location decision are those that contribute most to geographic differences in unit cost, as is shown in Figure 1, where B would be a preferable location to A even though the main item of cost, labour, is dearer there than at A: materials and marketing are proportinately less important over-all but, in this hypothetical case, vary in cost much more markedly than does labour.[12]

## Orientation to Markets and Materials

The above form of analysis is the basis for the familiar distinction between industries:

1. Oriented toward raw materials, as with saw-milling.

2. Oriented toward their markets, *e.g.* bread baking.

3. Termed 'footloose', having no particular orientation, *e.g.* some kinds of precision engineering.

These terms only have meaning in quite specific contexts and unless these are stated explicitly for each case, three confusions may arise, as may be illustrated by examining the terms 'market' and 'material' oriented. First, these terms relate to specific industries and therefore to the raw materials and markets that are peculiar to each: beet sugar factories and blast furnaces may both be described as raw material oriented, though the former are mostly found in the rural east of Great Britain and the latter are concentrated in industrial coalfield, orefield and port locations.[13] Second, two factors may operate in the same direction and it may be difficult to distinguish which is the dominant one: the coalfields of Europe remain important

centres of industry not primarily because of the local availability of fuel and other materials, which was the initial reason
for development, but because they provide important markets
and possess facilities such as transport, owing to the dense
population inherited from the past. The third and most
important possible confusion arises in a more subtle way from
changes in the scale of consideration. For example, grain
milling in the United Kingdom is scattered through the grain
growing districts and is also important at ports such as London
and Hull, where grain is imported. Since purchased grain
represents two-thirds to three-quarters of the total cost of
milling[14] and since considerable economies in transport can
be obtained in these locations, it is reasonable to describe milling as raw material oriented. However, at the international
level, the grain-surplus countries such as Australia and
Canada export grain to be milled in the importing country.
This happens largely because flour is more perishable than
grain but also because the transport of flour would require the
separate movement of the bran and other residues and hence
the provision of further handling facilities. At this scale,
therefore, grain milling is market oriented and we have the
seemingly paradoxical situation that apparently conflicting
descriptions of the location pattern are simultaneously true.

## Transfer Payments and Economic Rent

Let us suppose that the optimum location of the new plant
has been calculated in terms of the minimum unit cost of
production. A serious problem will arise if another firm has
performed a similar calculation and if the two optimum
locations coincide. Since the possibilities for multiple use of
sites are limited, by what means does one user command the
site in competition with the other potential user?

The value of land provides the mechanism for the allocation
of the site in question to one or other firm. Let us suppose that
the optimum location for firms A and B is Z and that for both
of them the next best location is Y:

|  | Profits per annum | |
|---|---|---|
|  | Y | Z |
| Firm A | £100 | £200 |
| Firm B | £90 | £150 |

The 'profits' shown exclude any payment for the use of the sites, which in the first instance are assumed to be free. In this case, firm B would earn an excess of £60 annually by locating at Z rather than Y whereas for A the excess would be £100. Firm B would be able to pay £60 p.a. to use site Z in preference to Y without being worse off, and would gain if Z could be obtained for less than £60 each year. Unfortunately for B, firm A could spend up to £100 annually and could therefore bid a higher price than B: if A pays £60 p.a., or just over, it will still earn £40 p.a. (or just under) more than at Y. If the demand for A's product is large, it may be necessary to establish two plants and the following situation may prevail:

|          | *Profits per annum* | | |
|----------|------|------|------|
|          | X    | Y    | Z    |
| Firm A   | £90  | £100 | £200 |
| Firm B   | £70  | £90  | £150 |

Firm B could pay £20 p.a. for site Y (£90 − £70) whereas A could afford not more than £10 (£100 − £90). A would then occupy sites X and Z and firm B would locate at Y.

For the individual firm, any payment for land represents an expense and is known as a transfer payment, *i.e.* the payment that is necessary to prevent some other firm, that may be in the same industry, from using the site. In the initial case of two firms and two sites, the transfer payment is £60 p.a. (or just over), for which sum firm A can prevent B from using the optimum site Z. However, firm A then obtains a 'surplus' of £40 annually (or just under), which is known as economic rent. Where three sites are available, X, Y and Z, the sum that A would have to pay to prevent B from occupying the optimum location (the transfer payment) would be £80 (£150 − £70) and the economic rent (or 'surplus') accruing to A would be only £20 p.a. with respect to location Y (£30 p.a. with respect to location X).

In principle, therefore, the lowest price for any parcel of land is set by the transfer payment that is necessary to retain the land in the most profitable kind of use. The highest price that can be charged is the transfer payment plus the whole of the economic rent, or surplus, that accrues to the enterprise with the greatest economic rent at that site. Whereabouts within these limits the actual price paid will fall depends upon the efficiency of the land market, the degree of knowledge possessed by the parties and the institutional arrangements of the society. In a perfectly competitive economy, any economic rent above the transfer payment would be absorbed in the rental for the site (or be compounded in the purchase price).

For any one plot of land, the price paid represents largely, if not exclusively, a transfer payment to prevent its use by some other firm. But taking all land and considering the possibility of transferring agriculture, industry and all population to the less hospitable parts of the globe—the Sahara and Antarctica, for example—virtually all land payments represent economic rent, the surplus that can be obtained by using the better favoured lands in preference to the poorer.[15]

## Opportunity Costs

The ability of firms to make transfer payments for the use of sites and to realize economic rent depends upon the opportunities that are foregone elsewhere, or the opportunity costs. For each firm and each type of activity, opportunity costs will vary according to the nature of the available sites and their location. Equally, the opportunity costs of an area in any one activity are measured by the alternative uses to which the same land may be put. Lancashire has already been cited as an area that specialized in one kind of industry largely because of the lack of suitable alternatives (p. 20ff.)—its opportunity costs were low—whereas in Scotland the opportunity costs of cotton textiles were high enough to warrant a change toward metal manufacture. The notion of opportunity costs is fundamental to economic analysis in general, for any decision to allocate scarce resources means that some alternatives must be eschewed. It is also the key to all questions of location, and provides us with the means of understanding the doctrine of comparative advantage.

This chapter began with the problem of location for a single firm. In principle, this problem is identical to that of determining the best use for any particular piece of land, except that a different quantity is treated as known.[16] However, in discussing transfer payments, economic rent and opportunity costs, some mention has been made of whole industries and large

D

areas and the reader should note that henceforth the discussion is primarily concerned with the distribution of industries rather than of the constituent firms. The former is, of course, derived from the latter but the terms of discussion change somewhat.

*Comparative Advantage*

This doctrine has a long history in the field of economics, having been evolved in the early debates on whether or not it was to the advantage of a country to engage in foreign trade; what benefits are there and who reaps them? We know that some trade is beneficial from the elementary fact that production does not all occur in one infinitely small spot: if any one place is to have a variety of goods available, some movement and interchange is necessary. Furthermore, we know that costs of production do vary from place to place and that owing to climatic, geologic, topographic and other physical factors some types of production are limited in geographic extent. The doctrine of comparative advantage provides the conceptual framework that enables us to relate patterns of trade and production and to analyze the basis for regional specialization of production.

A simple example may be taken to illustrate the argument. Imagine two countries, say Britain and Portugal, which are able to produce cars and cork. Both countries require both commodities, which can be readily transported at no cost. If workers cannot migrate from one country to another but can freely change from one occupation to another within the respective countries, we may visualize the situations that are shown in Figure 2.[17] The vertical axes of the graphs represent the annual output of one worker in tons and the horizontal axes a choice of locations arranged according to the annual output of a worker in car and cork manufacture. For each diagram, the corresponding figures (which are entirely imaginary) are shown on the right. There are two basic reasons why the efficiency of production may vary from one place to another. In the first place, the endowment of natural resources is unequal; in the imaginary case we are using, the climate of Britain is not very suitable for the commercial growth of cork. Second, the level of technical accomplishment may vary; compared with Britain, Portugal is not economically very advanced and is therefore ill-equipped for car production.

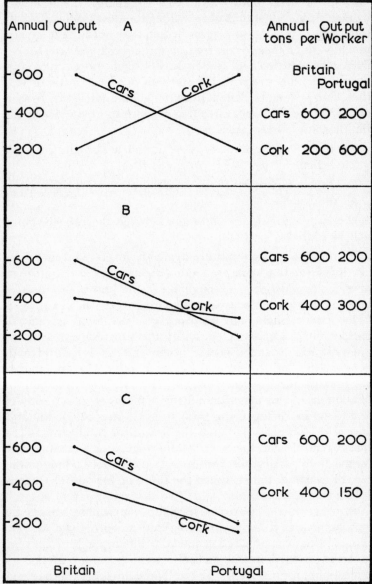

Figure 2. Illustration of the concept of comparative advantage

In Figure 2A, there is no doubt that if the British workers specialize in car production, exchanging their produce for Portuguese cork, both countries will benefit. Each British worker making 600 tons of cars foregoes a cork output of 200 tons, a ratio of 3:1: so long as Britain does not have to give as much as three tons of cars for one ton of cork, she will benefit from specialization and trade. In Portugal, an output of 200 tons of cars means sacrificing 600 tons of cork, a ratio of 1:3: therefore, Portugal will gain from trade if she can get more than one ton of cars for every three tons of cork exported. Hence, the limiting rates of exchange are:

3 tons of cars for 1 ton of cork, at which Portugal reaps all the benefit.

0·333 ton of cars for 1 ton of cork, at which Britain reaps all the benefit.

If the exchange rate is somewhere between the two, the gains will be shared.

Of the two options that are available to Portugal in Figure 2B, it is clear that cork production yields a larger output than does car production. Although she is the poorer producer of both goods, cork has an *absolute* advantage over cars in Portugal. (The reader might care to work out the limiting rates of exchange.[18]) Figure 2C provides the greatest problem, for not only is Portugal a poorer producer than Britain of both goods but in both countries the annual output of a workman in car manufacture is higher than in cork. In Britain, an output of 600 tons of cars means sacrificing 400 tons of cork, a ratio of 1·5 to 1: in Portugal, the ratio is 1·333 to 1 (200÷150). If cork is produced in Portugal, the loss of car production is less than would be the case were Britain to grow and manufacture it, and both parties will gain from specialization so long as the rate of exchange falls between the ratios of 1·5 and 1·333 tons of cars to one ton of cork.

In practice, the degree of specialization will be limited by two factors. It is highly probable that as Portuguese workers transfer from car production to cork, the output per man year in cork production will at some point begin to decline as diminishing returns set in (p. 48). The same is also probable in car manufacture in Britain. In these circumstances, specialization can occur only to the point at which the relative marginal productivities of the two industries are the same in both countries. Furthermore, where one country has a much smaller population than another, the smaller could be fully specialized on one product and yet be unable to supply all the needs of the larger one. In the imaginery example we have been using, Britain might have to produce some cork to supplement Portuguese production.

This much simplified account of the doctrine of comparative advantage may be extended to situations involving three or more countries and commodities without altering the fundamental conclusion that trade is worth-while for the least as well as the best endowed region or nation. Furthermore:

1. The production of any commodity (cork in Figure 2) may be located in the country or region which in *absolute* terms is the worst of the available places for the item in question.

2. Conversely, a region (Portugal in Figure 2) may specialize in the type of production for which, in *absolute* terms, it is least well endowed.

In both cases, the apparent paradox is due to the *relative* advantages and in particular to the opportunities that are or would be foregone. It follows that the real explanation for any particular pattern of localization, say cotton manufacture in Lancashire, may lie as much in the relationships of cotton to other types of enterprise in Lancashire and elsewhere as to relationships directly between cotton textiles and the factors of their production.

This point was clearly made by O. E. Baker in 1925 in a discussion of the world's potential supply of wheat. Wheat is an adaptable crop that can tolerate a very wide range of climatic and soil conditions and which is therefore forced to cede to other crops with more exacting needs much of the land that is good for its production:

> The crop or other agricultural product which is most limited in climatic or other physical requirements of production will, if the demand for it be sufficient, have first choice of the land. It possesses, so to speak, a sort of natural monopoly and consequently commands a price which gives it an advantage over other crops or products.[19]

In addition to the biological limitations on production one must add economic restrictions, including those imposed by the problems of marketing bulky or perishable goods, particularly when transport was less efficient than it is now.[20]

The doctrine of comparative advantage applies at all scales, from the specialization of the individual worker or enterprise to that of whole nations or continents. The concept of the 'urban economic base' is but a special case of the general one, analyzing the 'export' (or 'base') element of a city's economy:[21] it is comparable to the notion of a country's 'export base'. Political frontiers are therefore significant to the extent that the freedom to move goods (and other things) across them is impaired by tariffs and other restrictions. International frontiers are readily located and their effects can be identified with comparative ease. However, intra-national movement may be impeded by legal and extra-legal conditions as much as or more than international trade and migration. The Inter-State Commerce Commission of the United States was established and is maintained primarily to ensure free traffic between the States of the union. Differing railway gauges between the states of the Australian commonwealth have in the past been a serious hindrance to trade while the absence of all but rudimentary means of transport over much of China has for centuries caused parts of that country to have stronger affinities with external territories than with the rest of mainland China.

### Trade as an Alternative to the Movement of Labour and Capital

The inseparable connections between patterns of trade and patterns of location was stressed by Ohlin.[22] Furthermore, the movement of goods is an alternative to the transfer from region to region of capital and labour, the two factors of production that are at least partially mobile. Though the movement of goods, labour and capital may be substitutes one for another, the geographic consequences of one kind of transfer will clearly be different from those arising from another, on account of their varying impact on the location of production. For example, both India and Italy are in the process of economic development but India has been less successful than Italy partly because she cannot 'export' her problem in the form of migrants on a scale that is significant relative to her problems (Table 4). Italian migrants have gone in their hundreds of thousands to the United States and in large numbers to the countries of western Europe. Superficially, it would appear that this migration has altered the geographic balance of industry and commerce, less development having occurred in Italy and more elsewhere than would otherwise have been the case. The matter is almost certainly more complicated than that, for the emigration from Italy, especially southern Italy, may have been an important factor in aiding economic development by permitting the growth in available productive resources to keep ahead of population increase.[23] Therefore, no general statement about the nature of the effects of various transfers can be made; it is sufficient to note the connections between them, that the resultant geographic patterns are closely affected, and that this proposition holds good whether the scale of consideration is essentially local, regional or international.

TABLE 4

INDIA AND ITALY: movements of population and capital, 1956–61

|  | Population in 1960, million | Per caput income $U.S., 1960 | Net emigration 1956–61, million | Balance of payments, 1956–61, $U.S.m. | | |
|---|---|---|---|---|---|---|
|  |  |  |  | Current account | Capital account | Errors and omissions[2] |
| India | 431·7 | 116 | ( · )[1] | −3,834 | +4,075 | −241 |
| Italy | 49·4 | 512 | 1·7 | +2,077 | −1,281 | −797 |

Sources: U.N., Statistical Yearbook, Demographic Yearbook and Monthly Bulletin of Statistics.

1 Official statistics record a negligible movement of people: for 1956–59 a total of 12,492 departures and 11,944 arrivals. The net emigration may be greater than recorded but is not significant in relation to India's population.

2 Ideally, the net current and capital accounts should both be equally large but of opposite sign (positive for inflow and negative for outflow). The net 'errors and omissions' covers unidentified transactions not included in the main accounts.

If the movement of factors of production is a substitute for the movement of goods and the resulting geographic patterns differ, one effect is similar whichever item is mobile. The free movement of goods tends to equalize the prices of commodities in all parts of the world and hence tends to equalize the remuneration of the factors of production. Similarly, the migration of labour (or capital) will have the effect of bringing wages (or interest rates) nearer to a uniform level, tending to equalize the prices of goods and services. This tendency towards geographic uniformity of prices and earnings may be, and in many cases is, masked by the fact that other forces have a stronger effect in widening geographic differentials (p. 76).[24]

## The Optimum and the Margin

The concept of an optimum location has been attacked by E. M. Rawstron[25] as signifying little, for in practice it is impossible to know what the optimum location is because circumstances change during the life of a plant, extraneous factors like personal satisfaction have a part to play in location decisions, and knowledge is imperfect. There is an additional and more rigorous reason that Rawstron did not discuss why enterprises are unlikely always to choose the optimum location. The concept of perfect competition tacitly assumes that knowledge is freely and instantly available to all persons without any effort, a proposition that is patently absurd in the real world. If a firm investigates the alternative locations available for a new plant, an expense is incurred that will increase the more thoroughly the enquiry is made. These expenses must be set against the capitalized benefits expected to accrue from the choice of a good location or the best available location. If the benefits are small in comparison with the costs of ascertainment, the firm in question will not press the investigation very far and will select a location that may well not be as good as others which were available but were not investigated. The decision would be entirely rational and could be an optimal *decision* even if the selected location were not the very best that was available.[26] Furthermore, any investigation of alternative locations takes time, and time may be precious. Wilkinson Sword, a Sheffield firm, developed a stainless steel razor blade that achieved a remarkable sales success in the United Kingdom during 1962 and 1963, when demand far exceeded supply. The firm, anxious to take advantage of its success before competitors could get a real footing in the market, was glad to lease a factory at Cramlington, Northumberland, which the Board of Trade was building in advance of demand and which could therefore be available quickly. Immediate occupation was more important than an optimum location. An inquiry among twenty-eight branch factories established in Northern Ireland in recent years showed that in seven cases ready availability of a works was a principal reason for going there; in three other instances this factor was mentioned as a subsidiary consideration.[27]

Thus, Rawstron argued, it may be more useful to consider the geographic limits within which an enterprise can be successful than to seek to know the best possible location. As a conceptual problem, the definition of the geographic limit of possible production is as difficult as the definition of the optimum place for the enterprise. However, the empirical evidence with which to plot boundaries is much greater than that available for seeking the optimum location. Whether one takes an agricultural product like milk or an industrial one like steel, a map can in principle be made to show the actual distribution of production within a given area at a particular time. As a first rough approximation, the line that just encloses the area of production may be taken as the economic margin, beyond which profitable operations are not feasible. With agricultural goods, the approximation may be a close one, for individual farms are comparatively small enterprises and are therefore numerous, giving a large number of observations. With industrial undertakings, there are many fewer plants and therefore the boundary based on the plotted distribution may correspond but poorly with the real economic margin of production.

To attempt to equate the geographic limit of production with the economic margin can only be justified for a long-established product for which the conditions of competition with other products have not changed in the recent past. The same is true of the boundaries between different kinds of land use. Wherever a product or use of land is newly introduced and has had inadequate time to spread widely (p. 77), or where competitive conditions have changed radically, there is likely to be very little correspondence between geographic limits and economic margins.

The simplest form of economic margin is found in agriculture, under the idealized conditions that von Thünen conceived for his isolated state, in which the soil was uniformly fertile throughout and the farmers were all rational and equally able.

Under these conditions, quite sharp boundaries would exist
between systems of cultivation, boundaries that could reasonably be represented as lines. But the real world consists of
variable terrain and climate, and nurtures people of various
abilities and the economic margin of cultivated land is therefore
normally marked by a few scattered holdings which are
peculiar in their natural endowment, location with respect to
communications or in the ability of the farmer. Furthermore,
the boundary between two forms of cultivation is even less
precise, because the line must be drawn where the two products in question are judged to be equally important, a judgment that may be based either on the areas of land involved or
the contribution to farm revenue. Thus, a geographic margin
separating two forms of activity represents the average conditions compounded of the experience of several or many
separate economic units any or all of which may or may not
be in a state of equilibrium at the time of the investigation. This
is a special case of the general problem in economics of attempting to derive generalized information on operating structures,
based upon empirical data, to test hypotheses about the
behaviour of firms.[28]

TABLE 5

THE RESPONSE OF COTTON TO THE APPLICATION OF
POTASH FERTILIZER

| POTASH (*kilogrammes per hectare*) | | COTTON (*kilogrammes per hectare*) | |
| --- | --- | --- | --- |
| *Application* | *Increment* | *Yield* | *Increment* |
| None | — | 585 | — |
| 17 | 17 | 1,012 | 427 |
| 34 | 17 | 1,353 | 341 |
| 50 | 16 | 1,500 | 147 |
| 67 | 17 | 1,657 | 157 |

*Source:* M. Lamer, *The World Fertilizer Economy*, 1937, p. 71.

The terms 'margin' and 'marginal' have a precise meaning
that must be made clear. The above table shows how the
application of potash fertilizer affects the yield of cotton, from
which it will be seen that with each increase in the rate of
application there is a corresponding rise in output per hectare,
but that the increment of yield tends to decline as more

fertilizer is applied.   A rational farmer will increase the application of fertilizer until the extra cost incurred by the last
application (the marginal cost) is balanced by the revenue
obtained from the extra output (the marginal revenue).

The comparison of the marginal addition to output with
the marginal cost incurred by a firm may readily be translated
into spatial, or geographic, terms.   If the demand for a particular product, say wheat, increases there is likely to be an
expansion of output.   This may be achieved either by an increase in the yields, through the application of more fertilizer
and general technical improvement, or by an extension of the
cultivated area.   In the latter case, the marginal wheat land is
that which has last been brought into cultivation.   If other
things remain equal, the land last brought into use will be the
first to be taken out of wheat cultivation if the demand for this
grain should fall.   Other things are not always equal and change
in one direction is often less easy than change the opposite way.
For example, rubber trees do not begin to yield until at least
five years from planting, after which year output rises to a
maximum at twelve to thirteen years and can be maintained
thereafter for several decades.   At a time of expanding demand,
new land will be brought into use and old plantations will be
replanted.   A succeeding phase of prolonged low demand and
poor prices may result in a reduction in the planted area but
this reduction will affect the remaining old plantations, where
operating costs are high, more than the new ones.   Thus, the
margins for expansion and for retraction may be located differ-
ently and the term 'margin' should properly be qualified to
show whether a particular geographic margin is defined in
terms of marginal increase or decrease in the area devoted to
the product(s) in question.

An alternative way of defining the margin for the production
of a particular commodity or group of commodities is through
the net income that is produced.   Those farms or factories that
only just cover their costs, leaving little or no return on the
capital and enterprise of the owner(s), are regarded as marginal
producers.   This kind of enterprise, especially in farming, is
often a family business where a high value is put upon independence, for the sake of which a low income is accepted.
Family firms of this kind are remarkably tenacious in two ways:

they remain in business when by 'rational' economic standards they should be liquidated; they often persevere with the same type of production irrespective of shifts in relative profitability, owing to the lack of capital available to invest in new equipment and an ingrained suspicion that change might lead to disaster. The persistence of small farms in central Wales is an example,[29] while in the industrial and commercial sectors the tenacity of family firms in Europe is remarkable; 'the small family firm in Western Europe seems to have a staying power that makes it long outlast its period of profitability'.[30]

The concept of marginal farming is therefore commonly associated with poor standards of living, an association that is reasonably correct when one is thinking of land which is marginal to any kind of farming. But in terms of individual products, the marginal producers who will curtail (increase) production in response to a fall (rise) in price are often those who occupy good land and command a good income, for they can more readily adapt their production to changing market conditions. Paradoxically, therefore, many farmers in Wales, for example, who occupy marginal farmland (as defined by the level of income) are not marginal milk producers since their response to price changes is somewhat insensitive.

A further complication arises in the following way. In the above discussion of geographic margins it has been assumed that changes in output are marginal to the particular industry as a whole, e.g., as with small variations in the total wheat area. This is legitimate when the industry in question comprises a very large number of separate firms but may not be relevant if many units of production are controlled by one company. In this case, the geographic distribution of activity will change according to considerations affecting the marginal activities of the companies in question. A recent example is the closure by Harland and Wolff of their Govan yard, which was one of the more modern shipyards on the Clyde.[31] The rationalization of Harland and Wolff's activities rendered the works redundant even though in terms of the shipbuilding industry as a whole there were other yards which more obviously merited the description of being 'marginal' in a time of contraction. (See also pp. 94–5 for a discussion of the effects of the size of firm.)

*Intensive and Extensive Margins*

A firm situated at or near the optimum location is likely to employ a combination of productive factors different from that employed by another firm producing the same commodity but located near the margin. A simple case is that in the semi-arid wheat and barley producing regions of the United States and Australia, yields per hectare are about one-quarter of those in Western Europe, the major importing region. In the arid areas, a larger quantity of land and machinery is required to obtain a given output, whereas in Europe more labour is used. With respect to land, the arid areas engage in extensive culti-vation whereas in Europe the output is described as intensive. The limit beyond which wheat cultivation cannot extend into drier areas is called the extensive margin; the limit beyond which wheat production cannot be intensified by raising yields to meet competition from other uses, such as horticulture, is the intensive margin. But what is the extensive margin of wheat production is at the same time the intensive margin for millet or for cattle ranching. Conversely, the intensive margin of wheat cultivation is simultaneously the extensive margin of horticulture or urban land uses. This concept of the intensive and extensive margins of production relates to the amount of land used to obtain a given final product and must not be confused with the yield of crops or livestock per unit area of farmland. For example, passing from a major consuming area such as the Ruhr either eastwards or southwards, the yield per hectare tends to fall.[32] However, there are regions, such as that around Naples, where the crop yields are very high but where much of the produce exported to the industrial regions of Europe is processed, into tomato *puré* for example. The volume of final product afforded by a hectare is quite small and the agriculture is said to be extensive with respect to land, though judged by the inputs of labour and materials the farming would be described as intensive. In the present context, therefore, extensive agriculture is not necessarily one where first yields are low nor is intensive agriculture necessarily one where first yields are high, though this is usually the case. The horticultural region of Naples–Salerno is in the region of Europe where land is used extensively in respect of the main European markets but where the per hectare yields of crops can be very high: on the world scale, the meat and dairy industries of New Zealand are comparable.[33]

*Movement of Margins*

The geographic margins of production for any particular commodity may shift in response to changes which affect:

1. The cost of production of the commodity in question, due either to technical developments in the production process or to changes in the prices of inputs such as labour and fuel.

2. The demand for the commodity.

3. The production of, or demand for, products elsewhere in the world such that a readjustment of production areas occurs and affects the commodity under consideration.

There is a great variety of ways in which changes occur under the first heading, ranging from the discovery of methods for using coal as coke in iron production to the development of plant and animal varieties to cope with particularly rigorous conditions. One example from the United Kingdom will suffice to illustrate the kind of change that is constantly occurring:

> A recent enquiry, carried out in Scotland, has confirmed that the greatest extension of the limits of afforestation took place at the time when improvements in methods of ground preparation were made, *i.e.* at the advent of turf planting in the nineteen-twenties and subsequently when the development of the tracked tractor made the use of modern forestry ploughs possible in the late nineteen-forties. Ploughing, combined with phosphatic fertilizers and the exotic Sitka spruce, has made the raising of promising plantations possible over many acres of grass-land hitherto considered marginal. More recently still the combination of draining and cultivation with more elaborate fertilization and the use of the undemanding Lodgepole pine promises to extend still further the afforesta-tion limit on peat of such poor quality that it is hardly tackled for forestry in any other country except Ireland.[34]

An example of the second consideration, changing demand, may also be taken from Scotland. A new cement works was opened in 1963 at Dunbar, East Lothian, with an annual capacity of 0·4 million tons, which represents half the cement used in Scotland at that time. Before the plant was opened, about two-thirds of the cement consumed was imported from England. The construction of this works was prompted by the rapidly growing regional use of cement, the fact that demand was great enough to warrant a plant sufficiently big to obtain most of the economies of scale of production and the transport savings that could be realized.[35] Similar circumstances prevail in the spread of modern steel-making capacity into countries, such as India, that are experiencing rapid economic development. Demand may also decline, as has happened in the case of tin-plate produced in hand-mills during recent decades: modern strip mills and cold reduction plants make tin-plate more cheaply owing to the large scale of operations and they also produce an article of superior quality. The more primitive pack mills that have occupied over fifty locations in South Wales and western Gloucestershire were widely scattered from Carmarthen to Lydney; they have been driven out of business, the geographic area of their economic production having contracted to vanishing point, while the six modern plants are concentrated at Ebbw Vale and in the vicinity of Swansea.[36]

Changes in the supply of, or demand for, other products in other parts of the world may have repercussions on the area or commodity that is the focus of interest. During the last quarter of the nineteenth century, the whole agricultural economy of the British Isles was subjected to severe problems of adjustment owing to the rapid increase in imports of food and other agricultural products. The influx of grain, wool, meat and dairy produce in particular was a major cause of agricultural depression and also stimulated a change of emphasis to fresh milk, high quality fatstock, vegetables and sugarbeet, for example. The adjustment affected the country as a whole but also had differential effects on certain regions, the arable areas generally being the harder hit and having to undergo the greater transformations.[37]

*Marginal Shifts and the Level of Yields*

Changes in the area devoted to particular agricultural products may take place at either the intensive or the extensive margin of production for the product in question, or at both simultaneously. Where adjustment does occur simultaneously at the two margins, one of three combinations may be found.

1. Expansion at both the intensive and extensive margins.
2. Contraction at both.
3. Expansion at one and contraction at the other.

The last of the three cases is illustrated by the spread of commercial cultivation during the second half of the nineteenth century into the temperate plains areas of North and South America, Australia and elsewhere, releasing the flood of imports that so radically changed the agriculture of Western Europe. The belts of production conceived by von Thünen expanded very rapidly, each belt migrating away from the main centres of consumption, principally Western Europe. The world geography of production and trade was dramatically altered and individual localities experienced a sequence of uses which represented one cause of the phenomenon known as 'sequent occupance'.[38]

There is thus no simple relationship between changes in the area under a particular crop or devoted to livestock and changes in yield per hectare. During the last century, the notion gained currency that an increase in the area planted with wheat or barley, for example, meant a decline in average yield. This was a reasonable proposition for the circumstances of the time, when in the world as a whole the marginal land being brought into use was progressively drier and poorer. The idea was apparently confirmed by H. D. Vigor, who analyzed the relationship between wheat yield and the area in wheat in England, using county data for the period 1885–1908.[39] The area devoted to wheat *fell* greatly in that period (due primarily to imports of foodstuffs) and Vigor concluded from his analysis that the observed *increase* in yield had been greater in those counties with the larger decline of area in wheat. This he attributed to the selective withdrawal of the poorer wheat land within each county, although he commented that the decline in planted area did not appear to be concentrated in those counties with a low yield. However, the adjustments in area may as probably occur on the good as on the poor wheat land, with the consequence that in more recent times no apparent correlation exists between crop-area changes and yields in the United Kingdom.[40]

An attempt has been made to discover whether shifts in the location of production of various grains in the United States have had a material effect upon yields. The method is illustrated by the hypothetical figures in Table 6, where A and B represent two localities producing wheat in two different years. Between 1900 and 1960, the total actual output has risen by 15 tons (190 − 175) though the total area in wheat has remained constant. How much of this increase can be ascribed to the general rise in yields resulting from improved farming and how much to shifts of production (which in this case have been from the higher to the lower yielding region)? If there had been no change of yield at A and B, the changing location of production would have caused a decline in output of 12·5 tons (175 − 162·5); had the area remained constant and the yields in the two areas risen as shown, production would have been increased

TABLE 6

THE EFFECT OF LOCATION SHIFTS ON YIELD AND OUTPUT OF WHEAT

| '*Actual*' Results | A | B | |
|---|---|---|---|
| 1900 | | | |
|     Yield, tons per hectare | 1·0 | 1·5 | |
|     Area in wheat, hectares | 100 | 50 | |
|     TOTAL OUTPUT, tons | 100 | 75 | 175 |
| 1960 | | | |
|     Yield, tons per hectare | 1·2 | 1·6 | |
|     Area in wheat, hectares | 125 | 25 | |
|     TOTAL OUTPUT, tons | 150 | 40 | 190 |
| '*Hypothetical*' results | | | |
|     Output in tons with area of 1960 and yield of 1900 | 125 | 37·5 | 162·5 |
|     Output in tons with area of 1900 and yield of 1960 | 120 | 80 | 200 |

by 25 tons (200 − 175). The changing geographic distribution of production in this hypothetical case therefore caused a fall in output which was more than compensated by the increase in production occasioned by improved techniques and strains of

E

wheat. It is, however, inadmissible to conclude that the location shifts accounted for a reduction in output of exactly 12·5 tons, since the location and yield changes were occurring simultaneously and the net improvement of 15 tons is not derived from 25 minus 12·5. Nevertheless, the method shows the *maximum* possible effect of the two changes taken separately.

Applied to the States of the American Union for the years 1900, 1930 and 1950, this method produced conflicting results according to whether crop area or yield was held constant and according to which year was chosen as the datum. Between 1900 and 1950, the average actual yield of wheat rose from 0·92 tons per hectare to 1·16 tons. Using the 1900 yields, location shifts between states accounted for an increase in average yield of only 0·05 tons per hectare; if the 1950 yields were used, location shifts caused a decline in yield of 0·06 tons. The authors concluded that inter-state shifts of location were unimportant as a factor affecting average yields, though they further concluded that re-location within the states accounted for a decline in wheat yield of 0·04 tons per hectare between 1900 and 1950.[41]

*Elasticity of Supply and Demand*[42]

The higher the price of a commodity, the less of it will normally be consumed; conversely, demand will rise with each successive reduction in price. Similarly, only the very efficient producers or those in very favourable locations will be able to make a profit when prices are low but if prices are high additional enterprises will be set up and established firms will expand their output. There is a unique point at which the schedules of potential total supply and potential total demand interesect and this point determines the price of the commodity in question. (In more sophisticated cases, there may be more than one point of equilibrium but this need not concern us.) If for any reason there is a change in the pattern of demand, the schedule of prices that people are willing to pay for particular quantities may rise or fall and the equilibrium level of production will either be elevated or depressed. The point of intersection of the supply and demand schedules will also change if the supply schedule should be altered.

The magnitude of change in production (or consumption)

associated with a given alteration of price is measured by the elasticity of supply (or demand). The concept of elasticity can as readily be explained with reference to production as to consumption. Suppose that wheat fetches £20 per ton and that at this price 1,000 tons is grown annually. If the price falls to £10 per ton, some producers may find that wheat is no longer a profitable crop and the output may fall to 800 tons per annum. Proportionately, the reduction in output is much less than the price fall and the output is said to be inelastic. If wheat production fell below 500 tons annually, the proportionate decline would be greater than the price abasement and production would be elastic. The elasticity of supply can be given a numerical value as the ratio between the proportionate changes in price and production. (The elasticity of demand is obtained similarly, as the ratio between relative price and consumption changes.) The average of the initial and final prices (or quantities) is taken as the base and the difference between this and the initial price (or quantity) is expressed as a proportion of the base value. The elasticity is the ratio of the two relatives. For example, if the price of wheat falls from £20 to £10 per ton and output declines from 1,000 tons the elasticities are calculated as follows:

|   | Wheat ouput tons | Proportionate change in output | | Proportionate change in price | | Elasticity |
|---|---|---|---|---|---|---|
| 1. | 800 | $\frac{100}{900}$ $(=0\cdot111)$ | ÷ | 5/15 | $(=0\cdot333)$ | 0·3 |
| 2. | 500 | $\frac{250}{750}$ $(=0\cdot333)$ | ÷ | 5/15 | $(=0\cdot333)$ | 1·0 |
| 3. | 400 | $\frac{300}{700}$ $(=0\cdot429)$ | ÷ | 5/15 | $(=0\cdot333)$ | 1·3 |

Any value above unity represents an elastic response of production, as in case 3; an inelastic response is indicated in the first case, where the elasticity is below one. Without entering into all the refinements of this concept, two points must be noted:

1. The elasticity of supply (or demand) measured in the above manner applies in principle only to an infinitely small

segment of the supply (or demand) curve and it will therefore normally vary from one part of the curve to another.

2. The short-term response may differ from the long-run change.

Some of the factors affecting demand are discussed in Chapter 6 and we may therefore concentrate on questions of supply. Changes in the production of any one commodity are affected by factors other than variations in its price and the price elasticity of output. It may be that the cost of production is also variable within quite wide limits, at least in the short run, due to:

1. Changes in the price of inputs such as fertilizers and labour.

2. Changes in the quantity of inputs used.

3. The deferment or advancement of capital investment and major maintenance.

Operating costs may fall or rise in concert with changes in the price of the final product, or in a varying relationship thereto, and hence the relevant concept of the elasticity of supply is given by the ratio of the proportionate production change to the proportionate change in the net revenue per unit of output. Rubber production in Malaya during the period 1929–33 provides an apt illustration of this relationship (Table 7).[43]

TABLE 7

MALAYA: rubber prices, production and costs, 1929–33, based on data from eight estates

|  | 1929 | 1930 | 1931 | 1932 | 1933 |
|---|---|---|---|---|---|
| Gross proceeds, pence per Kg. | 21·5 | 13·4 | 7·2 | 5·4 | 6·7 |
| Total cost, pence per Kg. | 12·9 | 11·4 | 7·2 | 5·2 | 5·4 |
| Index of output | 100 | 102 | 108 | 120 | 108 |
| Hectares in rubber | 32,040 | | | 33,164 | 33,121 |
| Index of daily wages | 100 | 80 | 70 | 56 | 60 |
| Hectares supervised by one European | 352 | | | 706 | 690 |

Source: P. T. Bauer, 'Rubber production costs during the great depression', Economic Journal, 1943, pp. 361–9.

The response of output to price changes is also affected by technical relationships in the production process. An extreme example is provided by the petroleum industry in which natural gas is obtained in large quantities as a by-product of oil extraction. Of the gas that is produced in association with oil, 32 per cent. is re-injected into the earth to maintain the underground pressure, so easing the process of winning the oil, 41 per cent. is used for various useful purposes and the remaining 27 per cent. is surplus.[44] As the supply of gas is conditioned by the output of oil, an increase on the low price for gas will call forth no increase in gas output from the oil wells (the output of fields which yield only gas, *e.g.* the Lacq region of France, may well respond to price changes). However, the use of pipelines and ocean tankers for the transport of natural gas is opening up a big market for it in the industrial regions of the world and demand is likely to continue to increase more rapidly than the supply. The time will come, therefore, when gas and oil may be regarded as true joint-products, comparable to the meat and wool that are obtained from sheep. The pricing of joint-products presents tricky problems in the allocation of costs between the goods in question, problems for which there is no complete solution, and consequently the concept of the price elasticity of supply of one of a pair of joint-products is unreal: the proper formulation is the elasticity of the joint supply with respect to changes in the joint price. This idea may be applied in a modified form to much agricultural production. In rotation farming, one crop—say clover or sugarbeet—may give a very low direct return but, by enhancing the fertility of the soil or by using resources which would otherwise be idle, increase the profits of the whole farm. A very small response to price changes may then be observable.

Where two or more products are alternatives to each other, the output of one may not change in response to a rise or fall in price if similar price variations have affected the other products. G. R. Allen thought that he had found a curious situation in Saskatchewan, Canada, where for the period 1914–34 a fall in wheat prices was associated, in the short run, with an increase in the area sown to wheat. It appears that this association was due to the fact that when wheat prices fell, the prices realized by the products that were alternatives to wheat fell by as much or even more.[45] In this case, the true measure of the elasticity of supply is the proportionate change in wheat output in relation to the proportionate change in the price of wheat relative to competing crops.[46]

In the great majority of cases, the response of output to relative price changes is 'normal', in the sense that a long-run higher price relative to other commodities will in time call forth an increase in production, and an abasement of the price will result in a diminished output (production techniques remaining constant). However, where the opportunities for other products are limited on account of the physical environment or social and technical conditions, and where the population is immobile and therefore does not migrate readily in response to changing economic circumstances, the relationship between price and output may be 'perverse'. An example is provided by the experience of the Lesser Antilles when the price of sugar on the London market during the last quarter of the nineteenth century fell from 7·1d. per kilogramme to 2·1d. and then, with the exception of the boom during the First World War, fell to 1·2d. in the early 1930s.

> Throughout the Lesser Antilles, the planters sought new crops to replace the hitherto dominant cane. . . . Those islands which could find alternative crops, adopted them. However, the planters of St. Kitts-Nevis, Antigua, and Barbados had such discouraging experiences with alternative crops that they again turned their attention to sugar.

These islands are characterized:

> by much level land, by low to moderate rainfall with frequent droughts, and by exposure to high winds. These conditions have discouraged or prohibited the growth of limes, cacao, bananas, nutmegs, and other crops which have replaced sugar eleswhere.[47]

The consequence has been a rise in sugar production in these three islands, using much improved techniques, while sugar output elsewhere has fallen substantially.

Close parallels have been reported in Nigeria. Palm kernels were not much used by the Africans in the 1930s but were exported in large quantities and, in some parts of the forest belt of the South, provided a substantial source of income to the farmers:

if a fall occurs in the price offered by the European firms, there is no immediate curtailment of the quantities offered for sale, but efforts may even be made to increase their volume so that the money income derived therefrom may be maintained at the same level.[48]

In contrast, the Nupe of the Middle Belt had developed a highly diversified cash-crop agriculture in which:

the adjustment of crops grown to fluctuations in their market prices appears, perhaps in consequence of the wider choice available and the great development of exchange, to be more flexible and deliberate than in the main ground-nut and cotton belts of northern Nigeria.[49]

The production of rubber provides another example of 'perverse' behaviour arising from institutional causes. For plantations specialized in rubber production, a fall in price may be associated with an increased output (Table 7) while peasant farmers who tap rubber as a supplementary source of income may respond in a 'normal' way to the same price change. During a period of low prices, the peasant producer may cease tapping his trees and devote himself to other occupations, which are not available to the plantation.[50] The response to price change may then vary geographically if land holding patterns differ from place to place.

*Conclusion*

In thinking about the location of any one firm, we may conceive of both the optimum location and the geographic limits within which the enterprise may be viable but earning lower profits than would be obtained at the optimum place. In a perfectly competitive economy, any deviation from the optimum would result in profits being less than 'normal' and this would not occur. With the various imperfections that do exist, there may be a wide range of possible locations yielding very similar results. Consequently, within the economic margin there is scope for many extraneous, non-economic, factors to affect the detailed siting of a plant. In such a case, the future profits may be less than could be obtained elsewhere.

But if a rational analysis of location is made, and if the same is done for various land users, conflicts of interest may arise if several optima coincide. These conflicts can be resolved by the application of three closely related ideas. The opportunities that are foregone in using any site for one purpose rather than another determines the power each use has to compete for the site in question. Hence, we have the concept of economic rent, which, in conjunction with the notion of transfer payments, explains the logic of geographic variations in the price of land. These geographic variations in the price of land are an important part of the mechanism for allocating land between various uses. Another part of the mechanism is provided by the doctrine of comparative advantage. From the comparative advantage argument, we can see that location and trade are two closely related aspects of the distribution of activities on the face of the earth. However, because goods are exchanged, the production of a commodity in any particular place is much affected by the terms on which trade will take place: one part of this wider issue is the response of production to changes in price. The idea of price elasticity is therefore another fundamental part of the conceptual framework.

Underlying the whole of this chapter is a single basic concept, namely, that the economy of the world or any constituent part tends toward a position of equilibrium. Although many dynamic changes have been mentioned, such as the growth of population and technical innovation, the mechanisms that have been discussed are all tending to restore a stable situation. In practice, of course, this is never achieved before some new disturbance is experienced. It has also been tacitly assumed throughout most of the discussion that the main problem, in a static situation which does not change in the short run, is: how are activities distributed among places on the earth's surface, i.e., how is a cake of fixed size divided? The next chapter explores some of the ways in which these ideas must be modified, for there is good evidence that in some respects the economic system is not tending toward equilibrium. In an era of rapid economic development, many of the more important, and difficult, problems are concerned with the geographic distribution of new activities (how and where does the cake increase in size) and these problems in dynamics are not necessarily answered by using concepts in statics applied to short periods of time.

## REFERENCES

1 A. Weber, 1957, *op. cit.*, (Chap. 2).

2 E. M. Hoover, 1948, *op. cit.*, (Chap. 2).

3 The reader interested in comparisons with the United States is referred to R. C. Estall and R. O. Buchanan, 1961, *op. cit.*, (Chap. 2).

4 National Institute of Economic and Social Research, 'The plastics industry; a comparative study of research and innovation', *Economic Review*, November 1963, p. 26.

5 G. Maxcy and A Silberston, *The Motor Industry*, 1959, p. 31.

6 The number of variables is further increased when the scale of output, volume of sales and price of product are also treated as variable factors.

7 S. B. Saul, 'The motor industry in Britain to 1914', *Business History*, December 1962, pp. 22–44.

8 G. Maxcy and A. Silberston, 1959, *op. cit.*, p. 13.

9 S. B. Saul, 1962, *op. cit.*, p. 25.

10 A. Nevins, *Ford: The Times, the Man, the Company*, 1954, p. 408.

11 E. M. Rawstron, 'The distribution and location of steam-driven power stations in Great Britain', *Geography*, 1951, pp. 249–62: 'Changes in the geography of electricity production in Great Britain', *Geography*, 1955, pp. 92–97. G. Manners, 'Some location principles of thermal electricity generation', *Journal of Industrial Economics*, 1962, pp. 218–30: 1964, *op. cit.*, (Chap. 2).

12 E. M. Rawstron, 'Three principles of industrial location', *Transactions and Papers*, Institute of British Geographers, 1958, pp. 135–42.

13 W. Smith, 'The location of industry', *Transactions and Papers*, Institute of British Geographers, 1955, pp. 1–18.

14 In Northern Ireland, grain represents 77·0 per cent. of the value of sales (Northern Ireland Development Council, *Fifth Report 1960–61*, Appendix). The equivalent proportion for the Spillers Group in the United Kingdom is 62·5.

15 For a fuller discussion, see: R. G. Lipsey, *An Introduction to Positive Economics*, 1963, pp. 299–303.

16 M. Chisholm, 1962, *op. cit.*, (Chap. 2), pp. 41–43.

17 The assumed conditions may be stated more rigorously as:
    1. Perfectly competitive circumstances prevail in the markets for the factors of production and the final goods. (This implies no costs of transfer.)
    2. Unit cost of production is invariable with scale of output.
    3. There is a fixed supply of the factors of production (labour, land and capital) in both countries.
    4. Techniques of production, consumer tastes, the efficiency of labour and the distribution of income among the factors of production do not change.

18 1·5 tons of cars for 1 ton of cork, at which Portugal reaps all the benefit. 0.666 tons of cars for 1 ton of cork, at which Britain reaps all the benefit.

19 O. E. Baker, 1925, *op. cit.*, (Chap. 2), p. 31.

20 For a general account of regional industrial specialization in one country couched in terms of comparative advantage, see: E. M. Rawstron, 'Industry', in J. W. Watson and J. B. Sissons (eds), *The British Isles: a Systematic Geography*, 1964, pp. 297–318. An analysis of the best kind of industry for a particular location is provided by W. Isard, *et al.*, *Industrial Complex Analysis and Regional Development*, 1959. An example of a single industry in many locations is provided by K. Warren, 'The Sheffield rail trade, 1861–1936: an episode in the locational history of the British steel industry', *Transactions and Papers*, Institute of British Geographers, June 1964, pp. 131–57. For an analysis that takes account of both variable location and form of development, see P. A. Stone, 'The economics of housing and urban development', *Journal*, Royal Statistical Society, 1959, pp. 417–76.

21 R. B. Andrews, 'Mechanics of the urban economic base', various articles, *Land Economics*, 1953–56. J. W. Alexander, 'The basic–nonbasic concept of urban economic functions', *Economic Geography*, 1954, pp. 246–61. C. T. Stewart, Jr., 'Economic base dynamics', *Land Economics*, 1959, pp. 327–36.

22 B. Ohlin, 1933, *op. cit.*, (Chap. 2).

23 V. Lutz, *Italy: a Study in Economic Development*, 1962.

24 G. M. Meier, *International Trade and Development*, 1963, Chapter 7.

25 E. M. Rawstron, 1958, *op. cit.*

26 M. B. Nicholson, 'Probability and economic decision taking', *Manchester School of Economic and Social Studies*, 1959, pp. 221–40.

27 D. Law, 'Industrial movement and locational advantage', *Manchester School of Economic and Social Studies*, 1964, p. 136.

28 The reader is referred to any of the standard textbooks on economics for a discussion of the theory of the firm. A simple theoretical discussion of the problem as it relates to the determination of scale economies is provided by R. G. Bressler, Jr., 'Research determination of economies of scale', *Journal of Farm Economics*, 1945, pp. 526–39. On the determination of agricultural margins, see L. E. Gibson, 'Characteristics of a regional margin of the corn and dairy belts', *Annals*, Association of American Geographers, 1948, pp. 244–70: R. O. Buchanan, 'Some reflections on agricultural geography', *Geography*, 1959, pp. 1–13.

29 Welsh Agricultural Land sub-Commission, *Mid-Wales Investigation*, Cmd. 9631, 1955.

30 T. Scitovsky, *Economic Theory and Western European Integration*, 2nd printing, 1962, p. 129.

31 *Modern Transport*, 9th May 1964.

32 See map in S. van Valkenburg and C C. Held, *Europe*, second edition, 1952, p. 102, reproduced in M. Chisholm, 1962, *op. cit.*, (Chap. 2), p. 108.

33 P. Hall, 1966, *op. cit.*, (Chap. 2), Introduction.

34 M. V. Edwards, 'Marginal aspects of modern British forestry', *Advancement of Science*, 1962, p. 340.

35  *The Times*, 18th September 1963.

36  W. E. Minchinton, *The British Tinplate Industry*, 1957, map facing p. 1.

37  M. Chisholm, 'Agricultural production, location and rent', *Oxford Economic Papers*, 1961, especially pp. 342–52. G. McCrone, *The Economics of Subsidising Agriculture*, 1962, pp. 30–42.

38  M. Chisholm, 1962, *op. cit.*, pp. 189–90. P. Hall, 1966, *op. cit.*, Introduction.

39  H. D. Vigor, 'The increased yield per acre of wheat in England considered in relation to the reduction of the area', *Journal*, Royal Statistical Society, New Series, 1910, pp. 396–402.

40  L. Moore, 'The effect of changes in crop acreage on yield', *Farm Economist*, 1960, pp. 383–85.

41  D. G. Johnson and R. L. Gustafson, *Grain Yields and the American Food Supply*, 1962, especially pp. 20–22.

42  R. G. Lipsey, 1963, *op. cit.*, pp. 80–98, has a good account of the concept of elasticity.

43  See also: K. O. Campbell, 'The inelasticity of supply of wool', *Economic Record*, 1955, pp. 311–18.

44  C. Issawi and M. Yeganeh, *The Economics of Middle Eastern Oil*, 1962, p. 11. The data refer to 1959–60 and represent the average of the Middle East producers plus Algeria, Venezuela and the United States.

45  G. R. Allen, 'Wheat farmers and falling prices', *Farm Economist*, 1954, pp. 335–41. For discussion, see *Economic Journal*, 1956, pp. 271–87 and 1957, p. 144.

46  M. J. Brennan, 'Changes in cotton acreage in the southeast—implication for supply functions', *Journal of Farm Economics*, 1958, pp. 835–44. R. M. Stern, 'The price responsiveness of primary producers', *Review of Economics and Statistics*, 1962, pp. 202–07.

47  O. P. Starkey, 'Declining sugar prices and land utilization in the British Lesser Antilles', *Economic Geography*, 1942, pp. 210 and 212.

48  D. Forde and R. Scott, *The Native Economies of Nigeria*, 1946, p. 232.

49  *Idem.*, p. 183.

50  E. W. Zimmermann, *World Resources and Industries*, 1951, p. 394.

# CHAPTER 4

# Scale and Variability

By the law of diminishing returns (p. 48), each additional unit of input yields a smaller increment of output than the previous one until the point is reached that the marginal cost equals the marginal revenue. This point represents an equilibrium situation in which an individual or a firm maximizes net income. The principle operates with respect to additional dressings of fertilizers, to extra storeys on blocks of flats, to increases in the depth of oil and water wells and to a whole host of phenomena. Implicitly, it provides the basis for the notion of equilibrium, in the sense that any force will generate its own countervailing reaction. There is a close parallel with the Newtonian law of dynamics, that for every action there is an equal but opposite reaction.

However, there are important circumstances in which the law of diminishing returns does not operate, where an increase in inputs results in a proportionately greater increment to production; increasing returns are then said to obtain. Figure 3 (p. 72), illustrates the matter in a simple way. The law of diminishing returns is represented for each of three firms, A, B and C, by that part of the output-unit cost curve which lies to the right of the respective nadirs (a, b and c), for on this section of each curve an increase in output causes unit cost to rise. But over the range of outputs to the left of the nadirs, unit cost falls with an expansion of production. Although diminishing returns operate eventually, over a considerable range of experience the reverse situation occurs, giving marked economies of scale.

Economies of scale may be considered in relation to the individual plant, the firm or the industry as a whole.[1] They may also be conceived as occurring internally within a plant (factory, farm, etc.), firm or industry, or externally.

The precise distinction between these two forms of scale

economy is best deferred until p. 76 and meantime the account can most usefully begin with scale economies internal to a plant and then proceed to external economies as they relate to plants, firms and industries.

## Optimum Scale

Some discussion is first needed of the idea of an optimum level of output or scale of production. The optimum level of production may be defined in either of two ways: first, as the output at which profits are maximized; second, as that level of production which gives the lowest average unit cost. As E. A. G. Robinson has pointed out,[2] the scale of output which maximizes profit may be affected by elements of monopoly or other imperfections in the economy. For this reason, it is preferable to consider the optimum output as that which minimizes the average unit cost of production, in which case the optimum scale of output is determined essentially though not entirely by technical considerations. By adopting this approach, one deliberately ignores the fact that in the real world a location decision involves an assessment of manufacturing and marketing costs in relation to the size of available market and the price that can be charged. As has already been stated (p. 32), the scale of plant and choice of location are mutually interdependent variables in an economy which is imperfectly competitive. Only in conditions of perfect competition is it conceivable that the optimum location and scale of plant (firm or industry) would be obtained automatically. Thus, whereas previously location has been discussed without reference to the scale of output, we shall now renounce any consideration of location as it affects the size of units.

## Internal Economies of Scale in the Plant

The reader who wants a full treatment of the reasons why large-scale production may be cheaper than the output of small plants or firms is referred to the work of Robinson,[3] for only a brief summary can be included here. Any process of manufacture or the provision of a service can be divided into a large number of sub-processes or stages. This can be seen vividly on a visit to any motor-car assembly plant, where each worker has a quite specific and limited task to perform. As a natural result, workers acquire dexterity and can therefore comfortably achieve many times the output of a novice. The division of labour confers two secondary advantages. If a worker concentrates on only one job, then it is unnecessary for him to waste time transferring from one bench or machine to another to perform a succession of tasks. Furthermore, it becomes possible and economic to devise equipment that will perform the individually specialized operations: for example, in a dairy there are machines for washing and sterilizing the bottles before other ones fill them with milk and place the cap in position. Such aids may of course be very simple, as in the case of electric drills for tightening bolts in the assembly of cars, or highly elaborate, as the rolling mills used for converting incandescent steel into bars or strips.

The production capacity of a machine, or of a worker with mechanical aids, performing specialist operations is much greater than that of a worker who does many jobs with simple tools: the multiplication of workers and machines is necessary so that each task may be done by specialist equipment. But this in itself produces some serious problems because the skill of engineers has not been sufficient to ensure that all machines in a sequence of production have the same capacity. In car manufacture, it appears that scale economies on the assembly line are exhausted at about 100,000 units per annum, whereas a line for the manufacture of cylinder blocks will still yield economies up to 400,000 units annually and in the press shop the optimum is not reached until production is running at 1,000,000 units each year.[4] Thus, the optimum combination of these three processes would be two press shops, five cylinder block lines and twenty assembly lines turning out some 2,000,000 units annually. Economies of scale are exhausted for some operations earlier than for others and these will therefore be duplicated, perhaps many times over, with the overall economies that can be obtained being conditioned by one or two key processes.

In addition to the above economies of manufacture within an individual plant, large size may confer other benefits. The manager of a small works is likely to be a jack-of-all-trades and he may be master of only one or two. An expansion of the business would enable him to employ an accountant, production manager or personnel officer, and the efficiency of the administration could thereby be increased. The bigger a firm is, the more credit-worthy it is likely to be and therefore the more readily may finance be available, possibly at advantageous rates. In the marketing of its products, a large plant may obtain favourable transport terms and be able to spread the cost of advertisement and promotion. Likewise, bulk buying of materials may yield discounts owing to the suppliers' lower unit cost of handling. Finally, in an age that is increasingly based upon scientific discoveries and the application of technical developments, a small organization may be unable to afford laboratories and research equipment whereas a larger one may reap many benefits from such facilities.

Exactly the same arguments apply to firms comprising several plants. It is quite common for economies in the actual manufacturing processes to be exhausted before managerial, sales and research economies have been fully exploited. Thus, it is quite usual for a firm to have two or more manufacturing plants, even though similar or identical goods may be made in each plant: petroleum companies in the United Kingdom, particularly Shell and B.P., have several refineries scattered round the coast. With the oil refineries in Britain, the factor that limits the size of the installations is not the exhaustion of scale economies in refining but the cost of distributing the refined products. To concentrate the output into fewer plants would yield further processing economies but, evidently in the estimation of the companies, these would be more than off-set by the greater costs of the longer distribution hauls and other disadvantages. In this case, as in others, the limit of scale economies is set by diminishing returns and we are apparently back to a situation of equilibrium.

Two things modify this conclusion: the range within which scale economies operate may not always be so limited and therefore may not be readily exhausted, and technical and economic change may mean that a new and larger optimum scale is called into being before expansion up to the old optimum has occurred. This can be illustrated by the recent history of gas manufacture in Great Britain. Before the last World War, the unit cost of manufacturing and distributing gas made from coal varied from about £283–£309 per 50,000 cubic metres of gas in undertakings with an output exceeding 28 million cubic metres annually to £381–£486 in those making 1·4 million cubic metres or less.[5] The majority of the smaller works were located in comparatively small towns and expansion thereof would have meant laying pipelines across considerable tracts of countryside. At that time, the extra cost incurred in so doing, allied to the varied ownership of the plants, effectively prevented the economies of scale in manufacture from being more fully exploited. With the post-war nationalization and improvements in the manufacture of steel pipes for high-pressure transmission, the laying of regional gas grids became an economic proposition and was pressed ahead vigorously. As a consequence, nearly 500 of the 1,050 gas works in Great Britain nationalized in 1949 had been closed eight years later;[6] by 1962, the number of active plants had fallen to under 360. During the early 1960s, the bulk import of liquid methane from oil and gas fields overseas began and Imperial Chemical Industries, Ltd., succeeded in developing a new process for making town gas from the light by-products of oil refining by a process known as steam-naptha reforming. These and other more recent developments are likely to bring the number of gas plants in the country down to a comparative handful in the foreseeable future, each one of huge capacity.

The reader will recognize that similar considerations apply to the electricity supply industry, which has already been referred to (p. 34), the manufacture of steel, cement and motor vehicles and the refining of crude petroleum, to name only a few of the major manufacturing industries of the world. The recognition of scale economies and the measurement of their magnitude does, however, present grave problems of definition, comparability of circumstances and the adequacy of statistics. For this reason, reliable estimates can be made only for the comparatively few industries whose products are similar, either between firms at any one time or over a run of years.[7]

In the British gas industry, economies of scale have been associated in recent years with a rapid decline in the number of plants. The reason for this is that demand has until recently been fairly stable and fewer but larger works have been substituted for many small ones to produce roughly the same total amount of gas. Were the demand for gas to have been rising, as now has begun to be the case, the reduction in the total number of plants would have been less, as some of the smaller units which have in fact been closed would have been enlarged or replaced by additional new works. In the event of a very rapid increase in consumption, larger producing units would be associated with a constant or increasing number of works. Great Britain's electricity generating capacity showed an increase in the number of stations to a maximum of 500 in 1929, whereafter a fairly continuous decline occurred until 1949, when the number stood at 331: during this period, scale economies outpaced the growth in demand. Between 1949 and 1962, the supply of electricity trebled but the total number of stations in use fluctuated around the 330 mark.

Looking at the world as a whole, the number of works in most industries is expanding as population and incomes grow, even though individual plants may be becoming larger. Thus, whether or not economies of scale are associated with a reduction in the number of plants depends upon the relationship between (i) the rate of growth in consumption and (ii) the rate of technical change leading to scale economies in manufacturing or processing.

When considering changes over time in the size of plants associated with economies of scale, two kinds of shift must be clearly distinguished. The first may be illustrated by reference to Figure 3, in which curves A, B and C represent the average unit production costs for three firms making some standard commodity, X. Owing to the variable circumstances in which each firm finds itself—the age of its equipment, cost of supplies, size of available market, skill of its workers, etc.—the cost-curves are not identical. For each firm, there is an optimum level of output up to which expansion is profitable owing to the operation of increasing returns but beyond which diseconomies outweigh any further savings from a larger scale of working. For each firm, therefore, scale economies consist in moving *along* the cost curve to the optimum point. If we are interested in the industry as a whole, we may imagine a line just enclosing the individual curves, shown by the pecked line in the diagram.[8] For the industry as a whole, economies will be gained if firms shift *from* curves such as those represented by

F

A to ones signified by C. Such a shift will normally imply the adoption of more elaborate machinery and processes, the further mechanization of processes, the use of different labour skills and other changes in the production-function. The British gas industry is an example of shifts from one production-function to another; hypothetically, three obsolete plants represented by A in the figure can be replaced by one modern plant, C, to give the same output at lower unit costs.

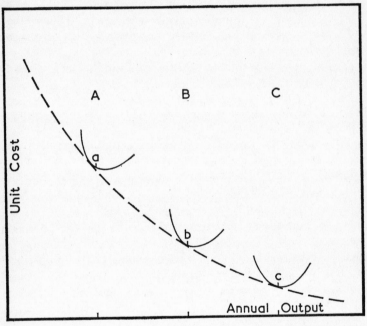

Figure 3.   Unit cost of production in relation to scale of productive unit

Some kinds of process lend themselves much more readily than do others to standardization and mass-production. Scale economies are much more evident in brewing than in butchery, in paper than in patisserie manufacture. There is therefore a spectrum of industries ranging from those in which scale economies internal to the plant are negligible to those in which they dominate the cost structure.

If scale economies are considerable and are widespread among all types of industry, one would expect there to be clear evidence in the increasing size of factories. In practice, the interpretation of the available statistics has stimulated a fierce controversy that has left the whole topic in a somewhat confused state.[9] Confusion has arisen from the problem of choosing a criterion for measuring size and from the difficulty of interpreting the findings. Size of factory can be measured in terms either of employees or of output and the two do not necessarily give the same picture, especially for comparisons over time. For example, in the period 1946 to 1959, the Billingham plant of Imperial Chemical Industries, Ltd., doubled the value of its output while reducing its labour force from 15,000 to 14,800.[10] The most readily obtainable data refer to employment and this is probably the most useful criterion to use for geographic purposes. Changes in the national average size of plant are affected by:

1. Changes in the size of plant in individual industries.

2. Changes in the proportion of industries with different sizes of factory.

From the available evidence, it appears that in terms of employment the average size of factory is increasing only slowly in a number of industrially advanced nations. Great Britain is somewhat exceptional in having a marked increase in the average size over recent decades; details are shown in Table 8.

TABLE 8

GREAT BRITAIN, 1935–61: the percentage distribution of employees in manufacturing industries, in establishments employing more than ten persons

| SIZE-GROUP OF ESTABLISHMENT | PERCENTAGE OF TOTAL EMPLOYEES | | | | | | |
|---|---|---|---|---|---|---|---|
| | 1935 | 1947 | 1949 | 1952 | 1955 | 1959 | 1961 |
| 11–24 | 5·4 | 4·0 | 4·2 | 4·2 | 3·4 | 3·3 | 2·7 |
| 25–49 | 8·5 | 6·9 | 7·2 | 7·2 | 6·6 | 6·7 | 6·4 |
| 50–99 | 11·7 | 10·5 | 10·2 | 10·2 | 9·7 | 10·5 | 11·0 |
| 100–249 | } 39·0 { 18·7 | 18·1 | 18·0 | 17·3 | 17·4 | 16·4 |
| 250–499 | 15·6 | 15·9 | 15·4 | 15·0 | 14·8 | 14·8 |
| 500–999 | 13·9 | 13·9 | 14·2 | 14·1 | 14·6 | 13·5 | 14·2 |
| 1,000–1,999 | } 21·5 { 12·3 | 11·8 | 11·9 | 12·8 | 13·2 | 13·2 |
| 2,000–4,999 | 11·4 | 11·7 | 11·5 | 12·3 | 12·4 | 12·6 |
| 5,000 and over | 6·7 | 6·7 | 7·5 | 8·3 | 8·2 | 8·7 |
| | 100·0 | 100·0 | 100·0 | 100·0 | 100·0 | 100·0 | 100·0 |

Sources: Ministry of Labour *Gazette* and *Annual Abstract of Statistics*.

In this country, the increase in size is general to all major industry classes other than textiles and coal mining, in both of which technical advance has resulted in a declining number of employees per plant. It is probable that in other countries the size of plant in most industries is growing but that the industries in which smaller plants predominate are increasing their total employment rapidly enough to cause the change in over-all average to be small.

Economies of scale may be realized either by an increase in the size of a plant carrying out all the processes or by the sub-contracting of jobs to specialist factories. In the latter case, scale economies are realized for individual processes without being apparent in the size of factories as measured either by employees or by output. This point is demonstrated by the following table.

TABLE 9[11]

UNITED STATES, 1947: manufacture of motor vehicles and parts

| | All companies | Vehicle assembling companies | Other companies (components) |
|---|---|---|---|
| Number of companies | 779 | 8 | 771 |
| Number of plants | 963 | 130 | 833 |
| Value added by manufacture ($m.) | 3,577 | 2,150 | 1,427 |
| Value added per plant ($m.) | 3·71 | 16·5 | 1·61 |
| Value added per company ($m.) | 4·59 | 268·7 | 1·85 |

Scale economies may thus cause two seemingly contrary tendencies to occur simultaneously. Individual plants may become larger, as has happened with steel works, refineries and assembly shops, for example. Such growth is checked by the habit of sub-contracting specialist jobs to component suppliers who may individually be quite small. The geographic interest of this situation may be explored in several directions. The geographic literature abounds with descriptions and analyses of the localization of industry, in which an attempt is made to assess the extent of and reason for the concentration of diamond working in Amsterdam, the clothing trades of New York and London and the steel trades of the Ruhr, for example. The quantitative techniques of description mostly stem from the work of P. S. Florence,[12] who devised indices based upon the proportion of the employment in industry A in an area X in relation either to the proportion of total employment in area X or to total employment in industry A in the whole country. In this way, it is possible to describe any area as highly specialized or not, and any industry as highly localized or not, in relation to the regional or national economy. The technique may be applied to data on the value of output (either gross or net) but in practice employment returns have been used more widely. This form of description and the less sophisticated ones that are more common ignore the possibility that two industries with similar degrees of apparent geographic concentration may be composed of units differing greatly in size. The extent to which any given degree of localization or specialization arises from one plant employing 10,000, ten plants each of 1,000 or one hundred plants each of 100 employees has very important economic, social and geographic implications.

Size as such tends to be treated as one factor that influences the siting of works, since the availability of adequate flat land, water supplies, harbour facilities, etc., restricts the range of choice in siting for large plants compared with the options available for diminutive ones. But there are other important aspects of the matter that are often overlooked. A factory employing 10,000 workers directly supports some 20,000 persons: taking account of the necessary service trades of retailing, schooling, entertainment, etc., the total population supported by the one works is likely to be 40,000.[13] In effect, a town of that size could be a one-industry, one-*plant* settlement whose whole prosperity would depend on the one major employer. This situation exists at Corby, Northamptonshire, where Stewart and Lloyd (steel tubes) employ 75 per cent. of the male labour force, and at Hatfield, Hertfordshire, where a similar proportion of the workers depends upon De Havilland's aircraft plants. The modern situation of a town whose employment is dominated by a single firm has strong parallels in history: sorely distressed by the condition of the 2,000 workers who depended on his cotton mills at New Lanark, Robert Owen set about social reform during the Napoleonic Wars; the workshops of railway companies were for long the main employers in Swindon, Didcot, Ashford (Kent) and elsewhere, while some Scottish whisky distillers also built settlements for their workers before Bourneville and Port Sunlight were thought of. Unless the employment of a town is to be dominated by a single works, a big plant must be located in a large centre of population or else workers will be obliged to commute considerable distances. Changes in the size of manufacturing unit therefore have important implications for the size of communities, the range of employment opportunities therein and the geographic extent of commuting.

Internal economies of scale thus have a close bearing on the number of plants in an industry and hence on the geographic pattern of its distribution. Furthermore, the size of individual works intimately affects the life of the employees as one factor determining the complex inter-relationships of community size, journey to work, range of job opportunities and the stability of income in the community.

## External Economies of Scale

The concept of external economies has in recent years caught the imagination of many economists, primarily because it seems to provide an important mechanism to explain the processes of economic growth. The result has been a copious flow of articles and books that either discuss the nature of the concept or press it into service in various guises. The account that follows is based very largely on a summary of the arguments published by H. W. Arndt.[14]

If we consider any one industry, say the manufacture of refrigerators, an increase in capacity may be occasioned by an expansion in demand. (The new capacity may result from the expansion of one of the existing firms or the entrance of a new one.) Hitherto, all manufacturers have made a particular component themselves but with the advent of the new manufacturing capacity it becomes worthwhile for all the firms to subcontract to a specialist for the supply of motors, switchgear or whatever it may be. In this way, all the firms gain and for the industry as a whole the saving is said to be internal; but for each constituent firm, the saving results from external causes. The distinction between internal and external economies therefore depends entirely upon the viewpoint adopted.

Similarly, economies may arise for any or all firms if demand anywhere in the economic systems rises. Arndt illustrates the point in terms of potatoes and fertilizers: if the use of potatoes increases, an expansion of potato cropping will enhance the use of fertilizers and this may make cheaper fertilizer production possible. Scale economies in fertilizer manufacture have not been fully realized hitherto: resources will therefore be released, providing a stimulus to consumption elsewhere in the economy.

Finally, external economies arise from the provision of facilities or the better use of what exists. This is particularly evident in the case of transport and services such as electricity, water supply and sewerage: but the principle applies with equal, though perhaps less evident, force to education, entertainment, banking and insurance, etc. A diverse range of activities will all benefit from the fact that other firms are in the vicinity using these facilities in common; the absence of these other firms would render uneconomic the provision of the physical and social 'infrastructure' upon which each depends. The regional existence or otherwise of technical colleges and training facilities is a material factor in the location of businesses within the United Kingdom.

As with internal economies of scale, two kinds of shift in external economies must be recognized: movements along the regional production-function and shifts from one function to another. The latter is undoubtedly the more important and has strong repercussions upon the relative rates of growth of regions, for often new developments—of manufacturing techniques, transport, education, financial institutions, etc.—are applied first in those areas which already are the more advanced, thereby temporarily but successively enhancing their advantages. There are three reasons why this should be so.

## Source of Innovation

The first is that an area or country that is technically advanced is more likely to be the source of innovations than is a less fortunate part of the world. This will result from the stimulus of felt needs, the possibilities for original work conferred by the available resources of libraries, laboratories and learned societies and by the generally high standard of education and technical accomplishments. New techniques cannot in any case spread overnight and the progress of diffusion is often impeded by the poverty of communication and downright jealousy, which in modern times is protected by patent rights. It was at Coalbrookdale in 1709 that Abraham Darby first successfully smelted iron with coke made from coal and in the immediately succeeding years—

> knowledge of the process appears to have spread only within the circle of Darby's relatives and personal friends. . . . It appears probable, indeed, that until about the middle of the century the process was confined to Shropshire and the adjoining district of Bersham. . . . The setting up in 1760 of the great works at Carron, and of the large furnace at Seaton, near Workington, formed an outstanding advertisement for the new process, and after this time it was rapidly adopted at works in Staffordshire, South Yorkshire, Northumberland, and elsewhere.[15]

Nevertheless, as late as 1806 there were still eleven charcoal furnaces operating in Great Britain, compared with 162 coke furnaces;[16] the spread of the new technique was barely completed inside a century *within* one country, which was then the most advanced industrial nation in the world. Europe did not get its first coke furnace until the 1790s and as late as 1850 over half the iron made in Western Europe was smelted with charcoal; one charcoal furnace survived at Ria, in the Pyrenees, until 1914.[17] Charcoal iron is still made in some parts of the world, India for example.[18]

With the spread of literacy and general education and improvements in the means of personal communication, the diffusion of technical knowledge can now occur much more rapidly than formerly. In an interesting study of the tinplate industry, W. E. Minchinton observed that:

> Three methods of diffusion have been of importance. Knowledge of the methods employed have (*sic*) been transferred from one country to another by travellers' reports, by the migration of skilled workers, and by the export of machinery. . . . In practice, of course, no such sharp differentiation existed between the methods used—in the earlier periods industrial spying was often the essential preliminary to the migration of skilled workers while

today the reports of experts often precede the placing of orders for equipment from foreign countries and assistance from skilled foreign workers is usually required at first— but for analytical purposes the distinction can be validly made.[19]

The sale of equipment, licences and technical knowledge in the twentieth century means that techniques can spread around the world with considerable expedition.

However, too much must not be made of the trend toward quicker diffusion. During the earlier part of the industrial revolution, the place at which an invention occurred was not necessarily the locality in which it was first exploited. For example,

> The cotton industry began in the East Midlands with the arrival in Nottingham of James Hargreaves and Richard Arkwright in 1768, after the destruction of Hargreaves' spinning machine in Lancashire. The spinning jenny and Arkwright's roller spinning machine represented the culmination of many attempts to produce machinery to supply the rapidly increasing demand for cotton yarn, and Nottingham thus became the cradle of the two most important inventions in cotton-spinning machinery at that time.[20]

For a few halcyon years, Derbyshire–Nottinghamshire rivalled Lancashire as the chief cotton spinning region of Great Britain. Conversely, one may observe that commercial and military secrecy are not a prerogative only of former times and that consequently spying is not a quaint pastime only of people less civilized than ourselves. The transfer of technical, and especially military, knowledge between the western alliance and the communist world has been severely restricted since the last World War; likewise, within each bloc the transfer of techniques has been impeded—the French programme of nuclear research is being conducted parallel to the British and American work in the same field. In civil affairs, too, patents can be used to restrict access to innovations and limit their spread.

If an industry experiences a phase of rapid innovation, new techniques and equipment may be available long before existing plant has finished its useful life. The new methods may not then be adopted first in the main established centres of the industry owing to the reluctance of factory owners to scrap what is obsolete but working. This appears to have been one of the reasons for the shift of the cotton industry from New England to the southeast of the United States during and since the end of the last century. The owners of the southern mills installed the latest designs of equipment in their new factories while in the north old machinery was dispensed with only reluctantly. The result was that unit costs of manufacture were lower in the south than in the north.[21]

## The Demand for Innovation and the Capacity to Supply

Even where knowledge is freely available, it takes time for new techniques to spread owing to the time and cost of providing the necessary equipment and the fact that obsolete gear may still have many years of useful life after being fully depreciated. This factor of time is apparent in the provision of transport facilities, fuel supplies, telephone communications, water and sewerage, for these represent major civil engineering projects that are greedy of resources.

Given that resources are limited and that therefore the spread of an innovation takes time, the normal pattern is for the new technique to be applied first where the demand for it is greatest and where, therefore, the return on the investment will be the highest. This generally means that those areas which are already more developed tend to be the centres from which diffusion takes place. In a summary form, S. Godlund has shown this for the evolution of the railway network in Western Europe.[22] The repetition of the sequence can be clearly seen in the history of transport development in Britain,[23] particularly in the way that the distribution of motorways in use or planned five years after the first long stretch was opened in 1959 repeats the pattern of the railways fifteen years after the railway era began in 1825.[24] The broad outlines are strikingly similar and the differences of detail can readily be explained. For example, in South Wales and Co. Durham, the railway network was unusually dense to cater for the local iron industries and the export of coal. On the other hand, the absence of a motorway link between the north-east and the Midlands is explained by the improvement of the A1 road almost to motorway standards.

The provision of successive transport media may thus

confer important cumulative advantages on certain regions within a country. To some extent, this is also true *between* nations, for, compared with France or Western Germany, a country like Nigeria has only a skeletal system of all-weather roads. Economists have been very concerned about the provision of transport and other facilities in the less developed parts of the world as a pre-condition of and stimulus to economic development: but it is now being realized that a much wider view must be taken, for the skill and knowledge of the populace and the attitudes they adopt are probably far more important factors. All over the world, development programmes are hindered by the inadequacy of educational achievement, suspicion of new techniques, curious ideas of honesty and other social impediments. The difficulties that are thus created are liable to deter firms from investing in the less developed regions and hinder the operations of those that are established by expatriate or indigenous enterprise. There is thus a fundamental external economy in the quality of the labour force and the efficiency with which all institutions work. The trouble is that the acquisition of education, efficiency, etc., takes time and, further, that the standard in one place is only relative to standards elsewhere, which are constantly improving. It has taken Japan nearly one hundred years of sustained effort to transform herself from a 'medieval' society into a modern nation that is becoming accepted as one of the foremost industrial states with her own fund of invention and innovation. Even Russia, with a long history of contacts with Western Europe, much greater resources than Japan and a higher relative plane of development at the time of the revolution in 1917, is only now beginning to feel a reasonable equality with America and the 'free' world in her standard of development.[25]

## Private versus Social Return

Two kinds of demand may be distinguished, that which is 'effective' and that which is merely 'potential'. A hungry but penniless man has a potential demand for food that will remain unrealized for want of the money or other means to convert his desire into an effective demand. During the terrible famine experienced by Ireland in the 1840s, thousands of people died from hunger and disease while some foodstuffs were being exported from the island and Parliament at Westminster, pledged to Free Trade, vainly expected private merchants to supply the people's wants by normal trade. The purblind English government ignored what the merchants knew: the peasantry had not got the wherewithal.[26] Exactly the same principle applies in many spheres. For example, the construction of communications or the provision of electricity in underdeveloped regions may not be attractive to private enterprise because profits will be low, at least in the comparatively short run, even though eventually enormous benefits to the populace will be the result.

When a private individual or firm builds a factory or a road or engages in any of a very wide range of activities, a private cost is incurred, for which some compensating reward is expected. It used to be assumed that society as a whole would be richest (in the widest sense, including welfare and money income) if each individual sought to maximize his own welfare. We can see how false this is by considering smoke control in major cities. For the individual, the cheapest form of space heating is often raw coal, but this fuel emits into the air noxious gases and solid matter. In cities like Pittsburgh, London and Osaka, the result of the uncontrolled use of fuels has been a severely polluted atmosphere which, in particular meteorological conditions, can hasten the death of many persons whose respiratory system is weak, as well as causing much continuing damage to buildings, clothing and vegetation. The long-term collective or social welfare will be enhanced by controlling the use of the offending fuels but this will mean an increased private outlay because the less damaging fuels and other means of smoke abatement are costly.[27]

The fact that private and social costs and benefits do not always or even generally coincide provides an important clue to one of the apparent paradoxes of regional development. The less developed areas of the world are short of capital of all kinds and interest rates tend, therefore, to be higher than elsewhere, 'sometimes double comparable rates in advanced countries'.[28] However, the wages of labour are often much less than half those paid in the more advanced nations. The effect of scarcity on the price of capital is much less marked than is the consequence of excess supply for the remuneration of labour.

Much of the reason for this lies in the earning power of capital invested in the less developed countries; the private return is often comparatively low because the utility of any one investment is greatly affected by the lack of complementary facilities such as communications, education, electricity and commercial institutions. Although the long-term benefit to the society may be very great, the short-term advantages to the businessman may not be especially attractive. Owing to the existence of external economies in the more advanced parts of the world, the private return on capital invested there is often greater than in the less developed countries, at least for the comparatively short period of time that is considered for private investment. Consequently, the geographic disparities of development are apt to increase rather than diminish.[29]

Two kinds of remedy are available. The first is the deliberate effort of governments to re-distribute resources, from the richer to the poorer nations through international agreements and from the richer regions within countries to the poorer ones by means of subsidies, controls over industrial location, etc. (Chapter 8). The second is to allow, or actively to encourage, the operation of the 'deglomerating' forces that arise as the geographic concentration of population proceeds. The concentration of population leads to increasing scarcity, of land on which to build, of space for vehicles to move and park, of water supplies and fresh air, etc., and these scarcities ought to be reflected in rising prices.

## The Magnitude of External Economies

Either or both of these approaches requires some understanding of the magnitude and geographic extent of external economies and diseconomies. What is the minimum size and population density of a region and the level of development that will confer external economies, how great are these and at what point do diseconomies begin to outweigh the advantages of further development? The short answer is that we do not know. An important reason for this ignorance is that the conceptual and statistical problems are formidable in the extreme, not least owing to the probability that the minima and maxima are both becoming larger over time at a comparatively rapid pace. The concept of external economies provides a plausible explanation of the world-wide tendency for urban populations to be agglomerated in relatively small areas, for these areas to attract a disproportionate share of population growth and for the more advanced areas to grow richer more quickly than the poorer. However, we cannot assume that this is the explanation without a much closer examination of the mechanics of growth than has yet been made.[30]

Nevertheless, some fragmentary work has been done that illustrates the nature and magnitude of external economies. The annual expenditure per head of population on rate fund services (education, parks, libraries, etc.) for the eighty-three county boroughs in England and Wales has been examined for the period 1930–31/1936–37: the results are summarized in the following table.[31] The cost per person fell as the county borough became bigger until the optimum was reached at between 100,000 and 150,000, whereafter the average cost rose. K. S. Lomax examined the individual heads of expenditure for each year and tested the data for correlations with the wealth or poverty of the cities and the quality and quantity of services provided, and concluded 'that expenditure per head is a function, primarily, of population'. Each inhabitant therefore enjoyed an external economy from an increase of population up to 100–150,000 and thereafter an external diseconomy from greater size.

TABLE 10

ENGLAND AND WALES, 1930–31/1936–37: annual expenditure per head of population on rate fund services, eighty-three county boroughs

| Size-group 000 | Average population 000 | Average expenditure per head £ |
|---|---|---|
| 75 and less | 60 | 8·16 |
| 75–100 | 89 | 8·02 |
| 100–150 | 126 | 7·91 |
| 150–300 | 229 | 8·41 |
| 300 and over | 621 | 9·84 |

A second example is provided by the collection of milk from farms in England and Wales in 1956–57. The Milk Marketing Board organizes the off-farm collection, each farm being allocated to a particular transport contractor who collects the milk daily and delivers it to the local depot for pasteurizing and onward delivery to the consuming centres (or for manufacture). The contractors' operations are costed annually by the Board and payment is based on these costings. The records of 384 contractors have been analyzed to discover what factors influenced the average cost per litre of milk collected and it was found that approximately 84·5 per cent. of the variation in average cost could be 'explained' by three variables:

1. The quantity of milk collected per vehicle kilometre.
2. The quantity of milk collected per farm.
3. The distance annually run by the vehicles.

With the last two variables held constant, the effect of the first, quantity of milk collected per vehicle kilometre, is shown in Table 11. The implications of this table may be seen by referring to those contractors collecting 9·1 million litres or more annually. A particular collection route may pass very few dairy farms and yield only 14 litres of milk for each kilometre run by the lorry, in which case each litre cost 0·832d. to collect. If the dairy farmers doubled their output, or if the number of dairy producers increased so that 28 litres were collected per vehicle kilometre, the cost of collection would fall to 0·369d. per litre. Each successive increase in the quantity collected per vehicle kilometre would yield a further, though proportionately declining, economy of collection. In principle, therefore, each farmer would enjoy an external economy from an increase in the total amount of milk collected along a

TABLE 11

ENGLAND AND WALES, 1956–57: computed costs of milk collection from farms in pence per litre

| Litres collected per vehicle kilometre | Contractors collecting | |
|---|---|---|
| | over 9·1m. litres p.a. | 2·2–9·1m. litres p.a. |
| 14 | 0·832 | 0·840 |
| 28 | 0·369 | 0·371 |
| 42 | 0·247 | 0·248 |
| 56 | 0·194 | 0·195 |
| 71 | 0·165 | 0·166 |
| 85 | 0·148 | 0·148 |
| 113 | 0·128 | 0·128 |
| 141 | 0·117 | 0·117 |

contractor's route, though in practice such savings are garnered by the Milk Marketing Board in the first instance and are averaged among all the producers.[32]

The two examples that have been cited above should be regarded as illustrations of the principle of external economies rather than as providing any basis for generalizing about their magnitude and the range of conditions over which they operate.

*Scale Economies and Industrial Localization*

Scale economies may be manifested by the agglomeration of unlike or like (and related) enterprises: London has a diverse range of industries that are unrelated to each other except by the common use of facilities such as transport and insurance; nevertheless, within London there are strongly localized industries such as clothing and furniture that depend upon close links between the constituent firms.[33] Thus, the effect of scale economies upon the localization of a particular industry may be manifested in (i) the existence of a few very large works, or (ii) the regional concentration of small or medium-sized firms each of which is specialized on a limited range of processes.

This latter phenomenon probably was important in the emergence of Lancashire as the pre-eminent cotton manufacturing region of the United Kingdom. It has already been argued (pp. 20–3) that Lancashire had little natural advantage for cotton textiles in relation to Scotland and elsewhere except in the sense that other opportunities there were less favourable than in other regions. But Lancashire probably acquired an important man-made advantage in the form of external economies for individual factories, based upon the scale of the industry and the consequential scope for specialization of activities. As J. Jewkes[34] has shown, it was between 1841 and 1884 that in Lancashire the separation of processes into distinct factories became really pronounced, though it was not complete until the First World War. Up to about 1850, plants engaging in both spinning and weaving were more important than works concentrating on one or the other activity and so the full benefits of scale economies had not then been reaped. Hence it was possible for the comparatively very small cotton industry in

Northern Ireland to flourish from its inception in 1777 up to about 1825, whereafter its fortunes declined in the face of growing competition from Lancashire.[35] The larger Scottish branch of the industry survived considerably longer, until the 1860s, when shortage of cotton (whether real or anticipated) induced businessmen to concentrate on the metal trades.

For a full discussion of the operation of external economies in causing the agglomeration of like and related factories, the reader is referred to the work of Florence,[36] who has examined the matter exhaustively. He devoted much attention to the Birmingham region of England and the large range of inter-related metal and component industries found thereabouts; however, the principle is universally applicable.

## Problem of Variable Employment

The regional agglomeration of industries, aided by the operation of scale economies, is but one manifestation of the general principle of regional specialization which has been discussed in terms of comparative advantage (pp. 40–4). Agglomeration is one of the ways in which the income of individual businesses and of society as a whole can be maximized in the long run. Nevertheless, such regional specialization clearly implies a number of less advantageous side-effects, of which the most important is the impact on the local economy of short-term variations in the employment offered by an industry that normally provides a great part of the available work. This is a problem that concerns regions of all sizes: a town with a narrow employment base is as much affected as a region or nation that is similarly situated. The only important distinctions to notice between regions of different sizes are:

1. That on a local scale, workers can compensate for the loss of work with one employer by changing the pattern of their daily journey to work and seeking employment elsewhere. At the regional or international level, migration may be necessary if other jobs are to be sought and adjustment is therefore more difficult.

2. A single-industry town may in fact rely upon a single large works, whereas a regional or national economy relying on a single industry normally has several or many separate plants and/or firms. This distinction is significant in that an

G

individual works is more likely to experience variations in its activities than is the industry of which it is a part. Thus, a small region dominated by one works is likely to suffer greater employment variations, at least in the short run, than is a larger area depending on several firms in the same industry.

A secular increase in employment in an industry that is highly localized creates no notable problems that differentiate the area from any other subjected to development. While the industry in question prospers, like shipbuilding and coal in Britain during the nineteenth century, the regions that are specialized thereon prosper also. Problems arise when employment begins to decline and are acute in proportion to (i) the rate of decline, and (ii) the percentage of a region's employment accounted for by the declining industries. Faced with competition from abroad and rapid technical innovation, cotton textiles, coal and ships provide declining employment in the United Kingdom and these industries are highly localized and locally provide much of the available work.

Cyclical variations in business activity also have important repercussions upon the fortunes of various regions. The shortest periodicity that is significant is the annually recurring, regular and predictable fluctuations that occur with the passage of the seasons. The motor industry traditionally experiences an upsurge of demand in the early part of the year, partly due to the increase in pleasure motoring in the northern hemisphere during the spring and summer months, as this raises the incentive to buy a new vehicle, and partly because 'new' models are put on the market. The latter factor may result in the complete closure of a works in the autumn to allow re-tooling for the new models, with consequential short-term unemployment. Coal mines are busiest in the autumn and winter as that is the period of maximum demand, whereas seaside resorts tend to be deserted then and to swarm with visitors in the summer.[37]

Longer period fluctuations affect industries supplying capital goods and equipment that has a long life. The purchase of such goods may be deferred during a period of economic recession and consequently the industries that are affected tend to have a very variable level of activity. Shipbuilding is one such industry and structural engineering (for bridges, steelwork for buildings, tunnels, etc.) is another. Cyclical fluctuations lasting several years are common but cannot be predicted so readily as the shorter-term seasonal variations of trade.

Other kinds of variations are even less predictable. '... the difference between the consumption [of coal in Britain] during a very mild winter and spring, and that of a severe season, is likely to amount to upwards of ten million tons.'[38] But long-range weather forecasting is a notoriously hazardous game of guesswork. In addition to unpredictable natural causes of variation, man-made interruptions to trade and production must be reckoned. Because of the increasing interdependence of all parts of the economy, any interruption may have wide repercussions. The British steel industry has been suffering from the problem of strikes by small groups of key personnel and at various times in the recent past the great works at Port Talbot and Ebbw Vale have been so closed. During 1963–64, the refusal to work of a few hundred men threw some 20,000 others out of employment at the Port Talbot works and the nearby tinplate plants depending on a regular supply of sheet steel. Motor vehicle manufacturers were sufficiently worried by the prospective shortage of steel to place orders abroad, where surplus capacity existed. In this context, therefore, serious local economic problems arise from the existence of a single large works which dominates local employment.

The combination of regional specialization and the inter-linking of productive processes, particularly in the context of variable and not always predictable levels of employment, leads to three further considerations that will be examined in turn. These are:

1. Defence against local fluctuations through the diversification of regional economies.

2. The fact that economic fluctuations are exacerbated by the operation of the 'multiplier'.

3. The geographic extent of interdependence.

*Diversification*

As a counter to the hazards of dependence on a limited range of employment, public bodies and central governments in the United Kingdom, United States and elsewhere have been much interested in programmes for diversifying the occupational range of selected regions. In the United Kingdom, diversification has provided an essential theme to the efforts to help the north-east, Scotland, South Wales and other areas. Diversification is desired for any or all of several reasons:

1. Some industries employ mainly men or women and the localization of any one industry may imply an imbalance of job opportunities between the sexes. For example, the north-east coast of England has a concentration of employment in coal-mining, shipbuilding and heavy engineering, all industries employing mainly male workers. Since the 1930s, the range of female employment has been widening but the rate of development has been inadequate to bring the ratio of female to male employment anywhere near the national average, as is shown by the data for the Northern Region in Table 12. In this table (Column E), the importance of female employment in the textile areas of Lancashire and Northern Ireland stands out.

TABLE 12

UNITED KINGDOM, 1961: the relationship between male and female employment measured by 'activity'* rates

| Standard Region | Labour force (000) | Activity rates in per cent. | | Ratio of activity rates: D as % of C |
|---|---|---|---|---|
| | | Male | Female | |
| A | B | C | D | E |
| Midland | 2,236 | 81·6 | 42·0 | 51 |
| East and West Ridings | 1,885 | 80·2 | 39·3 | 49 |
| North Western | 3,003 | 79·7 | 42·0 | 53 |
| London and South Eastern and Southern | 8,106 | 79·3 | 40·8 | 51 |
| Scotland | 2,155 | 76·6 | 37·6 | 49 |
| North Midland | 1,565 | 76·0 | 36·8 | 48 |
| Northern | 1,302 | 75·0 | 32·4 | 43 |
| Wales | 970 | 69·6 | 27·5 | 40 |
| South Western | 1,266 | 66·6 | 30·9 | 46 |
| Northern Ireland | 483 | 63·0 | 33·6 | 53 |
| UNITED KINGDOM | 22,973 | 77·1 | 38·4 | 50 |

Source: National Economic Development Council, Conditions Favourable to Faster Growth, (H.M.S.O.), 1963, p. 16.

* The activity rate is the estimated number of employees (employed and unemployed) as a percentage of the total population over the age of 15.

2. Where employment is highly seasonal, it may be desired to attract other occupations in which the seasonal peak of demand comes during the slack season of the first-established industry. This is in fact very difficult to arrange and where it is possible it implies either that each individual will seasonally change occupation (the traditional basis for toy manufacture in mountainous areas, the work being done by agriculturalists in the winter months) or that different sectors of the population will be unemployed at different times of the year.

3. The more usual motive is to reduce the percentage of workers in the locally dominant industries, thereby rendering fluctuations in their employment less serious for the region in question.

These aims of location policy are of course distinct from, though closely related to, the general intention of maintaining a high level of activity and growth in the economy as a whole. Furthermore they imply the idea of 'balance' between employment in various industries, that no region (or nation, for that matter) is economically healthy unless its economy is 'balanced'. This doctrine has a wide currency in the literature on regional problems and economic development. The two fundamental problems are to define first what one means by 'balance' and second the size of area to which the concept is to apply. The nature of this problem is illustrated by the data in Table 13, showing employment in metal manufacturing in England and Wales in 1961. The employment exchange of Swansea had 2·6 per cent. of its employment provided by the one class of industry, which was equivalent to the proportion for England and Wales, but was only one-seventh that of Southwest Wales. If Swansea is to have a 'balanced' or 'diversified' employment structure, is Southwest Wales or England and Wales to be chosen as the norm? Clearly, it would be ridiculous to suggest that the proportion of employment in metal manufacture in both Swansea and Southwest Wales should equal the national average, for by applying the same criterion everywhere to all industries a uniform spread of occupations would result, so denying any concept of varying locational advantages.

The concept of regional diversification and the balance of employment is therefore imprecise and must be treated with caution. In principle, regional diversity should only be

TABLE 13[39]

ENGLAND AND WALES, 1961: employment in metal manufacture*
in relation to total employment

| Area | Total employment 000 | Employment in metal manufacture, 000 | Employment in metal manufacture as % of total |
|---|---|---|---|
| Swansea employment exchange | 51·0 | 1·3 | 2·6 |
| Southwest Wales | 195·8 | 37·4 | 19·1 |
| Great Britain | 22,490·0 | 637·1 | 2·8 |

\* Census class V (metal smelting, founding, rolling, tinplating).

pressed so far as is necessary to provide an acceptably low level
of employment fluctuation, a suitable range of choice of jobs
and a rate of growth of employment that is deemed reasonable.
It is entirely rational to balance the short-term losses arising
from fluctuation against the long-term benefits of specialization
and to attempt to strike a compromise: indeed, this is good
economic reasoning though it depends on many subjective
assessments. However, it must be clearly recognized that one
policy cannot wisely be pursued to the exclusion of the other.
Furthermore, in the present context, there are three different
ways in which diversification may be viewed.[40] An individual
factory may make diverse products that are related either by
the materials used or the processes employed, thereby spreading
the risk of fluctuations in demand. Or a firm controlling several
plants may choose to make a wide range of quite unrelated
goods in their various establishments, each of which is highly
specialized. Finally, the economy of a region may be diversified either by having works that individually make a wide range
of goods or by having specialized factories over a wide spectrum
of products.

Variability in economic conditions may be split into two
parts. There is the problem of *risk*, where the degrees of
probability of various outcomes can be predicted with con-
considerable precision: the risk of experiencing drought or
flood can be calculated quite easily if the relevant data are
available. On the other hand, one speaks of *uncertainty* when the
probabilities cannot be calculated: when speculation forces
up the price of a commodity, as happened with sugar in 1963
following a reduction in Cuban output and the emergence of

Russia as a buyer, the possible outcomes are uncertain. The operation of these two conditions is universal but can be seen more readily in the case of agriculture than industry. The day by day, season by season variation of the weather is apparent to us all and vitally affects most agricultural pursuits. The hazards presented by plant and animal pests and diseases—whether locusts or boll weevils, foot-and-mouth disease or rust—are also familiar. Nor does it take an acute observer to notice that the prices of agricultural products are much less stable than is the case with industrial goods. Prices are highly variable largely because of the following combination of circumstances. If the supply of food increases suddenly because harvests have been good, we would expect prices to fall and to some extent consumption will rise. But the capacity of the stomach is limited and therefore even a large fall in price will not stimulate a big increase in demand. Conversely, a shortage and consequently high prices will not check the willingness to buy food. Demand is said to be inelastic. Similarly, it may take suppliers several years to adjust their output to changed market conditions, since the production cycle is rarely less than a year and for tree crops may be as long as ten years. Supply is therefore inelastic. In both cases, inelastic supply and demand relate to the short periods: over longer periods, a permanent shift in relative prices may induce the substitution of one foodstuff for another and both supply and demand may then be quite elastic; the success of 'broiler' chickens as a cheap form of meat in the United States and now in Europe is a case in point. However, it remains true that the agricultural sector is notorious for the short-term and unpredictable variability, i.e., uncertainty, of product prices, this being one reason for state intervention to reduce fluctuations in farmers' incomes.

As Table 14 illustrates, the farmer has a choice between seeking the long-term maximum income, which may mean great annual variations, or a more stable but lower income based on diversification. Usually, some form of mixed farming is practised wherever the climatic conditions reasonably permit. In many areas, however, the range of economic products is limited, owing to drought or cold in particular. Except for restricted areas where irrigation is possible, much of Australia's interior can sustain commercially only sheep, cattle or wheat and the

TABLE 14

CALIFORNIA, FRESNO–MADERA AREA: estimated net income and income variability for farms of 227 hectares, the farm area being equally divided among the crops

| Crop combination | Average net income 1953–57, dollars | Variability of income as % of average |
|---|---|---|
| Cotton | 89,000 | 36 |
| Cantaloupes | 74,000 | 76 |
| Sugar beet | 28,000 | 55 |
| Alfalfa | 22,000 | 42 |
| A-A-A-C-C-Ca. | 53,000 | 28 |
| A-A-A-C-C-Sb. | 45,000 | 23 |
| A-A-A-C-Sb-Ca. | 44,000 | 28 |
| A-A-A-C-Sb. | 37,000 | 21 |
| A-A-A-Ca. | 35,000 | 45 |
| A-A-A-Sb-Ca. | 34,000 | 39 |
| A-A-A-Sb. | 24,000 | 35 |

Source: H. O. Carter et al., 'Risk and diversification for California crops', California Agricultural Experiment Station, Circular 503, 1961, p. 11.

scope for diversification is therefore severely limited: the same is true of the Virgin Lands of the U.S.S.R. and parts of the United States and northern Canada, to name only a few other examples. Toward the arid margin of agricultural use, the problems attending low average precipitation are multiplied by the greater variability of its incidence and periodic droughts are common. In these circumstances, a large scale of operation may be essential not only because of the low average yield but also so that financial reserves may be accumulated against the lean years. For example, from about 1880, squatters occupied much of western New South Wales, staking out claims for sheep runs. This colonization happened to coincide with a sequence of quite good grazing seasons but from 1895 to 1902 disastrous droughts occurred and many graziers were bankrupted. In general, the least long-term damage was sustained by the larger units and in particular by the pastoral finance companies, whose financial resources combined with the control of properties in various locations that were not all equally affected simultaneously enabled them to survive where others failed. The result was a permanent enlargement of the scale of individual holdings and of ownership to a level more appropriate to the natural conditions.[41]

A similar but less spectacular process has been observed in the Middle East, particularly in Syria. Initially, the land was held in owner-occupation by the peasantry but the highly variable climate meant that in some years they had insufficient provender and were forced to borrow from moneylenders, pledging their land as security. Interest rates being high, it was a lucky peasant who could clear his debt during the ensuing good years and by degrees the debts tended to accumulate as further harvest failures occurred. In time, the peasantry became tenants of the moneylenders and their economic status declined with increasing population, many peasants having no security of tenure and being forced to pay 'extortionate' rents. In the present day, these landlords are often castigated for causing the poverty of the peasantry. Yet in fact the very power of the landlords derives from the insecurity of livelihood offered by small holdings in such an environment.[42]

In this context, it is worth noting that although the fragmentation of farm holdings is usually regarded as a severe handicap to good husbandry, the scattering of plots does confer at least one incidental benefit. Where there are natural hazards such as hail or insect pests, the incidence of which is normally localized but is unpredictable, the fragmentation of farm holdings may mean that the risk of total destruction is reduced for each farmer.[43] In a self-sufficient community, this may be virtually the only form of 'insurance' that is available. Fragmentation usually occurs for reasons other than the spreading of risk and the 'insurance' effect is perhaps a minor advantage to set against the numerous problems created by the dispersal of farm plots.

The problems of variability therefore have a geographic expression in:

1. The mixture of enterprises undertaken within a single factory or farm.

2. The regional mixture of enterprises.

3. The geographic layout of productive units.

4. The scale of productive units.

This last consideration is intimately connected with the institutional arrangements available for providing credit. Where credit is easily available, small *operational* units are possible under conditions of great income variability; otherwise, the operational unit must be large in order to command sufficient financial reserves to tide over bad years. Conversely, if it is desired as a matter of policy to encourage small operating units—family farms for example—in conditions of great variability, a necessary condition is the provision of adequate credit facilities.

Problems of risk and uncertainty have teased economists and stimulated a body of highly sophisticated literature. Following the lead given by F. H. Knight[44] in 1921, and conforming to the central interests of economists, the discussion of risk and uncertainty has centred round the problem of how an individual person or firm should act in given situations in order to maximize either welfare or profits. For the solution of problems of this kind, economists have called in aid statisticians. By analogy with the sorts of problem encountered in games like bridge, games theory has been developed as a means for choosing the optimum of several alternative courses of action. A tool commonly used for solving the theoretical formulations is now known as 'linear programming', the essence of which is to convert a finite range of possibilities into mathematical terms for solution as equations. This approach to economic problems impinges upon matters of economic geography in two respects. First, variations in the geographic environment (*e.g.*, rainfall) may be built into the mathematical models as variable factors. Second, the solution of such problems depends upon an assessment of how probable one outcome is in relation to another and this general question of probabilities has an important bearing upon geographic problems.

*Probability*

Any location pattern of economic activities arises as the result of innumerable individual decisions taken over a longer or shorter period of time. In principle, therefore, any attempt to explain what has already occurred, or is likely to happen in the future, is an exercise in explaining a large number of separate actions. Unless one seeks refuge in some form of determinism, whether geographic determinism that postulates the control of human actions by the physical environment or historic determinism based on the working out of inevitable patterns of history, it is necessary to consider the circumstances in which decisions are taken. In practice, knowledge of the available alternatives is always imperfect; even if knowledge of the present were complete in all respects, the actual decision would have to take account of probable future developments during the relevant time period, which may be one year for a farmer planning the sowing of annual crops or twenty years for an industrial complex. Thus, in common with the historian, the geographer and the economist must ask themselves how probable each event was (will be) before it actually occurred (occurs) if they wish to understand the sequence of actual events and make sensible predictions for the future.

> When the historian asks himself about the probability of a past event, he actually attempts to transport himself, by a bold exercise of the mind, to the time before the event itself, in order to gauge its chances, as they appeared upon the eve of its realization. ... the path of historical research, like that of so many other disciplines of the mind, intersects the royal highway of the theory of probabilities. ... the majority of the problems of historical criticism are really problems of probability, but such that the subtlest calculation must own itself incapable of their solution.[45]

Though statistical techniques may not be applicable to many of these problems of historical probability, the significance of the mode of thought can be appreciated from an example. The motor vehicle industry in England has for several decades been localized at Coventry, among other centres. One of the reasons commonly given for this localization is the fact that in and around Coventry the manufacture of bicycles had become established by the end of the nineteenth century and that this industry was in economic straits just at the time when motor vehicle manufacture began to expand rapidly. Motor vehicles are akin to bicycles and require similar manufacturing skills and therefore, so the argument runs, the bicycle and related engineering firms were glad to adopt the new product and skilled labour was available for incoming firms.[46] An examination of this account raises a number of questions. In the first place, bicycle manufacture was not confined to Coventry, being also represented in Birmingham and Nottingham. Why did not motor manufacturing develop in Nottingham, which to all appearances had advantages similar to Coventry and Birmingham? The answer probably lies in the relative efficiency of Raleigh at Nottingham and bicycle manufacturers elsewhere combined with the varying proportion of local employment in bicycle manufacture (low in Nottingham, high in Coventry). Second, were there not industries other than bicycle manufacture that were also experiencing economic troubles at the relevant time and which, therefore, would have been interested in the new outlet? W. Smith argued that other kinds of engineering were less similar to cars than were bicycles: this proposition may be accepted but it merely demonstrates that other industries were less likely to adopt vehicle making—it does not prove that they could not.

The reader will perceive that a great deal of original research would be necessary to establish the factual situation and that at the very best one would be able to say that Coventry had a high (or low) probability of developing the motor industry. As M. Bloch has remarked:

> In any study, seeking the origins of a human activity, there lurks the . . . danger of confusing ancestry with explanation.[47]

We have come full circle to the concept of opportunity costs (p. 39), which strictly ought to be viewed in terms of individual decisions and which should enter into all assessments of probabilities.

Some recent articles in the *Annals* of the Association of American Geographers[48] embody concepts of probability as applied to geographic patterns of human behaviour and represent an advance from the accepted need to measure probabilities in the field of physical geography (climatic phenomena, floods, etc.). One article attempts to construct a model of regional growth based on a sequence of transport, industrial, population, etc. developments in Sweden, while another is concerned with patterns of marketing livestock in Africa in the context of varying market prices, length of trek and variability of climate and hence of the condition of the animals at the time of sale. If both articles display important defects, this shows how difficult of resolution are the problems and how little the progress that has been made to date.

## The Multiplier

The reader will recall the discussion of variations of employment within particular industries and the problems that arise when an industry with high variability dominates a particular region (p. 87). The effects of variability are accentuated by the operation of what is known as the 'multiplier', of which we have already had a glimpse (p. 89). If a hundred key men go on strike, the resulting unemployment may run to thousands in a very short time: the initial unemployment has been multiplied many times.

The concept of the multiplier was originally developed to help explain the behaviour of employment and income levels in the national economy as a whole, each nation being conceived as an isolated state which in the simplest case had no transactions with the outside world. If we imagine a condition of unemployment in any country, the government may decide to spend £10 million per annum on a programme of public works to stimulate the economy and so to increase incomes and employment, the funds being raised by means of a budget deficit. The annual sum of £10 million becomes an income for those who are brought into work and probably most of this income will be spent. Suppose the workers spend an extra £9 million each year on food, clothing, etc., they thereby create work and income for another group of workers who may in turn spend nine-tenths of their extra earnings, or £8·1 million. The initial outlay of £10 million annually directly created that amount of income (and related employment) but indirectly some multiple of that figure. What that multiple is depends upon two conditions:

1. The proportion of the extra income that is spent.

2. The necessity that the total new saving must equal the initial outlay (investment) that has been financed by a budget deficit.

In the case cited above, total new saving placed with

the government must equal £10 million each year and as each recipient spends nine-tenths of his extra income (his marginal propensity to consume is 0·9), equilibrium will be reached when total income has expanded by £100 million annually. Hence, the multiplier is 10, or the reciprocal of the marginal propensity to save, which is 0·1.[49]

The concept of the multiplier may be translated into geographic terms most readily through employment, though in the process some of the elegant precision of the original version is lost. If we imagine that the initial annual investment by government out of a budget deficit provides work for 1,000 people, the income that they spend may generate work for a further 900, who in turn make employment for 810, and so on. The limit to the multiplier effect will be set by the need for extra annual savings to equal the extra annual investment. Given this limitation, the reader will readily visualize that an addition, to, say, the road building programme in southern England will directly create work on the site plus additional employment in cement and gravel works (probably in the vicinity), in the manufacture of steel for reinforcing the concrete (probably in the north east) in the making of earth-moving equipment (anywhere in the country or even abroad) and in service and consumer industries all over the country. The establishment of a works of any kind will mean either the immigration of workers to the area or a decrease in local unemployment, or both, and in either case there will be an increased local demand for shopping facilities, entertainment, transport, etc. The result will be that if initial employment increases by 1,000, roughly 1,000 further workers will be provided with work, though not necessarily all in the same locality: the employment multiplier is roughly two (p. 75). A comparatively modest initial development will therefore expand as those industries that are closely tied to their markets congregate around the first development. The enlarged population cluster may then become attractive for industries which either are less closely tied to particular markets while being generally market oriented, for example mineral waters, or which are closely market oriented but need a large population to draw upon, such as theatres and quality printers. As the growth accumulates, each increment to population is likely to engender a multiplier effect. The multiplier does of course also operate in the reverse direction and once a decline in regional employment has begun it may become cumulative.

The multiplier is an attractive concept that is fraught with dangers. It has appeared quite extensively in the guise of 'urban economic base' studies, which attempt for particular city communities to isolate the 'export' sector of the local economy. By establishing the relationship between 'export' and 'non-export' activities it is hoped that the fortunes of the community can be predicted for changes in the activity of the 'export' sector. The concept of the urban economic base has been exhaustively described[50] and criticized[51] elsewhere so that it is relevant here to make only four cautionary points:

1. Whereas data may be adequate for the calculation of multipliers at the national level, the smaller the geographic area within a country the less satisfactory are the statistics (the problem is comparable to that of constructing regional or local income accounts).

2. The size of area chosen critically alters the results. The world as a whole is a closed economy with no exports or imports. As the unit considered becomes smaller, the proportion of 'export' employment must rise. Hence, the identification of 'export', 'import' and 'non-export' or local sectors changes with scale. This point has been aptly made for Lincoln, Nebraska, the economy of the city having been compared with southeast Nebraska, Nebraska as a whole and the United States.[52] (Cf. Table 13 on p. 92.)

3. Once the difficulties of scale have been resolved, there remains the problem of distinguishing which activities serve as 'exports' from the region in question (or as 'imports'). As trade and financial data are normally available only at the national level, bold estimation is required.

4. Finally, there comes the problem of whether all changes are to be regarded as autonomously induced from *outside* the region being studied, through changes in the demand for 'exports' or the supply of 'imports'? This convention has been adopted but is not entirely satisfactory. Taking the world as a whole, all changes are internal within the system and even in a small area changes may occur in the internal sector that will materially affect relationships. In a city the size of Tokyo

(8m. inhabitants), a change in fashion may mean the multiplication of hairdressing saloons and a reduction in expenditure
on cars or clothes imported from elsewhere. The change in
economic relationships would have arisen from internal, not
external, causes.

The multiplier is therefore a concept that must be treated
with great care, as may be seen from the discussion following
an estimate that the establishment of a steel works in the
New York–Philadelphia area with an annual capacity of 3
million tons and employing 11,666 persons would generate a
total local employment of 180,000 in ten years.[53]

*Geographic Extent of Interdependence*

Since one of the difficulties in using the multiplier concept
for regions smaller than nations is the fact that all regions have
external links, this chapter may fittingly be concluded with a
brief comment on the geographic extent of interdependence.
Even a cursory glance at world trade figures shows that there
is a world-wide movement of foodstuffs, raw materials and
finished manufactures. It would be tedious to labour this
point. However, an interesting related field of investigation
has been almost entirely ignored. Given the modern tendency
toward specialization of industrial production and the growth
of contract component supplies, with the consequential interdependence of firms, over how large an area can operations
economically be conducted? Clearly, proximity between suppliers and purchasers confers *some* advantages in terms of cost and
administrative ease and traditionally a city like Birmingham
has been congratulated for the advantages it offers by having
specialist suppliers close together. But there has been no full
and quantitative investigation of just how great the benefits are.
Furthermore, modern conditions of transport and communication almost certainly mean that the size of area within which
productive processes can conveniently be integrated is increasing quite quickly. That this is in fact happening is strongly
suggested by the changing pattern of the United Kingdom's
import trade shown in Table 15. There has clearly been an
increase in the relative importance of part-manufactured goods
since before the last world war; such goods comprise plastics,
metal components, metals for further fabrication and textiles

## TABLE 15

UNITED KINGDOM, 1935–38/1963: percentage distribution of imports valued c.i.f.

| CLASS OF IMPORT | Av. 1935–38 | 1952 | 1953 | 1954 | 1955 | 1956 | 1957 | 1958 | 1959 | 1960 | 1961 | 1962 | 1963 |
|---|---|---|---|---|---|---|---|---|---|---|---|---|---|
| Food, beverages, tobacco | 45·0 | 34·5 | 39·2 | 39·1 | 36·9 | 37·2 | 36·6 | 39·8 | 38·1 | 33·9 | 33·8 | 35·0 | 34·8 |
| Basic materials | 28·1 | 32·8 | 31·4 | 30·2 | 28·7 | 28·1 | 28·4 | 23·7 | 23·4 | 23·3 | 23·0 | 20·6 | 20·6 |
| Mineral fuels, lubricants | 4·8 | 9·8 | 9·4 | 9·8 | 10·6 | 10·7 | 11·5 | 11·7 | 11·7 | 10·6 | 11·0 | 11·9 | 11·6 |
| Semi-manufactures | 14·9 | 16·8 | 13·4 | 15·3 | 17·8 | 17·3 | 16·1 | 15·9 | 16·5 | 19·9 | 19·2 | 18·8 | 19·0 |
| Finished manufactures | 6·7 | 5·6 | 6·1 | 5·2 | 5·6 | 6·4 | 7·0 | 8·5 | 9·8 | 11·9 | 12·6 | 13·4 | 13·6 |
| Other | 0·5 | 0·5 | 0·5 | 0·4 | 0·4 | 0·3 | 0·4 | 0·4 | 0·5 | 0·4 | 0·4 | 0·3 | 0·4 |
| | 100·0 | 100·0 | 100·0 | 100·0 | 100·0 | 100·0 | 100·0 | 100·0 | 100·0 | 100·0 | 100·0 | 100·0 | 100·0 |

*Sources: Annual Abstract of Statistics, Monthly Digest of Statistics.*

H

for finishing, to name a few items. Unfortunately, comparable figures for exports are not readily available. Within the United Kingdom, it appears that the size of area in which it is possible to have close inter-relations between factories is expanding and the reader will find some of the fragmentary evidence recorded elsewhere.[54]

Suffice it to note that the increasing geographic extent and degree of interdependence means that the multiplier effect in any one locality is hard to distinguish because of the 'leaks' to other parts of the world. Hence, a recession in one part of the world has serious repercussions everywhere and the governments of the world are being forced to recognize their mutual interests in the maintenance of prosperity. But if distress can spread like contagion, so too can prosperity and the multiplier can be used as one of the agents for increasing the general welfare. For this to be realized, however, deliberate government interference in economic matters is undoubtedly essential and hence the rôle of governments is an essential element of the economic system, as is shown in Chapter 8.

*Conclusion*

This chapter has sought to examine some of the ways in which, in a dynamic economy, there may be disequilibria of a persistent or recurring kind in the spatial pattern of activities. One of the counts on which the doctrines of perfect competition is vulnerable is the question of scale economies. If one of the basic propositions of perfect competition, that there be many firms supplying a given commodity, is to be valid, it follows that scale economies must be negligible in relation to the volume of sales in a given market. Otherwise, the number of competing firms will be small. Because scale economies do exist, both internally in the firm and externally, a number of important geographic consequences follow. Scale economies internal to a plant are manifest either in very big factories carrying out many processes—such as a modern steel works—or in numerous small plants specialized to one or a few processes. In the former case, problems may arise from communities being highly specialized and dependent upon one works, or from the great distance of commuting. In the latter case, of interdependent specialization, the conditions are created for regional external economies of scale to operate in favour of the major agglomerations of population.

With both internal and external economies of scale, technical and other changes are causing constant movements *along* the production-functions and *from* one production-function to another. Such changes are excessively hard to measure statistically: even in assumed static conditions, regional production-functions have not been satisfactorily calculated, though such exercises have been undertaken for single industries. However, most innovations originate in the more advanced areas of the world and take time to spread to other areas. Therefore, by virtue of their advantage in time, the more developed regions are likely to continue to attract a disproportionate amount of new development in the absence of countervailing activity by governments.

In a dynamic situation, it is not realistic to try to construct a series of equations for simultaneous solution to give the spatial pattern of economic activities. Decisions of all kinds are taken at a point in time, each point forming part of a sequence of events that itself becomes history. Each location decision, even if taken in the light of perfect knowledge about the past, must be made in the light of uncertainty about the nature of decisions taken contemporaneously and to be taken in the future. Each decision that is taken affects the relative desirability of all locations, which may again be altered by future actions within the life of the factory, house, etc., for which a location is being sought. The evolution of geographic patterns is therefore to be seen as a sequence of decisions, the probability of each one being dependent upon the past and the expected future developments. In explaining the development of geographic patterns, one should consciously think of the field of probabilities at each stage, in an attempt to assess the extent to which the actual pattern deviates from a truly random one.

These probabilities are strongly conditioned by the ease with which adjustments to change are able to occur. It is therefore appropriate to examine in the next chapter some of the more important geographic aspects of the divisibility and mobility of the factors of production.

## REFERENCES

1 An industry comprises several firms (unless monopoly prevails) and each firm may control several factories, offices, farms or other enterprises, according to the industry in question.

2 E. A. G. Robinson, *The Structure of Competitive Industry*, first published 1931, re-issued with revisions.

3 *Idem.*

4 G. Maxcy and A. Silberston, *op. cit.*, 1959 (Chap. 3), pp. 77–81.

5 K. S. Lomax, 'Cost curves for gas supply', *Bulletin*, Oxford University Institute of Statistics, 1951, Table IV, p. 245.

6 G. Manners, 'Recent changes in the British gas industry', *Transactions and Papers*, Institute of British Geographers, 1959, p. 157.

7 For a survey of some of the problems and the results of enquiries, see B. Balassa, *The Theory of Economic Integration*, 1962, pp. 124–31. Also, F. T. Moore, 'Economies of scale: some statistical evidence', *Quarterly Journal of Economics*, 1959, pp. 232–45; A. J. Harrison, 'Economies of scale and the structure of the road haulage industry', *Oxford Economic Papers*, 1963, pp. 287–307.

8 R. G. Bressler, 1945, *op. cit.*, (Chap. 3).

9 J. Jewkes, 'The size of the factory', *Economic Journal*, 1952, pp. 237–52. G. R. Allen, 'The size of the factory in Sweden—a note', *idem.*, 1953, pp. 914–17. P. S. Florence, 'The size of the factory: a reply', *idem.*, 1954, pp. 625–28. J. Jewkes, 'Are the economies of scale unlimited?', in E. A. G. Robinson (ed.), *Economic Consequences of the size of Nations*, 1960, pp. 95–116.

10 J. W. House, 'Recent economic growth in North-East England. The rôle of four national growth industries', *Research Series* No. 4, Department of Geography, University of Newcastle-upon-Tyne, 1964, p. 35.

11 J. Jewkes, 1960, *op. cit.*, p. 101.

12 P. S. Florence, 1944, *op. cit.*, (Chap. 2). For a full discussion, see W. Isard, *et al.*, *Methods of Regional Analysis: an Introduction to Regional Science*, 1960, Chapter 7. An interesting example of the application of these techniques is P. G. Hall, *The Industries of London since 1861*, 1962.

13 This calculation is based on a total civil employment in Great Britain of 24.1m. in June 1963, of which 12.6m. could be described as 'basic' employment and the remainder as 'service' workers. The total population was 52.2m. Therefore, for each 'basic' worker there were three other people.

14 H. W. Arndt, 'External economies in economic growth', *Economic Record*, 1955, pp. 192–214.

15 T. S. Ashton, *Iron and Steel in the Industrial Revolution*, second edition, 1951, pp. 36–37.

16 *Idem.*, p. 99.

17 N. J. G. Pounds and W. N. Parker, *Coal and Steel in Western Europe*, 1957, pp. 106, 107 and 153. See also E. A. Wrigley, *Industrial Growth and Population Change*, 1961.

18 O. H. K. Spate, *India and Pakistan*, 1954, p. 657.

19 W. E. Minchinton, 'The diffusion of tinplate manufacture', *Economic History Review*, 1956–57, p. 350.

20 D. M. Smith, 'The cotton industry in the East Midlands', *Geography*, 1962, p. 258.

21 J. Blicksilver, 'Cotton manufacturing in the southeast. An historical analysis', *Studies in Business and Economics*, Georgia State College of Business Administration, No. 5, 1959.

22 S. Godlund, 'Ein Innovationsverlauf in Europa, dargestellt in einer vorläufigen Untersuchung über die Ausbreitung der Eisenbahninnovation', *Lund Studies in Geography*, Ser. B, Human Geography, No. 6, 1952. See also T. Hägerstrand, 'The propagation of innovation waves', *idem.*, No. 4, 1952.

23 W. T. Jackman, *The Development of Transportation in Modern England*, second edition, 1962.

24 W. Smith, 1953, *op. cit.*, (Chap. 2), p. 161.

25 For an interesting account of the diffusion of agricultural techniques, see G. E. Jones, 'The diffusion of agricultural innovations', *Journal of Agricultural Economics*, 1963, pp. 387–405.

26 C. Woodham-Smith, *The Great Hunger: Ireland 1845–9*, 1962.

27 The cost of smoke abatement plant for a modern steel works amounts to 'several million pounds'. *The Times*, 25th June 1964.

28 S. Enke, 1963, *op. cit.*, (Chap. 2), p. 113.

29 G. Myrdal, *Economic Theory and Under-developed Regions*, 1957.

30 M. Chisholm, 'Must we all live in southeast England? The location of new employment', *Geography*, 1964, pp. 1–14.

31 K. S. Lomax, 'The relationship between expenditure per head and size of population of county boroughs in England and Wales', *Journal*, Royal Statistical Society, 1943, pp. 51–59. See also O. D. Duncan, 'Optimum size of cities', in J. J. Spengler and O. D. Duncan (eds), *Demographic Analysis: Selected Readings*, 1956, pp. 372–85.

32 M. Chisholm, 'Regional variations in road transport costs: milk collection from farms in England and Wales', *Farm Economist*, 1957, pp. 30–38.

33 P. G. Hall, 1962, *op. cit.*

34 J. Jewkes, 1930, *op. cit.*, (Chap. 2).

35 E. Jones, *A Social Geography of Belfast*, 1960, pp. 34 and 41.

36 P. S. Florence, 1948 and 1962, *op. cit.*, (Chap. 2). For full details on the Birmingham area, see G. C. Allen, *The Industrial Development of Birmingham and the Black Country 1860–1927*, 1929. W. Smith, 1953, *op. cit.*, (Chap. 2), contains much useful data on the geographic patterns associated with external economies in several British industries.

37 S. S. Kuznets, *Seasonal Variations in Industry and Trade*, 1933.

38 G. Manley, 'Climatic fluctuations and fuel requirements', *Scottish Geographical Magazine*, 1957, p. 26.

39 S. H. Spence, 'Toward a new regional economic policy for south-west Wales', in G. Manners (ed.), *South Wales in the Sixties*, 1964, pp. 189 and 191.

40   E. C. Conkling, 'The measurement of diversification', in G. Manners, 1964, *op. cit.*, pp. 161–83. See also J. H. Dunning, *Economic Planning and Town Expansion: A Case Study of Basingstoke*, 1963, pp. 95–108.

41   N. Cain, 'Companies and squatting in the western division of New South Wales, 1896–1905', *Economic Record*, 1961, pp. 183–206. Compare: L. Hewes and A. C. Schmieding, 'Risk in the central Great Plains: geographical patterns of wheat failure in Nebraska, 1931–1952', *Geographical Review*, 1956, pp. 375–87.

42   D. Warriner, *Land and Poverty in the Middle East*, 1948, p. 85.

43   P. L. Lehrer, 'African agriculture in Kenya. A study of a changing system of subsistence farming', *Nigerian Geographical Journal*, June 1964, p. 31.

44   F. H. Knight, *Risk, Uncertainty and Profit*, 1921. For a recent survey of the economic literature, see M. B. Nicholson, 1959, *op. cit.*, (Chap. 3).

45   M. Bloch, *The Historian's Craft*, English translation, 1954, compiled from pp. 124, 125 and 129.

46   W. Smith, 1953, *op. cit.*, (Chap. 2), pp. 398–99. S. B. Saul, 1962, *op. cit.*, (Chap. 3).

47   M. Bloch, 1954, *op. cit.*, p. 32.

48   R. L. Morrill, 1963, *op. cit.*, (Chap. 2). P. R. Gould, 'Man against his environment: a game theoretic framework', *Annals*, Association of American Geographers, 1963, pp. 290–97.

49   If each worker saved £2 of every extra £10 of income (marginal propensity to save $= \frac{2}{10} = 0.2$), the multiplier would be $\frac{1}{0.2} = 5$ and the total income increase generated by the initial annual outlay of £10m. would be £50m. per year.

50   R. B. Andrews, 1953–56, *op. cit.*, (Chap. 3).

51   C. M. Tiebout, 'The urban economic base reconsidered', *Land Economics*, 1956, pp. 95–99. M. L. Greenhut, 'Comments on economic base theory', *Land Economics*, 1959, pp. 71–75. R. Artle, 'On some methods and problems in the study of metropolitan economies', *Papers*, Regional Science Association, 1962, pp. 71–87.

52   G. E. Thompson, 'An investigation of the local employment multiplier', *Review of Economics and Statistics*, 1959, pp. 61–67.

53   W. Isard and R. E. Kuenne, 'The impact of steel upon the greater New York–Philadelphia industrial region', *Review of Economics and Statistics*, 1953, pp. 289–301. For discussion, see the *Review*, 1954, pp. 308–14.

54   M. Chisholm, 1964, *op. cit.*, pp. 8–9.

# CHAPTER 5

# Divisibility and Mobility of Factors of Production

'It is usual to attribute economies of scale primarily—if not solely—to the lack of divisibility of productive units.'[1] Large-scale production is cheaper than small-scale operations where a particular piece of equipment cannot be designed with less than a certain capacity, as with the machine that bores motor vehicle cylinders. The building of a dam for the generation of hydro-electric power is another example, in which it is commonly necessary to erect a large dam with a big potential or to refrain entirely. In both these cases, the capacity is said to be indivisible. The principle applies in all spheres to some extent: there is a minimum practicable size of oil refinery, a lathe cannot usefully be bought piece by piece and a labour force can often only be increased by taking on a full-time employee, representing 40–50 working hours in a week.

It follows that a change in capacity, either as an increase or a decrease, cannot occur smoothly and continuously. Instead, productive capacity must change abruptly, the size of each step being conditioned by the magnitude of the indivisibilities. For example, a single steel works may produce three million tons of steel each year and a new plant of this size would represent about 10 per cent. of the United Kingdom's capacity, whereas in some clothing trades the potential output can be varied minutely through changes in hours of work and the number of employees. Where the indivisibilities are large, the precise matching of supply and demand is apt to present problems and periods of excess or deficient supply are liable to occur. In addition to the problems faced by firms in planning their future policy, the whole economic development of a country or area may be affected and hence the distribution of industry and population over the world.

The latter problem is illustrated by the hypothetical figures in Table 16. In countries A and B, the potential demand for electricity is rising by ten units annually: in A, the potential supply is represented by four hydro-electric projects each of which is capable of supplying ten units, whereas in B there is only one site but this has a potential capacity of forty units. In A, the actual supply of electricity can keep pace with demand but in B the construction of the facilities to meet the initial need would result in the under-use of the investment until the fourth year. This may render the investment uneconomic, thereby causing it to be postponed, perhaps indefinitely. If postponement occurs, the potential demand may not in fact grow as quickly in B as in A and this may cause further delay in the project.

TABLE 16

HYPOTHETICAL GROWTH IN SUPPLY OF AND DEMAND FOR ELECTRICITY

| | COUNTRY A | | | COUNTRY B | | |
| YEAR | Potential demand | Potential supply | Actual supply | Potential demand | Potential supply | Actual supply |
| --- | --- | --- | --- | --- | --- | --- |
| 1 | 10 | 4 × 10 | 10 | 10 | 1 × 40 | 0 |
| 2 | 20 | 4 × 10 | 20 | 20 | 1 × 40 | 0 |
| 3 | 30 | 4 × 10 | 30 | 30 | 1 × 40 | 0 |
| 4 | 40 | 4 × 10 | 40 | 40 | 1 × 40 | 40 |

Peru is an example of country experiencing the problems represented by B in the above table:

The possibility of utilizing the power potential of the two great bends of the Mantaro River to generate electricity was foreseen 20 years ago by a Peruvian engineer, but the need at that time was much less [than now]. The area, as it still is today, was rugged and remote; and no one was then interested in capitalizing such an initially expensive scheme.

But the picture has changed. The Lima-Callao urban area now houses two million people and continues to grow. New industries and factories are springing up like mushrooms and the demand for electrical power increases every year. The total potential of the Mantaro River is so great that it would be able to meet this demand for the foreseeable future and still have reserve power in hand. . . .

The first phase of the scheme, with its 330,000 kw installation, also includes all the civil engineering work up to a surge chamber for the second phase, which, with additional machinery, will step up the power to 660,000 kw when required. Further stages, up to the total estimated potential of 2,500,000 kw can then be added as the area is opened up and the demand for electrical power increases.[2]

The size of the project, even the first part alone, is shown by the fact that in 1964 the total installed generating capacity in Great Britain was 36,562,000 kw and that only 10 plants had an individual capacity exceeding 400,000 kw. The population of Peru is about ten million compared with 52 million in Great Britain and her *per caput* income is only about one-seventh of the British level.

In contrast, the folded Atlas Mountains of northwest Africa, close to the sea, provide many comparatively small river basins each of which can be developed independently of the others. In the early 1950s, there were in French Morocco nine river development schemes for irrigation and hydro-electric power and four further projects were planned.[3] The possibility of undertaking successive comparatively small schemes has been one factor favouring comparatively steady development in Morocco.

We may therefore conceive of indivisibilities creating a series of thresholds to growth and development. The Mantaro scheme in Peru has had to wait until the 1960s largely because the demand for electricity was previously inadequate to justify it; thereby, the development of the economy has been slower than might otherwise have been the case. Once the threshold has been crossed and the scheme is functioning, a high rate of growth may be expected, at least until the capacity of the hydro-electric installations is fully used and the next threshold reached. There is therefore a very important inter-relationship between the size of the thresholds and the rate of economic development. If an economy has been growing slowly and prospectively will so continue, even a small threshold may not be crossed because there will be a prolonged period of under-use of the resource. Conversely, rapid growth in demand makes it possible to undertake big schemes since the new facilities will be fully used within a short time.

*Divisibility: Land and Capital*

In a literal sense, the natural endowment of soil, minerals, climate, etc., ('land') can be exploited in very small units or very large ones, and in this sense land as a factor of production is nearly infinitely divisible. In the same way, capital, as money, can be split into minute amounts and is therefore also highly divisible. In practice, any development of land resources involves an application of capital and conversely, most applications of capital require a complementary use of land. Hence, the relevant consideration is the minimum scale of joint development that is warranted in any particular circumstances. This minimum may be conceived as the least magnitude of exploitation that will ensure that all costs are recovered, including interest on the capital sum invested. This minimum represents an indivisibility, the size of which is conditioned by three major sets of consideration:

1. The kind of development—factory or irrigation scheme.

2. The technical accomplishments of the place and the time.

3. The nature of the physical environment.

From the discussion of scale economies in Chapter 4, it appears that over a wide range of manufacturing industries the minimum size of viable enterprise as measured by output is increasing, possibly quite rapidly. Already, in a large range of basic industries, such as steel, oil refining, vehicle assembly, textiles and plastics, the minimum economic unit represents a large annual output, which may be too great for a small, underdeveloped nation to sustain.

Another major reason for indivisibilities resides in the physical environment and is particularly evident in the case of hydro-electric power development. The volume of the river, its seasonal regime and the configuration of the valley condition the size of dam that can usefully be built. The Kariba, Volta and Kainji schemes in Africa are all huge in comparison with those in Scotland, owing almost entirely to the physical conditions of the respective areas. The reclamation of the delta area of the Netherlands requires a vast array of interdependent engineering works the magnitude of which dwarfs even the remarkable achievement of draining the former

Zuider Zee, which in turn is a far larger scheme than the piecemeal embankment of parts of the Lincolnshire and Norfolk coasts.

The minimum size of factory or civil engineering project that is economic appears to be increasing, due to innumerable technical advances. In the past, when workshops were all small, a comparatively even pace of development was possible even in diminutive economies and an area was blessed that had rivers, marshland suitable for reclamation, etc., that could be tamed in small projects. The greater part of Western Europe has enjoyed this advantage. Now that much larger projects have become both feasible and economic, hitherto idle and unexploitable resources in Africa, Latin America and elsewhere can be developed and in the long-run may prove to yield a better return than the exploitation of smaller-scale resources elsewhere.

## *Divisibility: Labour*

In contrast to much capital investment, labour is highly divisible. Labour input can be varied in several ways:

1. In units of one whole-time worker.

2. By the use of part-time personnel.

3. The regular labour force may work over-time or short-time.

4. Casual labour may be employed.

5. A firm that has excess work in hand may sub-contract some jobs, which amounts, in effect, to a temporary expansion of the firm's capacity.

A long-term change in the level of a firm's activity calls for adjustment in the number of whole-time and part-time employees, whereas a temporary fluctuation is more appropriately met by changes in the hours worked: if the change is an increase in activity, subcontracting or the use of casual workers may be the appropriate solution. For seasonal variations, the use of casual workers and changes in the hours of work may be the best way of solving the problem.

Small establishments are more affected by problems of the divisibility or otherwise of labour than are large ones, for the evident reason that one day or hour of work represents a bigger proportion of the total labour input. Table 17 sets out some of the data for Great Britain showing the distribution of employment among large and small establishments in the year 1961. The importance of manufacturing establishments employing ten or fewer workers is not precisely known but they are thought to number about 140,000, possibly employing 0·5 million workers (in 1954, 545,000 were employed in manufacturing, mining and construction[4]). Agriculture is of course characterized by small units of employment: in 1961, there were 399,000 agricultural holdings in Great Britain employing 617,000 workers, or about one and one half persons per holding.

TABLE 17

GREAT BRITAIN, 1961: distribution of employment by size of establishment

| Size of establishment nos. employees | MANUFACTURING INDUSTRY | | RETAIL TRADES | |
|---|---|---|---|---|
| | Establishments | Employees 000 | Establishments | Employees 000 |
| 11–24 | 12,571 | 222 | | |
| 25–49 | 14,704 | 523 | | |
| 50–99 | 12,774 | 897 | | |
| 100–249 | 8,714 | 1,338 | | |
| 250–499 | 3,499 | 1,214 | | |
| 500–999 | 1,693 | 1,163 | | |
| 1,000–1,999 | 777 | 1,078 | | |
| 2,000–4,999 | 351 | 1,031 | | |
| 5,000 or more | 78 | 712 | | |
| TOTAL | 55,161 | 8,178 | 577,307 | 2,524 |
| Average number of employees per establishment | 148·3 | | 4·4 | |

Sources: *Ministry of Labour Gazette*, April 1962, p. 145. Board of Trade, *Report on the Census of Distribution and Other Services 1961*, Pt. 2, 1964, p. 2/25.

Agriculture and the retail trades are often characterized by a high proportion of part-time workers: respectively 11·7 and 26·4 per cent. in Great Britain in 1961. Seasonal and temporary workers accounted for a further 15·7 per cent. of the total labour force in British agriculture and these workers are mostly found in comparatively small areas of the country which specialize in crops that cannot readily be mechanized. The harvests of hops and fruit regularly draw large numbers of casual workers to Kent and Worcestershire. An alternative kind of adjustment in the agricultural sector is for teams of workers to travel regularly from one place to another engaged on contract work, as with sheep shearing in Australia and ploughing and grain harvesting in the United States.

In manufacturing and the service trades, subcontracting is common to cope with variable demand. As with the regular supply of parts or services, proximity between the parties is clearly advantageous. However, when supplies are obtained regularly, the chief saving conferred by proximity is in transport costs on the goods in question, whereas sporadic orders designed to cushion fluctuations of activity are more likely to involve close liaison and even supervision; hence, proximity will confer greater savings than for regular transactions. This is an additional factor encouraging the agglomeration of businesses, though, as we have already seen (p. 83), the magnitude of the savings that arise from agglomeration have not been measured.

The means of adjusting labour input to varying needs affects the distribution of income among persons, which in turn influences regional economies. One of the more obvious contrasts is that where over-time or short-time is worked, the effects on earnings are distributed among all the personnel, whereas to keep the weekly hours of work constant and change the number of employed persons means that the full brunt of fluctuations falls upon a few unlucky individuals. Work in British docks has traditionally been casual, the men reporting at stated times in the hope of getting work and, in the absence of employment, receiving no pay or only a small sum. The docker's life has always in the past been insecure and social problems have abounded in the dock areas. In contrast, railway workers normally enjoy security, even though their average wages may not have been much different from that of the dockers, and the urban areas inhabited by them are socially quite distinct from the dock areas.

*Mobility of Factors of Production*

Two kinds of mobility must be distinguished: movement of

factors between occupations or uses, and of factors between places. The former may be termed inter-industry and the latter geographic mobility. To appreciate the effect of mobility or the lack of it on geographic patterns, it is necessary to return briefly to some basic economic reasoning.

If the output of the whole world, or of any particular part of it, is to be at a maximum for any given level of techniques, the marginal product of any factor (say labour of a particular quality) must be equal in all uses and all places. (If in fact the marginal output of a particular worker varies from job to job or within the same job from place to place, then a transfer from a job or area of low marginal product to one of high marginal product will raise the total world or national production by the difference between the two marginal products.) A logical consequence of this proposition is that capital and labour should be fully mobile in both the geographic and the inter-industrial senses and that land should be fully mobile between uses (by definition, land is geographically immobile). Given these conditions, there will be a maximum degree of specialization, or localization, of production according to the principles of comparative advantage (p. 40). If there are any impediments to the free mobility of the factors of production and of products, the ideal distribution of activities will be upset; the greater the impediment, the greater may be the deviations from the ideal. Furthermore, any change in the degree of mobility of the factors of production, especially of one factor relative to the others, will materially affect location patterns. Hence, marked contrasts are likely in the localizing influence of the factors of production according to time and to place.

Although the world as a whole may benefit from the maximization of production made possible by the greatest feasible mobility of factors of production and of goods, individual, sectional and national interests may be threatened. For example, in countries such as the United States and Germany the marginal product of labour is far higher than in Turkey or China and therefore migration 'ought' to occur from the latter to the former countries. If the transfer were large, the standard of living in the advanced countries would be depressed and some classes of worker, say building labourers, would be affected more severely than others. Therefore, in practice, nations often restrict the international and intranational mobility of labour and capital to protect specified interests, and thereby location patterns are affected. These political impediments to mobility will be largely ignored for the present (see Chapter 8) and attention will be concentrated upon non-political, economic considerations.

## Mobility: Land and Capital

By definition, land is immobile geographically but it may be highly mobile between uses. One annual crop can readily follow another and any change of use is reversible, *i.e.*, if wheat follows potatoes, potatoes can succeed the wheat in the third year. However, a large number of land uses involve the application of greater or lesser amounts of capital—in the form of buildings, services such as water supply and roads, etc.—so that a change of use is much easier in one direction than in another: agricultural land usually can be built upon much more easily than residential areas can be converted to farms. Although in some cases land can be highly mobile between uses, it is more common for mobility to be inhibited by the nature of the plant erected on the property or by the long production cycle required for many agricultural enterprises. The inter-industry mobility of any plot of earth therefore is affected by:

1. The range of uses for which the land is suitable.

2. The nature of any works that have been, or would have to be, carried out to enable the land to be used in a particular way.

A massive building such as Shell House beside the river Thames, reputed to have cost over £30 million, or any of the skyscrapers in New York, clearly is a much more permanent fixture than the pre-fabricated dwellings erected on bomb-damaged sites immediately after the last war. Although it is always technically possible to remove fixed plant and equipment, the cost is considerable and will not normally be entertained until the original works have been fully depreciated and the cost of maintenance and operation is so high, in relation to the possibilities of redevelopment, that rebuilding becomes worthwhile. Therefore, where buildings or other fixtures have a long useful life, the use of the territory on which they have been put cannot readily be changed for twenty, fifty or even more years. Even if the initial development were optimal at the time it occurred, it is almost certain to be increasingly non-optimal as redevelopment becomes imminent. There must therefore always be some element of imperfection in the pattern of land use.

An apt example is provided by the problem of housing the growing population of southeast England. The official expectation is that in the area south of a line from the Wash to the Solent some 3.5 million extra persons will have to be provided for between 1961 and 1981. A substantial part of this increase could be housed in the suburbs that sprang up around London between the wars if these were rebuilt to higher densities. But for the present the government has eschewed this partial solution on the ground that these inter-war dwellings still have many useful years of life. Most of the population increase will have to be housed outside the existing conurbation and an ill-adjusted pattern of land use will survive for many years yet.[5] The same consideration applies to the location of industrial works. Once a factory has been built, be the location good, bad or indifferent, the enterprise will normally stay in that location, until it closes either because of bankruptcy or because obsolescence requires the works to be replaced. The locational pattern of an industry will then evolve as new capacity in new locations replaces the old, at a rate that will be conditioned very largely by the pace of technical development and the consequential tempo of obsolescence and change in locational advantages.

However, the complete removal of a plant does occur occasionally, as when Ford at Old Trafford, Manchester, found that its site was too congested and moved to Dagenham in the early 1930s. In other cases, new capacity is installed on the site of the old even though the initial locational advantages may have disappeared and no *ab initio* investment would be expected there. The Consett steel works is such a case, being the last representative of the numerous iron works that in the 1840s sprang up along the western edge of the Durham coalfield, at that time using local Coal Measure iron ore and coking coal. The persistence, or inertia, of this plant must be due to the fact that at each relevant point of time it was preferable to invest *in situ* rather than elsewhere, as the marginal product of the capital investment there was higher than would be the case if the works were transferred, because of the existence of plant, facilities, labour, etc.

Another consideration is the extent to which a given structure can be adapted to various uses. The nature of the problem is evident in planning a new town which is to have an ultimate population of say 250,000. Does one build the city centre as it is ultimately to be right from the beginning, in which case the central facilities will grossly exceed the demand for many years? Or does one build a part of the centre in its permanent form and leave space for subsequent expansion? The second solution will for some time leave a desert separating the centre from the residential areas unless temporary dwellings are erected on the land earmarked for future central uses, dwellings that could be dismantled in ten or twenty years' time. If this were done, the process of evolution that has continued over centuries in most cities could be planned to occur in decades. To the knowledge of the writer, this solution has not been adopted anywhere in the planning of a new town. However, until it or some equivalent answer is tried, there will remain grave problems in planning new towns much in excess of 80,000 and this is probably an important reason why in Britain official thought is only now tentatively accepting the idea of planning towns of 250,000. The inflexibility of the uses of buildings affects the scale of settlements that can be created in a given time and hence the location of population and industry. The same problem arises with any programme of development that requires a rate of change in land uses in excess of the rate of natural obsolescence of the structures: for example, the planning of a new university on a virgin site presents a microcosm of the issues involved in building a new town.

It is clear that the concept of economic rent (p. 37) provides but an imperfect mechanism for allocating land uses even in the most favourable circumstances. Further imperfections in the land market arise from the multiplicity of forms of tenure and of usufruct rights in land and its attachments. A freeholder may not develop his land to the full because he sets greater store by the maintenance of the existing

I

state (say, a house with large garden) than by increasing his income (by, for example, building flats over the garden). Change of use will then wait upon his death. Where land is held under leasehold and the leases have comparatively short currency—say twenty-one years—redevelopment in the light of changing needs can occur more regularly and certainly. Leases of ninety-nine years or longer are comparable to free-hold but are liable to create their own peculiar problems. In Great Britain, for example, the ninety-nine year leases on a great deal of property built in the Victorian era are now falling in and the lessees are finding that many landlords wish to redevelop the sites. The resulting displacement and/or increase of rents is providing a serious political and social problem where large numbers of leases are due to fall in at about the same time in a limited area, as in Swansea. A second example relates to the relocation of London offices. A Location of Offices Bureau has been established charged with facilitating the dispersal of office employment out of London and on the face of it, because central London office space costs a good deal more than equivalent accommodation in the suburbs, the policy should meet with success. But most of the suburban office accommodation is new whereas many firms in London occupy old property on lease and therefore are paying rents substantially below what they would have to pay were the leases to be re-negotiated. Of 167 firms in leasehold property in central London in 1963, 59 per cent. had over twenty years of their lease still to run.[6] The resulting discrepancy between rents actually paid and those that would be payable were leases to be re-negotiated is shown in Table 18 and the process of relocating offices is materially slowed down.

Mobility of land between uses is also impeded by legislation controlling land use; zoning ordinances for towns in the United States and the Town and Country Planning Acts of the United Kingdom, for example. Public bodies are em-powered to specify a particular kind of use for every parcel of land under their jurisdiction and this control effectively limits the range of options any owner or lessee has to change the use of his land. The purpose of such legislation is to preserve and enhance the public weal by deliberate limitation of the mobility of land between uses.

TABLE 18[7]

LONDON, 1963: actual and estimated rents for leasehold office accommodation in central London

| Rent per square metre per annum | Percentage actually paying rents shown | Percentage estimating market value of premises at rents shown |
|---|---|---|
| Up to 107/- | 12·6 | 0·7 |
| 108–214/- | 28·1 | 5·1 |
| 215–322/- | 34·8 | 14·0 |
| 323–429/- | 13·3 | 30·9 |
| 430–537/- | 4·5 | 30·1 |
| 538–645/- | 1·5 | 11·8 |
| Over 646/- | — | 7·4 |
| Ground rent | 5·2 | — |
| | 100·0 | 100·0 |
| Nos. of firms replying | 135 | 136 |

There are thus many hindrances to rapid change in the use of the earth's surface and change in one direction may be much easier than in the reverse way. This short to medium-term immobility arises primarily from the nature of the fixed capital that is applied to the land, capital that is geographically immobile and often cannot be adapted to other kinds of use. Since the greater proportion of capital is represented by physical plant and erections, capital is on *average* highly immobile. But at the *margin*, new funds that are seeking a profitable investment outlet are highly mobile in both the geographic and the industrial senses. Surplus funds will be invested where the (private) rate of interest is highest, that is to say, where the (private) marginal product of the investment is the greatest. The return to capital thus tends to be equalized between industries and places, though in fact parity is never achieved, if only because:

1. Different investors want to be able to redeem their investment in different periods of time.

2. The degree of risk attaching to investments varies from case to case.

3. People's assessments of the future are rarely identical and therefore two persons making the same investment will expect two different rates of return.

Moreover, the private return on an investment is seldom identical to the social return and therefore in many situations, especially in the less developed parts of the world, capital investment yields comparatively low returns even though capital is scarce (p. 82). The general mobility of capital between areas is thus reduced and on the whole capital tends to flow toward the more developed parts of the world unless countervailing action is taken, a phenomenon that provides a part of the mechanism of cumulative causation adduced by Myrdal to explain the progressive concentration of wealth, industry and population into a few comparatively favoured parts of the world (p. 76).

The ease with which funds can be transferred from one place to another depends primarily upon the extent to which banking facilities have been developed. Although the Greeks and the Romans had well-developed banking systems akin to modern facilities save only that they did not issue paper money, it was in Florence in the twelfth and thirteenth centuries that the foundations of the present system were laid. The Bank of Amsterdam was not established until 1609 and that of Hamburg followed ten years later. The English goldsmiths learned from the Dutch, and the Bank of England was founded in 1694: the Bank of France followed over a century later. The early banks, including the Bank of Amsterdam, were essentially places for the safe keeping of money and for the transfer of money from the account of one client to that of another. It was only slowly that the wider functions of transfer from branch to branch and bank to bank were developed and the business remained hazardous right into the nineteenth century. Between 1811 and 1820, for example, about 195 banks in the United States were bankrupted, and another 180 in the early 1840s; only with an Act of 1863 was the American banking system put on a reasonably firm foundation. Widespread and reliable international facilities are even more recent, institutions such as the World Bank and International Monetary Fund having been set up only after the last war.

The rapid evolution of financial institutions in the last 150 years greatly affects the rôle of capital as a factor in the location of economic activities: before capital was able to circulate freely, there was a strong tendency for any local accumulation of money reserves to result in local investment. For example, the greatness of Venice and Milan, Hamburg and Amsterdam during the so-called Middle Ages was founded on trade but part of the merchants' profits were invested in manufactures that would provide further opportunities for commerce. Owing to the difficulties of moving capital from place to place, combined with the problem of protecting investments during troubled times and the then current ideas of civic or national glory, this investment in productive enterprise mostly occurred locally. Trade fed manufacture and in turn manufacture fed trade, leading to cumulative growth in favoured areas but leaving other regions comparatively underdeveloped. The Po Valley of Italy and the lower Rhineland are two areas that benefited in this way. Of course, the sequence was not universal, for much investment, such as in churches, is materially 'unproductive'. Or, as in the case of Spain, specie imported from the New World led to inflation instead of productive investment.

During the eighteeenth and early nineteenth centuries, capital circulated quite freely within Britain, as the example of capital imports into Wales for the development of coal and iron resources shows (p. 23). But investment abroad was comparatively trivial, except in the colonies, which were regarded as extensions of the motherland whose power and wealth would be augmented in proportion to colonial growth. Only by the combination of Rothschild's innovation of fixing the interest rate in sterling and making dividends payable in London instead of in foreign capitals, with the victory of free trade concepts, with large-scale emigration and with the opportunity/need for investment in railways, mines, etc., did British capital begin to flow freely to non-colonies.

In the present day, the scale of investment in any area is increasingly dependent upon the power to attract funds and less and less upon the size of the locally generated investment surplus. Nevertheless, even within countries as advanced as Denmark and Norway, special steps are taken by government to increase the liquidity of financial institutions in some regions. The capacity to attract funds is a function first of the rate of return that may be expected and second of the chances that political changes will lead to expropriation, penalizing taxation of other disabilities. Hence, the political complexion and stability of a country is a material factor in whether or not it will attract foreign funds: when Cuba or Ceylon nationalizes plantations, banks, oil installations, etc., the future supply of investment funds from abroad is almost automatically sharply reduced. The uncertainties attending an investment in Vietnam or the Congo (Leopoldville) are high on account of the wars that rage or threaten, with the consequence that only the more lucrative investments will be undertaken privately or those deemed essential by the government concerned. On the other hand, a country that occupies a politically or militarily strategic position and which exploits this situation can win a disproportionate share of capital funds. When Russia agreed to finance the first stage of the Aswan High Dam, the western nations who had previously declined felt that it was necessary to accommodate Egypt for the later stages. India enjoys the distinction of having had three steel works built simulteneously by the British, Americans and Russians respectively.

International mobility of capital is also limited by the balance-of-payments problems of individual countries. A heavy outflow of capital funds that continues for any length of time may result in a balance-of-payments crisis for the country concerned. The domestic rate of interest is then likely to be raised and direct curbs may be placed on the export of capital, such measures being designed to correct the payments disequilibrium. Capital exports may also be checked if the balance-of-payments is in deficit on current account. Conversely, a country such as India must be able to increase its exports if foreign capital investments are to be serviced and repaid. Such exports constitute imports for nations like the United States and Germany, who may individually find that their balance-of-payments position is disturbed and that particular domestic interests, threatened by the rising tide of imports, may clamour for protection: Lancashire made her fortune with cotton in conditions of free trade and would now deny the same chance to Hong Kong, India and Japan.

Within the more advanced countries, capital has been able to circulate comparatively freely for many years and in these countries the location of employment and regional development generally is probably little affected by considerations of capital supply. Where the internal financial institutions are imperfect or rudimentary, capital remains comparatively immobile and is therefore a significant location factor.[8] At the international level, the movement of capital is subject to numerous complicated restraints but the recent development of institutions has eased some of the restrictions. Thus, at the international as well as the national level, it is the power to attract rather than to generate investment funds that will increasingly determine regional patterns of investment and development.

## Mobility: Labour

As in the previous analysis of land and capital, two kinds of mobility may be distinguished, mobility between places (geographic mobility) and kinds of work (occupational mobility). These two forms of mobility are far more closely inter-related in the case of labour than is true of land (which is geographically immobile) and capital. A man may leave Dagenham to look for a job in a car assembly plant at Coventry similar to his previous employment, in which case he is geographically mobile and occupationally immobile. Should he stay in Dagenham and take some other job, the description of his mobility is reversed. Finally, he may go to Coventry but get work on a building site, in which case he is both occupationally and geographically mobile at the same time. Thus, the two kinds of mobility may be alternatives (substitutes) or they may be complementary.

Fundamentally, mobility occurs in response to differences in job opportunities and earnings. That there are considerable disparities in average hourly earnings by kind of job and part of country is shown by Table 19, which indicates quite clearly one of the reasons for the substantial net migration into southeast England that has been observed for several decades. Reliable evidence on regional earnings for pre-war years is not available for the United Kingdom but in the United States the geographic variation in wage rates and earnings appears to be narrowing. In 1907, wage rates in manufacturing industries in the Far West were the highest in the country and were 30 per cent. above those in the Northeast but by 1945–46 the difference was only 15 per cent. (Table 20). A similar trend

occurred in United States agricultural wage rates[9] between
1866 and 1945, though the areas of low wages and high wages
have remained remarkably constant.[10] A sensible reduction in
geographic wage disparities has also occurred in France, where
the levelling mostly took place during the two world wars (see
Table 21).

TABLE 19

GREAT BRITAIN: average hourly earnings in engineering and other
metal-using industries, in pence per hour for January 1963, by standard
regions*

| REGION | TIMEWORKERS | | | PAYMENT-BY-RESULT WORKERS | | |
|---|---|---|---|---|---|---|
| | Skilled | Semi-skilled | Labourer | Skilled | Semi-skilled | Labourer |
| Midlands | 97·2 | 79·6 | 65·3 | 109·6 | 100·9 | 74·5 |
| Eastern and Southern | 95·8 | 90·3 | 72·7 | 96·2 | 101·8 | 75·3 |
| London and S.E. | 94·6 | 90·4 | 68·7 | 103·9 | 86·7 | 74·6 |
| South Western | 93·8 | 73·2 | 63·6 | 92·5 | 90·3 | 63·8 |
| Wales | 93·4 | 76·7 | 67·2 | 96·1 | 88·8 | 67·9 |
| North Western | 87·2 | 72·2 | 60·9 | 91·0 | 80·5 | 65·2 |
| Northern | 85·5 | 70·0 | 62·3 | 95·6 | 80·7 | 65·7 |
| Scotland | 83·7 | 73·0 | 63·3 | 93·5 | 82·2 | 69·9 |
| Yorks. and Lincs. | 83·5 | 74·4 | 61·7 | 91·6 | 83·4 | 65·1 |
| National average | 92·6 | 81·7 | 65·2 | 99·6 | 91·4 | 69·4 |

Source: Ministry of Labour Gazette, May 1963, p. 185.
* Overtime included.

TABLE 20[11]

UNITED STATES, 1907–1946: occupational wage rates in manufacturing
industries

| Year | Northeast | South | Midwest | Far West |
|---|---|---|---|---|
| 1945–46 | 100 | 85 | 101 | 115 |
| 1931–32 | 100 | 74 | 97 | 113 |
| 1919 | 100 | 87 | 97 | 115 |
| 1907 | 100 | 86 | 100 | 130 |

It is probable that within many countries the geographic
disparity of wages is becoming progressively less marked. In
comparing countries, however, there is some evidence that
incomes (and therefore earnings) are rising more rapidly in the

TABLE 21[12]

FRANCE, 1840–45/1954: by departments, the ratios of deciles of daily workers' wages

| Ratio of deciles | | 1840–45 | 1860–65 | 1892 | 1954 |
|---|---|---|---|---|---|
| Male | 9th decile ÷ 1st decile | 1·49 | 1·61 | 1·61 | 1·34 |
| | 8th decile ÷ 2nd decile | 1·23 | 1·37 | 1·36 | 1·20 |
| Female | 9th decile ÷ 1st decile | 1·67 | 1·72 | 2·03 | 1·27 |
| | 8th decile ÷ 2nd decile | 1·32 | 1·41 | 1·67 | 1·17 |

richer than in the poorer countries, a phenomenon that has obviously serious political implications. Whether or not this is the trend (and the evidence is far from conclusive), international differences in wage rates are far greater than the differences that normally exist within a single country. For example, a Turkish building worker employed in Western Germany can earn £3 instead of the 7s. a day he would get in his home country, or eight-and-a-half times as much.[13]

In considering whether to change occupations and/or move from one place to another, the majority of people consider the job opportunities and the relative levels of present and prospective income. They rarely examine closely geographic differences in the price level that may affect the amount that can be bought with the incomes being compared. For the most part, such comparison can only be made internationally since adequate data are rarely available for the different parts of a country. Differing international price levels frequently wipe out much of the nominal difference in income, as many migrants from Britain to the United States have discovered to their cost. However, within France:

> Everything leads one to believe that geographic variations in the cost of living at the end of the nineteenth century compensated only slightly for the differences in nominal wages at that time.[14]

Since then, the French cost of living has become geographically more nearly equal: for sixteen cities, the range in 1955 was from 103·7 to 94·9, Paris representing 100·0. For the comparable departments, annual earnings varied from Seine (Paris) as the highest at 100·0 to 60·6 in Vienne (containing the city of Poitiers, where the cost of living was 98·2). But

128          GEOGRAPHY AND ECONOMICS

compare the position in France with that reported for the
United States:

> An intercity comparison of both earnings and the cost of
> living indicates that the magnitude of the earnings
> differential among the large cities of the United States is
> three to four times that of the cost-of-living differen-
> tial. . . . The findings of this paper offer some evidence
> for the conclusion that the relationship is inverse, and that
> where earnings are low, the cost of living tends to be
> high.[15]

Many considerations other than earnings and living costs
must be taken into account before patterns of labour migration
and occupational shift can be analyzed properly.  The satisfaction to be derived from an occupation cannot be directly
measured in monetary terms, nor can the pleasures or otherwise of life in one place as against another.  Though it appears
that in the advanced countries both these factors militate
against rural, especially agricultural, pursuits and in favour of
urban ones, nevertheless agriculturalists as a class seem
prepared to tolerate a much lower income than their urban
brethren, as is shown by Table 22.  Young persons are more

TABLE 22

Probable Ratios of *per caput* 'incentive income' in Agriculture to Industrial
Wages, 1938

Probably over 75 per cent.
    Australia, New Zealand, France, China.

Probably 60–75 per cent.
    United Kingdom, Denmark, Germany (India, Burma,
    Hungary).

Probably 45–60 per cent.
    Sweden, Canada, Finland, Italy (Chile, Japan).

Probably 35–45 per cent.
    United States, Netherlands, Eire, Peru (Norway, Bulgaria,
    Portugal).

Probably under 35 per cent.
    Egypt, Mexico, Philippines, Thailand (Turkey).

*Source:* J. R. Bellerby, *Agriculture and Industry Relative Income*, 1956, p. 270.

Agricultural incentive income is the estimated income of labour and enterprise,
excluding income to other factors.

Countries in brackets are less certain than the rest.

mobile than older workers and sex also has an important bearing: in Western Europe, for example, rural areas offer fewer job opportunities for girls than for boys and therefore the girls are more prone to leave.[16] Nevertheless, women workers are less mobile on average, at least geographically, than are their male counterparts, as Table 23 (p. 141) indicates.

Also important are the expectations that people have as to what a new job or area may have to offer and these expectations may not accord very closely with reality. This is symbolized by Dick Whittington's belief that London's pavements were laid with gold: the optimist in us all will have it that even if others fail to find the gold, we will succeed—as indeed Dick did. Milan, São Paulo and Tokyo have their shanty towns, inhabited by many immigrants from the countryside who have found that their Mecca cannot provide them with all they expected, not even with work. The rate of urban growth is then related to people's expectations of employment and not to the rate at which jobs actually multiply and the concept of the urban economic base (p. 44) then has little relevance in trying to explain patterns of urban expansion.

Further factors affect the occupational and geographic mobility of labour but these can conveniently be discussed under separate headings.

## Occupational Mobility of Labour

Occupational mobility is likely to be greater the more nearly similar the occupations are and to be less in proportion to the dis-similarity. The geographic bearing of this proposition is illustrated by the advantages that Coventry is thought to have enjoyed because the sequence of industries, sewing machines–bicycles–motor vehicles, employed skills that could be readily transferred from one industry to the next (but see p. 97). In contrast, the northeast coast and South Wales have both experienced difficulty in diversifying away from the traditional coal and metal trades owing in part to the difference of skills between the 'old' and the 'new' industries. The history of shipbuilding in Britain aptly illustrates both relationships. Since there was an almost complete break in the development of shipbuilding techniques, the modern shipyards have not, for the most part, evolved directly out of the older ones making wooden vessels. During the early part of the last century, the advent of iron and steam required the use of techniques that were foreign to those of the traditional shipwright and many modern yards developed as entirely new enterprises or by the take-over of old yards by the new breed of engineer. Present-day shipyards are therefore more related to the location of iron and coal resources and the areas of engineering than to traditional links with shipbuilding in the pre-Industrial Revolution era. For all its former importance, the Thames estuary was unable to compete with the more fortunately endowed Mersey, Clyde and Tyne, where the main link with the days of wood and sail lay in the continued growth of sea traffic and therefore of locally based shipping companies which provided a market for the products of the yards.[17]

The long-term prosperity of a region will be more certain if the resident workers possess skills that apply to a wide range of industries or products than where the range of applications is narrow. Skill in foundry work or the use of a lathe can be turned to innumerable products whereas a riveter can hope for work only in a shipyard or on the erection of steel structures. If the demand for ships or structural steels falls, the riveter will find it much harder to find other work than will a machinist faced with a fall in the consumption of, say, spindles for electric motors. Part of the economic strength of the Midland and the London areas derives from the fact that the labour can be re-deployed easily in response to changing market conditions.

Is the number of skills particular to one industry or a small group of industries growing or declining in relative importance? (This question is quite separate from that of whether more or less skill is required.) To the knowledge of the author, no investigation of this problem has been carried out, though it is probable that the number of skilled jobs that is specific to one industry is declining in relative importance. A worker on a motor vehicle assembly line could as well assemble refrigerators or washing machines and modern production-control techniques employ basic principles with wide applications. Indeed, much of the art of industrial development depends upon the discovery and exploitation of first principles, a fact that underlies the following remarks about apprenticeship training:

> Theoretical knowledge must be accepted as an essential
> and integral part of the training of a skilled worker. Tech-
> nological change is now so rapid that rule-of-thumb
> methods are an anachronism. The worker must under-
> stand thoroughly what he is doing and why he is doing it
> that way so that he can adapt his knowledge to new
> needs without difficulty. . . .
> Restrictive lines of demarcation between related trades
> must be entirely removed. Not only would this permit the
> best use of available resources of skill, but it would give
> greater security of employment to the worker by making
> him less vulnerable to the ups and downs of demand in his
> own particular trade. Equally important, it would allow
> of a much greater amount of common training.[18]

At least in Britain, but presumably elsewhere as well, the
potential occupational mobility of the working force needs to
be much greater than it is and could be so if particular skills
were firmly grounded in general aptitude of wide relevance.
The rate of technical change is now such that a worker must
retain his capacity for learning throughout his working life.
Even if the occupational structure of an area remains constant,
the nature of the work actually done by the workers may within
a generation change out of all recognition.

Rapid technical change combined with the increasing facility
for occupational mobility that is implied by changing methods
of teaching renders a gross oversimplification the notion that an
area possesses great advantage from a 'pool' of skilled labour.
It is commonly argued, for example, that once a city like
Sheffield has developed silverware or cutlery as a speciality,
the existence of a body of workmen accomplished in these
arts is a strong inducement for any new firm to set up in the
area rather than elsewhere, as the requisite labour will be
readily available. This proposition implies that the labour is
geographically immobile (of which more below), that labour is
occupationally immobile and that *past* techniques will be of
value in the *present*. The last two assumptions have become
debatable, at least in rapidly developing economies, as is
illustrated by the problems experienced in operating a new,
highly automated works in Sheffield that was designed to

produce high quality alloy steel. In Sheffield, a renowned centre for this type of steel, the workmen were at first not very competent to operate the entirely new equipment.[19] This point has been recognized in a study of the changing locational advantages of Birmingham for motor vehicle assembly in the inter-war years:

> The fast changing technical requirements of production, and the emphasis on high productivity made raw, un-organized labour a positive locational advantage. . . . The Birmingham area's particular structural characteristics— and especially skilled labour—were thus, if anything, a deterrent to the expanding assembler of motor cars.[20]

A more extreme case, that of shipbuilding early last century, has already been mentioned (p. 129).

In fact, during Britain's industrial revolution:

> While new industries were still evolving their techniques and organization, untrained workmen were an advantage to the management and, for their own part, had hopes of rising to positions of seniority as yet unestablished. At the end of the eighteenth century most of the engine-men employed at Darby's ironworks at Coalbrookdale had been trained not by senior workmen, but by James Watt himself at Birmingham;  prior specialist training dis-qualified men for employment at Strutt's mills at Belper. Andrew Ure observed in 1836 that 'Mr. Anthony Strutt, who conducts the mechanical department of the great cotton factories at Belper and Milford . . . will employ no man who has learned his craft by regular apprentice-ship.' Skilled labour was at a discount at James Keir's chemical works, founded in the 1780s, at Tipton: un-trained labourers were in demand for new industrial processes. Traditional technological training through apprenticeship was increasingly superfluous. The Schools Inquiry Commission reported in 1868 large unused funds for providing apprentices with premiums, particularly in newly industrialized districts such as the West Riding of Yorkshire: 'The door of admission into all trades is wide open and needs no artificial help to keep it so'. These circumstances favoured countrywomen even more than men and they moved into the towns in greater numbers: their lack of training and skill in industrial processes was

no handicap and their success in industries which had once relied on skilled men caused Lord Ashley to lament, in debates on the Ten Hours' Bill, that they were 'gradually acquiring all those privileges which are held to be the proper portion of the male sex'.[21]

Labour's rôle in the location of British industry and in regional development appears to have changed though time to a remarkable extent. Before about 1750, traditional skills once acquired were quite potent in encouraging an industry to stay in one area and in inhibiting its spread. Between 1750 and about 1870, the rate of technical change was such that traditional expertise was often as much a liability as an asset. Then, from 1870 to shortly after the last war, the pendulum swung back, only to rebound since 1950, with the increasing tempo of change and the spread of new methods of learning skills. This general conclusion, which will not apply exactly to all industries and certainly not to all countries, is consistent with what we know of geographic mobility (p. 139-40). The over-all conclusion is that increasingly the prosperity of a region, as of a nation, depends upon how well equipped it is to accept and exploit technical change; fundamentally, this depends upon the attitudes of the people, for the Luddite lurks in us all. For example, the British shipbuilding industry is undoubtedly smaller than it would have been had demarcation disputes between the unions not hampered it in competition with Japanese, Swedish and German shipyards.

Herein lies the challenge to and opportunity for those regions that are lacking in mineral or other natural endowments attractive to industry or whose resource base is nearing exhaustion. If they can develop the potential for skill that exists among their people, they may be able to compensate for remote location and poor resources by developing capital and/or labour-intensive occupations, comparable to the watches, precision engineering and toys traditionally associated with Switzerland.

### Geographic Mobility of Labour

Geographic mobility of labour is manifest in a variety of ways:

| *Time-period* | *Size of group* |
|---|---|
| 1. Daily | 1. Single person |
| 2. Seasonal | 2. Family group |
| 3. Long-term but not intended to be permanent | 3. Mass migration |
| 4. Intended to be permanent | |

Almost any combination of time-period and size of group is possible and these combinations can occur both within countries and between states. In addition, there is the distinction between voluntary movement and that which results from coercion in one form or another. There is not space to treat separately involuntary movements such as the transportation of convicts to Australia or the forced exchange of population between Greece and Turkey after the First World War, and we shall assume that all movement is free. We shall further exclude the problem of daily commuting to work, a topic that has elicited a copious literature.[22]

One might expect geographic mobility to be greater where the income differences between areas are the most marked: by the same token, the poorest persons are likely to have the most to gain by migration. Empirical observation denies this easy correlation. An inter-war study of unemployed workers in South Wales showed 'that the chronically unemployed, *i.e.*, those unemployed for over a year, were about half as mobile as those unemployed for shorter periods'.[23] For a variety of reasons, those who most 'needed' to be mobile were the least able or willing so to be. The same point can be seen in the agricultural sector of Europe, for the greater rural exodi do not always occur from the poorer areas but often from those of intermediate income.[24] When the exodus from Ireland began in the summer of 1846 following the first potato failure and when it became evident that another was imminent, the *wealthier* peasantry were the first to go and the poorer only fled in destitution when the alternative was starkly evident:[25]

> The coincidence of areas of excessive pauperism and those of low rates of emigration was fairly close. From the south-west extremity of Ireland northward along the

west coast as far as County Galway this relationship held good, but farther north County Mayo was the exception to the general rule. Although the area of extreme conditions in the west is designated . . . as having more than 50 per cent. of its population paupers, this figure was frequently exceeded, notably in Ballinrobe, Ballyvaughan, Clifden, Listowel, Bantry, Scarrif, Kanturk and Newcastle, where over 70 per cent. of the population was indigent. Poverty of such proportions meant that virtually a half or even three-quarters of the population were not in a position to leave. The inability to go, because of lack of means, was cause for comment right through the famine; and clearly a pauper population could not pay the average fare of 50 to 60 shillings to Canada and not less than 70 shillings to the U.S.A.[26]

This situation has a close parallel in the definition of marginal land (p. 50). Just as marginal land, defined as that which most readily changes uses, is not necessarily yielding a poor return, so marginal labour is often not the lowest paid.

Emigration from Ireland before the famine years of the 1840s had been limited, among other reasons, by the cost of passages. During the eighteenth century, only some 5,000 persons sailed across the Atlantic each year, and these folk were mainly from Ulster, farmers of Scottish descent who possessed the means to better themselves. During the Napoleonic wars, a transformation occurred owing to the cessation of timber supplies from the Baltic and the consequential growth of English imports from Canada. These timber ships found a ready return cargo— Irish citizens—who could be transported profitably at very low fares, albeit in the most squalid of conditions. By 1844, the annual number sailing had risen to 68,000.[27]

The availability and cost of personal transport is clearly a crucial factor in any discussion of migration. In general terms, personal movement has become far easier in the course of the last century and a half. However, the cost of passenger transport is much affected by an important factor other than technical improvement and scale economies, for the standard of comfort expected by migrants today is so much greater than was tolerated even one hundred years ago that the real cost of passenger travel by sea and air, while less than formerly, has not fallen to the same extent as the cost of goods carriage.

K

Another variable factor is the amount of assistance accorded to migrants, either from private or from public funds. Before and during the Irish famine, some landlords helped their 'tenants' to emigrate, one at least even chartering a vessel for the purpose.[28] The railway companies of the United States and Canada during the last century assisted the passage of migrants in order to encourage the taking up of the land that had been granted to the companies, the exploitation of which was essential to the financial success of the railways. With the passage of the Empire Settlement Act, 1922, the British government negotiated agreements with nations of the then Empire for the assistance of those migrating from Britain, the governments sharing the cost equally.[29] These agreements have been renegotiated from time to time and currently, for example, an assisted Briton emigrating to Australia pays only £10 sterling towards his passage while other nationalities receive from the Australian government about £57 sterling in partial defrayment of their fare. In the period, January, 1947, to June, 1962, Australia received 933,000 assisted immigrants.

Numerous other forms of help may be provided. Australian immigrants may live in government hostels while seeking accommodation. In agricultural colonization schemes, the newcomer may be given work as a labourer on an already established holding for a year or two while he accumulates a little capital and learns how to cope with the new environment and when he gets a holding there may be a grant or loan of livestock and seed to enable him to start farming. Since the First World War, there has been a general tendency for governments to participate more actively in both internal resettlement schemes and in assisting international migration. Oddly enough, the latter phenomenon has occurred during a period in which governments have also taken greater powers to *prevent* emigration or immigration that they consider to be undesirable.

The propensity to migrate is affected by the amount of information that is available of opportunities elsewhere. In principle, the more freely information is available the more likely are people to feel the urge and the confidence to go, and the spread of literacy, the wireless and television should therefore stimulate geographic mobility. The migration of rural people to the towns does seem to be encouraged by an increasing awareness among the rural populace of urban opportunities, an awareness derived in part from the increased personal mobility conferred by motor vehicles and in part by the mixing of country and town children in schools that are situated in the towns. The exodus from Ireland was also facilitated by numerous agents who sold passage tickets (often fraudulently) and who simultaneously provided a channel for information (which was often coloured). However, where knowledge is imperfect it is also possible for exciting rumours to gain widespread credence, as the gold rushes to California, Yukon, New Zealand and Australia testify. The better is the fund of information, the greater is *rational* migration likely to be.

The problem of access to information has an important bearing on regional development within a country such as the United Kingdom. A broad distinction may be made between the more highly educated professional and executive class of worker and the remainder of the working population. For the former, there are well-organized channels of information, such as the 'appointments' column of *The Times*, whereby it is quite possible to know of job opportunities anywhere in the country. Travelling expenses for interview are commonly paid and there may even be a removal allowance paid by the new employer. Humbler folk must rely primarily upon the Ministry of Labour Employment Exchanges, which are able to apprise them of work available in the vicinity but are not geared to provide information for the whole country. Very little help is available for searching in other parts and for financing a removal, and to qualify for such aid as there is, a worker must already be unemployed. The present arrangements seem designed to immobilize that section of the working population which in many ways should receive differentially favourable treatment in order to equalize the opportunities for migration.

Migration within a country is also greatly affected by the amount and nature of the housing that is available. Immediately after the last war, accommodation in Britain was so scarce that most people durst not attempt to move lest they found themselves without a roof over their heads. As the supply of dwellings has eased, geographic mobility has been impeded by two other factors. Local authorities are permitted to subsidize their tenants, who may thus get remarkably cheap accommodation. In Scotland until very recently, many council tenants paid only 10s. or 15s. a week for an older house; if these families moved elsewhere, they would have to pay 30s. or 40s. at the very least and such an increase in rent has proved an effective deterrent to mobility. Similarly, the control of rents that was instituted during the last war still persists and creates a class of people who are paying less than the market price for their accommodation: they too need an especially big inducement to move. This kind of problem is highlighted by the case of Witton Park, Co. Durham, a village that sprang up during the last century west of Bishop Auckland on account of the establishment of an iron works. The plant closed between the wars and, the houses being squalid, insanitary examples of jerry-building, the county council wished after the last war to rehouse the inhabitants and raze the village. However, the rents are so low (the properties are owned by the National Coal Board) that the inhabitants have successfully refused to budge.

In addition to the above factors affecting migration, numerous others of a more sociological nature operate. Affinities or otherwise of language, colour and religion have a material effect in checking or encouraging movement in certain directions. Family or village associations often lead to the migration of a whole group of people once some members have taken the plunge.

Long-distance migration in a single move is rarer than short-distance transfers. In general, migration between any pair of places is inversely related to the distance that separates them, with the proviso that account must be taken of the intervening opportunities.[30] Isard quotes a number of examples[31] of this proposition and it is therefore only necessary to cite one case as an illustration. Of the 495 persons who left the parish of Asby, Sweden, between 1940 and 1944, 185 went less than 18 kilometres, 149 between 18 and 34, 42 between 35 and 51 kilometres and 49 between 52 and 68 kilometres. Thereafter, the maximum number for any seventeen-kilometre range was 16 persons.[32] A skew distribution with respect to distance is usual, though the range of distances involved and the median distance will vary in place and in time. In the case of Asby, the median distance of out-migrations in each ten-year period between 1840 and 1939, involving 7,730 people, was under 18 kilometres: for 1940–44, the median for 495 migrants was between 18 and 34 kilometres. By comparison, the median migration distance of 9,647 persons who had migrated to Oxford and were resident there in 1936 was between 90 and 101 kilometres.[33] The kind of migration will also affect the distances involved, as may be seen from the fact that in a study of the *residential* moves of families within Cleveland, Ohio, the median distance was found to be between 900 and 1,800 metres in the period 1933 to 1935.[34]

Due to changes in the factors that affect migration, one would expect that on a long-term view mobility should be increasing. It is exceedingly difficult to test this expectation owing to the deficiencies of the available statistics.[35] At the international level, it is impossible to measure total migration movements in relation to world population over a period of years and the experience of individual countries, being greatly affected by highly variable political conditions, cannot readily be used as the basis of generalizations. On the other hand, although internal migration is usually less well documented than is external movement, extraneous political changes have less effect on mobility patterns. The evidence that follows supports the idea that over time internal mobility is increasing.

Sweden has a unique record of population movements, based on annual parish registers. These show a steady decline in the proportion of persons who were born in their county of residence:[36]

| Year | Percentage of population born in county of residence | |
| | Rural areas | Urban areas |
| 1930 | 84·5 | 63·3 |
| 1860 | 95·1 | 74·9 |

Similar figures obtained in the French censuses show that the proportion of all persons residing in the department of birth is declining, from 78·6 per cent. in 1911 to 71·9 per cent. in 1946, and a sample survey in 1961 indicated that the trend had continued to that year.[37] In Great Britain, the percentage of the working population whose recorded place of work changed from one *standard region* to another within a twelve-month increased from 1·6 in 1952–53 to 2·4 in 1962–63.[38] In this country, the post-war era has witnessed a much higher level of worker mobility than obtained during at least part of the inter-war period, for between 1926 and 1935 the annually recorded movement of workers between *counties* (smaller than standard regions) was only about 1 per cent.[39] By contrast, geographic mobility in the United States appears to have remained nearly constant since 1870:[40]

| Year | Percentage of total population | |
|------|---|---|
| | *Born in state of residence* | *Born in state contiguous with one of residence* |
| 1950 | 73·5 | 10·4 |
| 1870 | 76·8 | 9·6 |

Statistics for annual change of residence show that there has been little change since 1950 in the degree of mobility: in March 1951, 92·7 per cent. of the American population resided in the same county as in March 1950, compared with 93·4 in 1962 who lived in the same county as a year previously.[41] The United States is probably atypical of the general trend owing to the exceptional mobility associated with immigration and the 'frontier days' of the nineteenth century.

An increasing degree of intranational geographic mobility reinforces the conclusion reached in examining occupational mobility, that the traditional view of labour as a factor in the location of economic activities must be modified (p. 131). In-creasing geographic mobility implies a reduction in geographic wage differentials, for which some evidence has already been offered (p. 125). (In the case of the United States, the reduced geographic wage differentials are probably due very largely to shifts in the location of manufacturing industry.) Conse-quently, wage differentials as a factor in industrial location and economic development generally within a nation are likely to become progressively less important. Increasing intranational geographic mobility also implies that the existing location of labour is becoming less important as a factor affecting industrial location patterns than formerly was the case. Therefore, where labour is willing to go becomes ever more significant. Traditionally, willingness to migrate has been largely con-ditioned by the job opportunities available but rising standards of living in an era of full-employment confer increasing scope for choice based on personal preferences of area, kind of society and access to open country or urban amenities. This kind of choice, once available to only a small section of the community, is now open to a larger and growing proportion of workers, particularly the highly trained. With rapid and sustained economic growth it is therefore probable that the relative growth of regions can be influenced by the deliberate policy of providing first-class facilities for shopping, entertainment, housing, etc., in those areas which it is desired to help.

Two cautions are necessary in applying the above reasoning to particular cases. Even within one country at a particular time there are marked differences in the degree of geographic mobility, as B. Wendel has shown for Sweden.[42] Using parish statistics for the period 1946–50 and making an ingenious correction for the areal extent of the administrative units, he found that mobility was high in the area Gävle–Örebro–Norrköping surrounding Stockholm, in much of rural northern Sweden and in the prosperous south of Scania around Mälmo. Mobility was generally low in the rural west and south but also in the vicinity of Göteborg, Sweden's second city. Likewise, the relative mobility of classes of workers is apt to differ from place to place, though data to measure these variations are scanty in the extreme. Table 23 shows that in the United States

TABLE 23

UNITED STATES, 1949–50: percentage of civilian population, March 1950, not residing in the same county as in March 1949

| Class of worker | Male | Female |
|---|---|---|
| Professional and semi-professional | 9·1 | 6·1 |
| Farm labourers and farm foremen | 7·5 | 3·4 |
| Service workers | 5·6 | 5·7 |
| Clerical, sales and kindred workers | 5·4 | 4·2 |
| Labourers, excl. farm and mine | 5·2 | — |
| Proprietors, managers and officials | 4·9 | 3·2 |
| Operatives and kindred workers | 4·4 | 3·4 |
| Craftsmen, foremen and kindred workers | 4·2 | 2·2 |
| Farmers and farm managers | 3·4 | 1·1 |
| AVERAGE | 5·0 | 4·5 |

Source: Bureau of the Census, Statistical Abstract of the United States 1952, 1952, p. 40.

male farm workers are nearly as mobile as professional persons and far more so than farmers and farm managers. In Western Europe, the 'upper' social classes are probably at least as mobile as in the United States but a sample study in France suggests that the difference between farmer and farm worker is much smaller there than across the Atlantic.[43] However, during the nineteenth century in Britain, it was the unskilled manual workers who dominated internal migration.[44]

## Movements of Capital and Labour as Alternatives?

It was suggested on p. 44 that geographic transfers of capital and labour could be regarded as alternatives that would yield dis-similar geographic distributions. This was too great a simplification.

If capital funds move from A to B, the transfer may take place without any movement of labour. Nevertheless, it is quite common for at least a few technical and advisory staff to super-intend the construction work that may be involved and to act as trainers of the indigenous workers during the first year or two of operation. This occurs even when funds from one advanced country are invested in another. Thus, capital transfers are usually accompanied by some transfer of labour, even though this is only a temporary migration.

On the other hand, any migration of labour (and of non-working folk) implies a corresponding movement of capital that may be substantial. At the very least, a migrant will take with him such capital as he possesses—savings and the money realized from the sale of assets such as a car and house. Indeed, some countries insist that a migrant must have a minimum sum of money, presumably as a guarantee against indigence. At his destination, it will be necessary to provide accommodation and facilities for work and leisure, and these provisions may be made either from local capital or by the import of capital, or both. The magnitude of the costs that may be associated with migration, other than the cost of travel, is indicated by the outlay of *public* money in grants and loans in Great Britain to provide one industrial job under the Local Employment Act, 1960. The average cost is about £1,000 per job but the most expensive projects may incur an outlay of £3,000. During the first year of the Act's operation, the distribution of projects was:[45]

| Cost to the Exchequer per job created | Number of factory projects |
|---|---|
| Below £1,000 | 147 |
| £1,000–£1,499 | 28 |
| £1,500–£2,499 | 9 |
| £2,500 or more | 3 |
| | 187 |

The Wilton chemical works of Imperial Chemical Industries, Ltd., represents a *total* investment of about £12,000 per worker, whereas in the clothing trades the *total* investment may be as low as £100–£150 per worker.[46]

The magnitude of these capital costs is partly conditioned by the scale of the migration. A single person will probably be able to find accommodation in the existing stock of dwellings and work in an existing factory, farm or office, and the marginal capital investment will therefore be negligible. However, when large numbers are involved, whole new communities must be created and the marginal outlay per migrant will be far higher.

If restrictions are placed upon the mobility of labour, one result will be to reduce, even if only slightly, transfers of capital. Conversely, if the transfer of capital is restricted, the movement of labour may be seriously affected:

1. If capital cannot be imported into a country that is receiving immigrants, the rate of absorption of the immigrants will be limited by the rate of local capital formation.

2. Would-be migrants are apt to remain where they are if they are prevented from taking with them their own capital.

We are thus able to understand some of the reasons why the waves of emigration from the United Kingdom to the United States during the last century were associated with increased investment activity in America and a decline in capital formation in Britain. Capital movements tended to occur simultaneously with, or shortly after, the major population transfers of 1844–54, 1863–73, 1878–88 and 1898–1907.[47]

As to the inter-related transfer of capital and labour between occupations, there is little to be said except that the rate at which the occupational structure of a country or region can change is in part conditioned by the fact that most of the capital stock consists of fixed plant, equipment and facilities of all kinds, of which the rate of physical replacement is one determinant of economic growth and change.

## Conclusion

Adjustment to changing circumstances may be impeded by two major classes of obstacle: large indivisibilities that create serious problems of adjusting capacity to demand; and the immobility of the factors of production. In general, it seems that the size of indivisibilities for many basic manufactures—steel, petroleum refining, plastics and chemicals, vehicles, etc.—is growing fairly rapidly. In developing countries it is therefore common in the early stages for many goods to be imported in small quantities and for many of these imports to be replaced by local manufacture as the demand expands. The rate of industrialization will be slow if demand rises sluggishly and if the indivisibilities are large. The same problem is manifest in the exploitation of natural resources if the development must be done on a big scale. However, modern engineering techniques make possible much larger projects than have hitherto been practical and consequently it is now possible to undertake projects of river control, irrigation, land drainage, etc., that could not be contemplated previously. The size of the threshold to development that can be tackled is getting bigger.

The mobility of resources, between kinds of activity and between places, has been curiously neglected in the geographic literature. The effect of any one location factor depends very much on its mobility relative to the mobility of all other factors. The relative mobility of land, labour and capital between uses, and of labour and capital between places, has changed greatly over time and varies widely from one locality to another. In particular, the notion that a localized pool of labour is an important inducement to the establishment in the area of further works of the same kind is untenable as a general proposition. It may be true in specific cases. But in each case it is a matter of the mobility of labour between jobs and places compared with the mobility of the other relevant factors, and there is no reason to suppose that the relationship is constant.

## REFERENCES

1 F. T. Moore, 1959, *op. cit.*, (Chap. 4) p. 233.

2 *The Times*, 4th March 1964.

3 J. M. Houston, 'The significance of irrigation in Morocco's economic development', *Geographical Journal*, 1954, p. 325.

4 Board of Trade Census. In subsequent censuses, the definition of 'small' firm has been changed to twenty-four workers or less.

5 Ministry of Housing and Local Government, *The Southeast Study 1961–1981*, 1964, p. 33.

6 Location of Offices Bureau, *A Survey of Factors Governing the Location of Offices in the London Area*, 1964, p. 19.

7 *Ibid.*, p. xi.

8 For a geographic account of the evolution of banking in one region, see J. Labasse, *Lex capitaux et la région. Essai sur le commerce et la circulation des capitaux dans la région lyonnaise*, 1955.

9 W. D. Weatherford, Jr., *Geographic Differentials of Agricultural Wages in the United States*, 1957.

10 For a comprehensive account of changes in *incomes* see F. A. Hanna, *State Income Differentials 1919–1954*, 1959.

11 M. Segal, *Wages in the Metropolis*, 1960, p. 84.

12 P. Madinier, *Les disparités géographiques de salaires en France*, 1959, p. 68.

13 *The Times*, 1st July 1964.

14 P. Madinier, 1959, *op. cit.*, p. 98.

15 J. P. Henderson, 'An intercity comparison of differentials in earnings and the city worker's cost of living', *Review of Economics and Statistics*, 1955, p. 407.

16 For example, of those born in the rural Swedish parish of Arnäs in the period 1896–1905, 36·5 per cent. of the men lived their whole life up to the age of fifty in the parish of birth, whereas only 26·1 of the females did. See B. Wendel, 'A migration schema. Theories and observations', *Lund Studies in Geography*, Ser. B, Human Geography, No. 9, 1953, p. 7.

17 D. Rebbeck, *The History of Iron Ship-building on the Queen's Island up to July 1874*, unpublished Ph.D. thesis, The Queen's University, Belfast, 1950.

18 Lady G. Williams, *Apprenticeship in Europe: the Lesson for Britain*, 1963, pp. 180, 182 and 183.

19 *The Times*, 11th October 1963.

20 M. E. Beesley, 'Changing locational advantages in the British motor car industry', *Journal of Industrial Economics*, 1957, p. 51.

21 F. Musgrove, *The Migratory Elite*, 1963, pp. 53–54, by permission of the publisher.

22 K. Liepmann, *The Journey to Work*, 1944. A. E. Smailes, *The Geography of Towns*, 1953. P. Self, *Cities in Flood*, 1957.

23 H. W. Robinson, 'The response of labour to economic incentives', in T. Wilson and P. W. S. Andrews (eds), *Oxford Studies in the Price Mechanism*, 1951, p. 220.

24 International Labour Office, *Why Labour Leaves the Land*, 1960, pp. 115–17.

25 C. Woodham-Smith, 1962, *op. cit.*, (Chap. 5), p. 214.

26 S. H. Cousens, 'The regional pattern of emigration during the great Irish famine, 1846–51', *Transactions and Papers*, Institute of British Geographers, 1960, p. 128.

27 C. Woodham-Smith, 1962, *op. cit.*, pp. 206–09.

28 T. W. Freeman, *Pre-Famine Ireland. A Study in Historical Geography*, 1957, p. 41.

29 G. F. Plant, *Oversea Settlement*, 1951, p. 82ff.

30 S. A. Stouffer, 'Intervening opportunities: a theory relating mobility and distance', *American Sociological Review*, 1940, pp. 845–67.

31 W. Isard, 1956, *op. cit.*, (Chap. 2), especially pp. 63–64.

32 T Hägerstrand, 'Migration and area', in D. Hannerberg *et al.* (eds), 'Migration in Sweden: a symposium', *Lund Studies in Geography*, Ser. B, Human Geography, No. 13, 1957, p. 87.

33 H. W. Robinson, 1951, *op. cit.*, p. 216.

34 S. A. Stouffer, 1940, *op. cit.*, p. 850.

35 P. M. Hauser and O. D. Duncan (eds), *The Study of Population. An Inventory and Appraisal*, 1959, pp. 486–543.

36 D. S. Thomas, *Social and Economic Aspects of Swedish Population Movements 1750–1933*, 1941, p. 46.

37 A. Girard *et al.*, 'Mobilité géographique et concentration urbaine en France. Une enquête en province', *Population*, 1964, p. 245.

38 *Ministry of Labour Gazette*.

39 H. W. Robinson, 1951, *op cit.*, p. 214. The figure given by Robinson is 0·5 per cent. of the total population.

40 Bureau of the Census, *Historical Statistics of the United States. Colonial Times to 1957*, 1960, p. 41.

41 *Ibid.*, p. 47 and *Statistical Abstract of the United States 1963*, p. 37.

42 B. Wendel, 'Regional aspects of internal migration and mobility in Sweden, 1946–1950', in D. Hannerberg *et al.*, 1957, *op cit.*, pp. 7–26.

43 A. Girard *et al.*, 1964, *op cit.*, pp. 229 and 233.

44 F. Musgrove, 1963, *op cit.*, p. 44.

45 Seventh Report from the Estimates Committee, Session 1962–3, *Administration of the Local Employment Act, 1960*, House of Commons, May 1963, p. 47.

46 J. W. House, 1964, *op. cit.*, (Chap. 4), p. 22.

47 B. Thomas, *Migration and Economic Growth*, 1954, chapters 10 and 11.

# CHAPTER 6

# Demand, Trade and Substitution

Articles are made and services provided only because they are wanted or are thought to be wanted. Normally, it is demand that begets production and only rarely does the availability of an article create the demand therefor. As remarked on p. 7, no study of the spatial distribution of productive activities can be complete without a full consideration of the demand factor. At the simplest level, the location of a factory will affect the volume of demand that can be tapped at any given cost in transport, advertizing and general office administration, and volume of demand will in turn condition the scale of output and hence whether or not scale economies of manufacture can be realized. To maximize profits in an imperfectly competitive world, easy access to a large market may permit scale economies to be achieved that will more than offset costs of assembling and processing materials that are greater than in other possible locations.

The real significance of demand runs deeper than this, for all production depends on the delicate relationship of supply–price–demand and any change in demand anywhere in the world is apt to have wide repercussions, as may any change of production. The factors that govern demand, and the geographic distribution of demand, may be studied for their own sake but in this book demand will be treated as one of the variables that influences the location of production.

We conceive of production as a flow of goods or services and we measure output in terms of unit quantities in a stated time (*e.g.* tons per annum). Consumption, or demand, must be viewed in the same terms: one consumes X oranges per day or week. Actual consumption represents only one point on the schedule of demand, which is a schedule of how much would be consumed at a series of given prices. In principle, one can construct a demand schedule for individuals and also as an aggregate for a whole nation or region. Aggregate actual consumption represents the point at which the schedule of aggregate demand intersects the schedule of total supply—hence is derived the price of the article.

## Price Elasticity of Demand

Fundamental to the analysis of demand is the metaphysical idea of utility. A hungry man will set great store by a plentiful repast but however great his initial appetite, there will come a time when the satisfaction derived from further eating wanes and, should he be greedy enough, nausea may supervene. The utility of additional food declines and may even become a disutility. The same principle applies with all goods and services. The first unit consumed is apt to be better appreciated than the last unit of the same commodity or service and a rational being will so order his private affairs that for the marginal outlay on one commodity (or service) he obtains a satisfaction equal to that obtained from equal marginal expenditures on all the other items he purchases. If the utilities of the marginal outlays are not equal, a re-disposition of the given expenditure will yield an increase in total satisfaction (though this is not a concept that is amenable to strict definition).

Any change in relative prices will alter the marginal satisfactions obtained from a given pattern of expenditure and is therefore likely to induce an alteration in the quantities of goods purchased. It follows that there is a price-elasticity of demand for any commodity, comparable to the price-elasticity of supply (p. 56). The elasticity of demand is much affected by the proportion of the consumer's total outlay that is absorbed by the commodity in question. Salt is a necessity of life which takes a minute part of expenditure in advanced countries and for which there is no substitute; demand is therefore price-inelastic. Housing, on the other hand, may take as much as one-quarter of a man's income and demand is very price-elastic. Demand is also affected by the fact that many forms of consumption require a complementary use of other goods or services: breakfast cereals are eaten with milk, tennis racquets can only be used with tennis balls. These are examples of joint demand (cf. joint supply). Finally, demand is strongly influenced by cross-elasticities or the possibility of substitution between articles of consumption. In the case of salt, there is no alternative commodity that competes and substitution possibilities are slender, whereas beef, mutton and pork are ready alternatives to each other and the demand for one meat is much affected by its price relative to the others.

In addition to demands for final consumption, there is a chain of what may be termed 'derived' demands. A motor-car comprises many thousands of parts, including tyres, leather upholstery and copper wires, to name only three, and therefore a car purchaser in the United Kingdom creates a demand for rubber (from Malaya perhaps, or synthetic rubber derived from Venezuelan petroleum) and for hides and copper which may be obtained respectively from Argentina and Zambia. Soap requires animal or vegetable oils for its manufacture, the production of wheat needs fertilizers and machinery and the use of electric light creates a need for glass for the bulbs. It is common for articles for which the demand is derived to represent only a small part of the cost of the final article and where this is the case the price-elasticity of demand will tend to be low. For example, the total consumption of rubber in cars is much more affected by the level of demand for cars than by changes in the price of rubber, as these have little impact on the price of the vehicles. However, individual tyre manufacturers find that their *share* of the market is much affected by their price (and quality) in relation to competing makes, even though total tyre sales are somewhat price-inelastic.

Few problems arise if both production and demand are price elastic since any disequilibrium between supply and demand will be rectified through quite small changes in price. If either or both demand and supply are inelastic, violent changes in price may be occasioned by small excesses or deficiencies of supply in relation to demand. For the producers and consumers, such price variation can be a serious economic hazard, particularly for the producer, who is often more dependent upon the commodity in question than is the purchaser, as with many mineral raw materials such as tin. Furthermore, if certain areas are specialized in the production of goods the price of which is variable, then the hazards of regional specialization are multiplied (p. 87).

Two broad classes of commodity are more affected by unpredictable price variations than any other, raw materials
for industry and foodstuffs. The evidence for this may be
seen in the columns of journals such as *The Financial Times*,
in which daily prices are quoted for substances like wool,
cotton, sugar and wheat whereas notices about changes in the
prices of manufactured goods and services such as transport are
sporadic.

Raw materials for manufacturing are generally in somewhat
inelastic demand owing to the fact that demand is derived and
is not greatly affected in the short run by changes in the price
of the materials. The demand may, however, be highly
variable: if there is a widespread boom in the industrial
economies, tin and copper, for example, are in great and
urgent demand. While a reduction in output of such raw
materials may occur in response to falling demand, an increase
in output may not readily be possible at short notice: new
mines might have to be sunk, for example. On the other hand,
variation in the yield of crops and animal products are often
great from one year to the next owing to the vagaries of climate,
pest and disease. Such uncontrollable changes in supply
combined with inelastic demand create conditions ripe for big
price oscillations.

In the case of foodstuffs, demand is inelastic because the
extent to which human beings can alter their intake of food,
either upwards or downwards, is fairly strictly limited by biological necessities. On the other hand, annual production
varies for the same reason that affects agricultural raw materials—unpredictable harvests. Agricultural production in
general is characterized by the large number of producers
engaged in the production of any one commodity and this
renders difficult, if not impossible, the planned control of output from year to year. Furthermore, if the conditions of climate,
terrain or equipment on farms limit the range of products that
can economically be produced, falling prices for any one
agricultural product may stimulate an increase in output that
will tend to accentuate the condition of excess supply (p. 60).

Although foodstuffs and raw materials generally are subject
to great changeability of prices, for particular commodities this
is not always so. For example, the retail price of broiler

chickens is less variable than is the retail price of most other meats, probably due to the organization of the broiler industry on 'factory' lines plus the comparatively short production cycle for chickens, whereby supply can be closely adjusted to demand. There may also be marketing agreements among sellers designed to reduce price fluctuations and to ensure 'orderly' selling, examples being the international trade in sugar and cocoa and the pre-war attempt to regulate the market for natural rubber (the success of such schemes is doubtful). If the marketing of produce is done through a monoposonist buyer, prices may be administered to reduce seasonal and annual fluctuations, as with milk in the United Kingdom and the major export crops of Nigeria. Or there may be long-term contracts governing prices and quantities, as with methane from the Sahara imported into the United Kingdom. Finally, if vertical integration of production is a feature of an industry, as with the mining of iron ore and the making of steel, short-term fluctuations in final demand will be reflected in changes in the output of the goods for which demand is derived and not in price changes.

Although it is generally true that manufactured goods vary in price less than do primary materials, this is really only true of intranational prices. Manufactures that are traded internationally appear to vary in unit price about as much as other goods entering international trade.[1] This may be due largely to the fact that exports abroad are commonly only a small part of total sales, often on individual contracts that are negotiated against the general trading prospects of the firm. If trade is slack, prices may be quoted below total cost but high enough to cover the variable (out-of-pocket) costs and contribute something toward the fixed or overhead costs. If trade is brisk, the foreign buyer may be required to pay well above the domestic price. (See Chapter 7.)

The marked stability of intranational prices for manufactures occurs despite the frequency of inelastic demand, which for a wide range of semi-processed materials and components is a derived demand. Several factors contribute to this seemingly paradoxical situation. Although the number of manufacturing establishments is very large, the extent to which commodities are differentiated in quality, design and pack is enormous,

L

wherefor the number of firms making identical goods is often quite small. This means that some form of market regulation, tacit if not overt, is comparatively easily organized, and is often exercised through the price leadership of one or two dominant firms. Second, the technical conditions of production and marketing render it easier, in the short run, to adjust output than to alter price. A change in the hours of overtime worked in a factory or an alteration of the total labour force, is comparatively easy to organize whereas price changes must be communicated to perhaps thousands of dealers and millions of consumers. Whereas a farmer can keep abreast of price changes which affect perhaps twenty or thirty products, although he may not be very efficient at so doing, an ordinary citizen would need to be aware of hundreds, if not thousands, of prices, to behave rationally. It is normal therefore, for short-term variations in the demand for industrial products to be met by output changes and not by price alteration.

This general statement does not apply equally to all manufactures. It is truest where the supply can most readily be altered to meet demand shifts and least true where the production cycle is long and where orders are individually negotiated. For example, many British shipyards were in 1964 quoting prices much below their previous levels in order to attract scarce orders, whereas the prices of many plastics hardly vary from one year to the next. Perhaps equally important, however, is the extent to which demand can be deferred.

### Deferred Demand

If hunger is satisfied, the satisfaction will last but a few hours and soon there will again be an urgent necessity to eat. The demand for food is therefore not one that can be deferred for any significant period of time. On the other hand, investment by a shipping line in a new vessel can be delayed for several years if the company judges that trading prospects are gloomy and that the existing stock of vessels will suffice. Therefore, although we initially conceived demand in terms of a continuous flow, it is more accurate to think of demand as a flow that may be continuous or sporadic. The demand for some commodities is extremely regular, as with food and water and, in lesser degree, clothing, domestic fuel, and non-durable consumer goods. The traditional antithesis is between these 'consumer' goods and investment goods—capital equipment of all kinds, from ships to factory buildings, bridges to hospitals— which have a long life. Expenditure on the latter class of things can be deferred for many years, even if it is not always wise so to do. A wide range of goods falls between these two extremes, in particular consumer durables like furniture, cars and television sets: the demand for these goods can be very fickle, though within a shorter time-period than affects basic investment goods.

### Some Geographic Effects of Variable Demand and Prices

The reader will recognize that the deferment of demand will have important effects. For a national economy as a whole, the multiplier effect on incomes and employment will mean that a deferment of demand will be followed by a downward spiral of economic activity. Conversely, when the deferred demands have accumulated and are translated into firm orders, a general boom is liable to ensure. These effects will be felt more acutely in those regions that specialize in goods for which the demand can be delayed than in the country as a whole.

In Chapter 4, some of the advantages and disadvantages of regional specialization were discussed and the hazard of variable economic activity was noted. The variation of income and employment associated with any particular degree of specialization is materially influenced by the type of activity and the characteristics of its market. For example, the economic recession of the 1930s resulted in considerable unemployment in the United Kingdom but the proportion of persons out of work varied widely from region to region. The severest effects were felt in the coalfield areas with much employment in capital goods—ships, structural steels, heavy machinery, etc.—particularly if an important part of the market was abroad. Recession in the engineering trades in the northeast and in Scotland reduced the local demand for coal and so exacerbated the decline in coal output occasioned by falling coal exports. In contrast, the midland and London areas, with a high proportion of industries catering for the home consumer markets, experienced much less hardship.

Specialized export economies are generally thought to give highly variable aggregate foreign exchange earnings, compounded of changes both in quantity and price. In practice, the matter is not as simple as that for a great deal depends on the nature of the commodity exported, the particular markets to which exports are sent and the form of the marketing organization. J. D. Coppock found that in the period 1946–58 the variability of export earnings bore no significant relation to the extent to which either one or three commodity groups dominated foreign earnings.[2] As an example, Venezuela obtained 92 per cent. of her export earnings from petroleum, but this commodity is produced and marketed under long-term agreements, in a vertically integrated industry to supply an end product the demand for which has been increasing at a fairly regular pace. Export earnings have therefore been remarkably stable, varying by 16·1 per cent. per annum, while the median variation for eighty-three countries was 19·4 per cent. Liberia, on the other hand, with 91 per cent. of exports provided by rubber, iron ore and diamonds, experienced an annual variation in earnings of 35·7 per cent.

*Income Elasticity of Demand*

The discussion so far has concentrated on comparatively short-run changes that represent shifts *along* demand curves. In addition, the whole schedule of demand may move in response to long-term changes in economic and social circumstances (cf. p. 71). One of the more important reasons for changes in the schedule of demand which results in reasonably systematic alterations in the pattern of consumption arises from changes in the standard of living. In the long-run, *per caput* incomes are tending to rise rather than fall and we may conceive of an income elasticity of demand that may be defined in terms which are similar to the price elasticity of demand. It is the ratio between the proportionate change in demand and the proportionate change in personal income in a given period of time (p. 56).

Howsoever rich a man may be, he cannot increase his ingestive powers and it follows that, once a sufficiency of food is available, the proportion of increments to income that will be spent on food is small. Adam Smith stated the principle and C. G. Clark[3] has collected an array of data to examine the nature of the relationship. For foodstuffs as a class, the available evidence shows that whereas some 75 per cent. of income at the very lowest income levels is spent on food (*e.g.*, China and Brazil), in high income countries such as Australia and the United Kingdom the proportion is less than one-tenth of that. There appears to be a saturation demand for foodstuffs and in the richer countries the *per caput* consumption, measured in physical quantity, does not now increase with further income rises. However, as personal incomes become bigger, there is apt to be an increasing expenditure on services associated with the selling of food, in the form of pre-packed, graded and washed foods and of pre-cooked dishes. Although the income-elasticity of food *consumption* may become negligible at high incomes, this may be less true of *expenditure* on food, if an increasing proportion of outlays is attributed to transport, processing and retail service.

Though the aggregate income-elasticity of demand for food declines with rising income, at any particular income level different commodities will have different income-elasticities of demand. The very poor have a highly income-elastic demand for staple foodstuffs like bread, rice and potatoes but at higher incomes these may become inferior goods the *per caput* consumption of which actually declines as other foodstuffs are substituted, such as meat, dairy produce and fruit and vegetables.

The same kinds of relationship between income and consumption can be seen to operate in other spheres. If the income-elasticity of expenditure on food tends to decline with rising standards of living, other parts of expenditure must show the reverse tendency unless savings steadily increase, for which there is little evidence. Clothing, housing and heating are the most important needs of life after food and consequently these items commonly have an increasing elasticity of demand over a considerable range of income. Only in the richer countries is there evidence that outlays on housing and domestic heating may be approaching saturation point, while for articles like clothing and domestic durables it seems reasonable to predict a continuing high and even increasing income-elasticity of demand at high income levels. But whereas the United States has probably nearly reached the saturation point for private motorcars, no other major country appears yet to be reaching this stage: in the United Kingdom, the rate of growth in vehicle ownership is expected to exceed population growth until at least the year 2000.

It is a common experience of the more advanced countries that as incomes rise the propensity to consume services increases. Personal travel, holidays and entertainment in particular attract an increasing proportion of outlays and it is quite probable that the income-elasticity of demand for these services will continue to rise into the foreseeable future.

If all demand were completely income-inelastic, very little economic development could occur as once people's initial wants were satisfied there would be little incentive to any additional effort. On the other hand, were all demand to have the same degree of income elasticity, economic growth would consist of the reproduction of the same goods and services in the same proportions as hitherto. In the real world, the pattern of demand does change as personal incomes rise—income elasticities of demand do vary—and this fact provides a powerful stimulus to economic development generally, at the same time as providing an important reason for changes over time in the structure of national and regional economies.

One of the more important effects is the decline in relative, and in some countries absolute, importance of employment in agriculture in the more advanced countries of the world. The income elasticity of demand for food is low and technical developments have been raising the productivity of agricultural labour. This situation contributes greatly to the fact that in the United Kingdom less than 5 per cent. of all jobs are in agricultural occupations whereas in Pakistan the proportion is more than ten times as great. An important geographic implication derives from the further fact that the location requirements of non-agricultural employments differ from those of the farming community: in particular urban situations are, for a variety of reasons, more favourable than rural ones. Hence, the modern phenomenon of urban and conurban growth.

Within the non-agricultural sector, changing patterns of demand are having significant effects. First is the changing ratio of manufacturing to 'secondary' and other 'tertiary' occupations, according to the type of economic development and the stage reached. In the more advanced countries, it is common for employment in professional services, administration and offices to rise more quickly than in manufacturing. Whereas the location of many kinds of manufacturing industry is greatly affected by the distribution of natural resources, this is much less true of the tertiary sector, for which market considerations tend to be paramount. Even within the manufacturing sector, a growing proportion of workers is 'unproductive', being concerned with design, marketing, administration, etc., tending to reinforce the significance for manufacturing industries of location in or near major market centres.

A changing pattern of demand is therefore instrumental in altering the relative importance of different activities, which necessarily have location requirements that differ. As economic growth proceeds, the importance of occupations that are closely tied to (dispersed) natural resources tends to decline whereas those that are oriented toward large urban markets tends to increase, thereby strengthening the forces that tend toward agglomeration (Chapter 4). This trend is accentuated by a more subtle effect of income-elasticity of demand, that is closely allied to technical development in general, namely, the growing sophistication of goods. Fifty years ago, a sewing machine would sew a plain seam but purchasers now expect also to be able to hem, stitch and buttonhole. Who would now buy a new Austin 7 car of the design that was so popular thirty years ago? Although demand for sewing machines, cars and other goods may reach saturation, there is a high income elasticity of demand for refinements thereto, comparable to higher degrees of processing of foodstuffs. Such refinements generally imply an increase in the amount of manual or machine work performed on a given quantity of materials. As time passes, therefore, the proportion of the final value represented by the basic materials—steel, plastics, leather, etc.—falls. At the same time, the final product may become more fragile and more costly than formerly to transport relative to transport costs on raw materials. Consequently, the advantages of location near raw material sources are lessened, implying an increase in the relative importance of other location factors—markets and the availability of specialist component supplies in particular. The tendency to agglomeration is thus accentuated.

Greater sophistication of the end products is only one reason for the generally declining importance of materials for industrial location. The other important factor is greater economy in the use of materials to achieve a given end, due to greater technical efficiency. A dramatic example is given in Table 24, showing that the quantity of coal needed to make one ton of pig iron fell by four-fifths in a century and a half. The more comprehensive data available since the First World War show that in the United Kingdom further economies have been made: between 1920–24 and 1955–59, the total amount of materials (ore, limestone, scrap and *coke*) needed to make one ton of pig iron fell from 4·21 tons to 3·36.[4] An additional factor conducive to greater economy in materials use is the extension of outlets for by-products that formerly were wasted: for example, blast furnace and oil refinery gases can be used for town gas supplies and the waste heat of electricity generating stations used for domestic heating.

TABLE 24[5]

ENGLAND: quantity of coal required to make one ton of pig iron

| Date | Coal, tons | Date | Coal, tons |
|------|-----------|------|-----------|
| 1919 | 2 | 1800–02 | 5 |
| 1899 | 2 | 1798 | 6 or less |
| 1869 | 3 | 1788 | 7 |
| 1840 | 3·5 | Mid-18th century | 8–10 |

The effect of such improvements in materials use combined with the changing structure of advanced economies is evident in the fact that in the period 1910–14 in the United States one dollar value of raw materials and fuels yielded $4·3 of gross national product whereas by 1950 the g.n.p. produced was $7·2.[6] A similar comparison for the industrial areas of Western Europe showed that for each £1 of raw material and fuel input £4 of gross manufacturing output were obtained in 1938 and £5·6 in 1954.[7]

*The Terms of Trade*

It was argued on p. 149 that variations in the price of goods may accentuate the risks attending a high degree of regional specialization of production, in that earnings may fluctuate much more than output. Such a situation would not matter greatly if the price of goods imported into the region in question fluctuated in concert with the export prices but, as we have seen, it is highly improbable that an exact matching of price changes can occur.

In discussing the concept of comparative advantage (p. 40), the fictitious example of the exchange of cars and cork between Britain and Portugal was used, in which, the goods were bartered. It is more realistic to express the transactions in monetary terms. Suppose that in the first year of trade, Britain's export of cars to Portugal at £100 equals the value of Britain's import of cork but that in the second year the price of cork has risen by 10 per cent., car prices remaining constant. In this second year, Britain's merchandise terms of trade have deteriorated and a given value of exported cars will buy less cork than formerly:

|  | Prices, year 1=100 | | Britain's terms of trade in year 2 relative to year 1 |
|  | Year 1 | Year 2 |  |
| Cars | 100 | 100 | $\dfrac{100}{110} \times 100 = 90 \cdot 9$ |
| Cork | 100 | 110 |  |

Portugal's terms of trade are represented by $\dfrac{110}{100} \times 100 = 110.$[8]

By the use of carefully calculated index numbers, it is possible to compare the average price change of imports into and exports from a country (or region) to obtain its terms of trade, or the terms of trade of one sector of the economy *vis à vis* the rest. Table 25 shows that national terms of trade for some countries are very stable but in other cases they fluctuate widely.

Calculation of the terms of trade of regions that are smaller than nations presents grave problems in that data are meagre. Nevertheless, the principle applies as forcefully for the smaller as for the larger unit and in some cases it is possible to make estimates of the terms of trade of a particular area within a

TABLE 25[9]
## TERMS OF TRADE VARIATION FOR SELECTED COUNTRIES, 1946–58

LOWEST VARIABILITY

| Country | Terms of trade | Export prices | Trade as % GNP |
|---|---|---|---|
| Netherlands | 2·4 | 6·9 | 100·6 |
| United States | 4·9 | 7·0 | 10·4 |
| Portugal | 5·1 | 8·8 | 44·8 |
| Italy | 5·1 | 6·9 | 30·4 |
| Eire | 5·1 | 5·6 | 68·2 |
| Canada | 5·1 | 5·5 | 43·7 |

HIGHEST VARIABILITY

| Country | Terms of Trade | Export Prices | Trade as % GNP |
|---|---|---|---|
| Ceylon | 16·7 | 15·6 | 72·0 |
| Nicaragua | 16·9 | 17·8 | 36·9 |
| Finland | 18·1 | 23·4 | 47·2 |
| Uruguay | 21·4 | 26·1 | 71·5 |
| Ghana | 23·9 | 27·6 | 70·4 |
| Malaya | 24·9 | 29·4 | 60·0 |

*Indices of variability

* The indices of variability approximate to the average year-to-year percentage variation suitably adjusted for long-term trends. The countries shown are those with respectively the lowest and the highest variability of the terms of trade out of a list of 41 countries.

state. For example, S. E. Harris[10] concluded that in the depression of the 1930s 'New England's terms of trade improved substantially' owing to the sharp drop in food and raw material prices relative to manufactured goods. The effects of the depression were, therefore, less severe there than they might have been. However, the terms of trade have subsequently moved against the region, contributing to the difficulty it has experienced in achieving and sustaining rapid economic growth. A sectoral example is also provided by data for the United States. For the period 1910–45, the average annual change in price as a percentage of the previous year's price for seventeen farm commodities varied from 11·6 to 35·2 per cent., whereas none of the major agricultural inputs varied by more than 6·2 per cent. on average. 'A sore point in agriculture has been that, while the price of farm commodities is very flexible, the prices of farm machinery, equipment, and supplies is (*sic*) not so variable.'[11]

The first effect of changes in the terms of trade is to redistribute incomes between the parties engaging in trade and therefore between geographic areas. Table 26 shows that the result can be quite substantial for a small country (or area) that relies greatly on external trade. The second effect follows, that changes in the terms of trade may excerbate problems of the balance-of-payments, as happened to the United Kingdom in 1964; during the first eight months, a worsening of the terms of trade by 2 per cent. contributed about one-fifth to the deterioration in the balance-of-payments.[12] Thirdly, multiplier effects may operate throughout the economy to accentuate recession or boom.

TABLE 26[13]

BELGIUM AND FRANCE: contribution of changes in the terms of trade on current account to changes in real national income *per caput* (in $ U.S. of 1913 purchasing power)

| YEAR | BELGIUM | | FRANCE | |
|------|---------|---|--------|---|
| | Actual income | Due to changes in terms of trade | Actual income | Due to changes in terms of trade |
| 1952 | 244 | +46 | 265 | −6 |
| 1938 | 238 | +22 | 267 | 0 |
| 1928 | 160 | −3 | 171 | −3 |
| 1913 | 165 | 0 | 171 | 0 |
| 1900 | 136 | +8 | 144 | +2 |
| 1872 | 66 | +2 | 96 | +1 |

+ Actual real income *per caput* greater than it would have been had current account terms of trade remained as in 1913.

− Actual real income *per caput* less than it would have been had current account terms of trade remained as in 1913.

The most readily measurable changes in the terms of trade are those that occur in the short run. Longer period comparisons involve formidable statistical problems and are in any case greatly affected by comparative technical developments and the discovery/exhaustion of natural resources. Therefore few useful generalizations can be made about long-run changes in the terms of trade. However, it is possible to analyze the general effects of transport improvements upon the terms of trade between low value goods on which transport bears heavily and high value commodities for which transport costs are comparatively low.

There is no need here to document in detail the fact that during the last 150 years the cost of transport has been declining in relation to the value of goods transported.[14] Three main reasons for the trend may be adduced:

1. The substitution of more for less efficient means of transport, *e.g.* the change from horse and cart to the internal combustion engine.

2. Technical improvements within the media of transport, including the realization of scale economies.

3. Changes in the composition of goods traffic toward articles of higher unit value and methods of handling giving greater 'transportability'.

These three factors may not operate universally and certainly may not continue indefinitely: for any place or time that transport costs are rising relative to the value of goods, the following argument must be reversed.

Suppose that there are two commodities, A and B, for which the f.o.b. works prices are respectively £8 and £96 per ton and on which the cost of transport for 100 kilometres is £2 and £4:

|  | A | B |
| --- | --- | --- |
| F.o.b. works price per ton | £8 | £96 |
| Transport cost per ton per 100 kilometres | £2 | £4 |
| Transport cost at 100 kilometres as % of delivered price | 20% | 4% |

If a radical improvement in transport occurs and costs are halved while the factory prices of A and B remain unaffected, the benefit would amount to a 10 per cent. reduction in the delivered price of A but only 2 per cent. on B. In the limiting case that transport became a free service, the proportionate effects would be respectively 20 and 4 per cent. Clearly, any general reduction in the relative cost of transport benefits most those commodities on which transport bears most heavily, *i.e.*, raw materials, fuels and foodstuffs (p. 191). This relationship is somewhat modified but is not vitiated by the fact that a reduction in transport costs may alter the f.o.b. works price of goods.

However, changes in transport techniques and costs do not apply uniformly to all commodities. In recent years, the greatest advances in transport have been in the bulk handling of standard commodities over considerable distances, as with the development of pipelines for petroleum and gas, huge 100,000 ton oil tankers and ore carriers, the pneumatic handling of grain and the 'merry-go-round' system of block trains for supplying coal to electricity generating stations. By comparison, advances in the handling of heterogeneous goods that originate and terminate in small lots have been most marked within the comparatively short radius allowed by road transport. Over long distances, the palletization of loads and the use of standard crates is making a modest contribution to the reduction of costs. The improvement of transport is therefore accentuating the ease with which basic materials can be transported over great distances relative to the ease of transporting the more valuable manufactures.

The net effect, therefore, is to extend the distance over which goods of low unit value can be transported relative to goods of high unit value. Therefore, the advantage of processing industrial raw materials at or near their sources is eroded and to an increasing extent materials can be transported to large industrial centres which:

1. Give access to markets, including markets for by-products.

2. Provide external economies of scale.

It also follows that as the local supply of raw materials is exhausted it is now less necessary for the industry(ies) affected to shift location to new sources, as happened in the charcoal era of iron smelting in England. Today, for example, the exhaustion of iron ore deposits in the Great Lakes area of the United States is being met by the import of Labrador and Venezuelan ore: the manufacture of steel remains in the same country, though its detailed location is changing, with a marked growth along the Atlantic seaboard. Similarly, Japan is now the world's third largest producer of steel but relies almost exclusively on imported material, much of which is obtained from Australia.

Thus are accentuated the tendencies toward agglomeration that have already been noted.

A second differential effect of cheaper transport is analogous to the one that has been discussed above. An area that is economically remote on account of distance, difficulties of terrain or the absence of well engineered transport facilities, will be affected in greater degree by any given percentage reduction in transport costs than will be the more fortunate regions where transport is a lesser item in the cost of external transactions. Reference to Table 27 will show that the foreign trade of Australia and New Zealand carries a very considerable cost of transport, the cheapness of the medium (ocean shipping) being offset by the great distances involved. Any general improvement of sea transport will clearly be more significant for these countries than for, say, the United Kingdom, the greater part of whose foreign trade goes much shorter distances. Two effects can be expected from a general decrease in transport costs:

1. An increase in the competitiveness of exports from Australia and New Zealand and probably an expansion thereof.

2. Greater competition from imports into the two countries to supply the local markets, which may result in the decline of some local manufacturing.

The balance of advantage to the region in question will depend largely upon the character of its trade.

TABLE 27

AUSTRALIA AND NEW ZEALAND: estimates of ocean freights as percentage of f.o.b. value of imports and exports (precious metals excluded)

| Year ending December 31st | New Zealand Import | Export | Australia Import | Export | Year ending 30th June |
|---|---|---|---|---|---|
| 1951–54 | 12·7 | 6·6 | 12·0 | 6·0 | 1951–54 |
| 1946–50 | 12·7 | 8·8 | 13·3 | 11·5 | 1946–50 |
| 1941–45 | 13·6 | 12·0 | 17·0 | 26·7 | 1941–45 |
| 1936–40 | 14·9 | 11·2 | 14·6* | 15·0 | 1936–40 |
| | | | | 17·2 | 1931–35 |
| | | | | 9·5 | 1929–30 |

Source: M. Chisholm, 'Shipping costs and the terms of trade: Australia and New Zealand', Applied Statistics, 1959, p. 197.

* 1937–40.

Australia and New Zealand have almost certainly gained from cheapening transport because a large part of their exports are basic materials and foods and imports are mostly manufactures. But if the remote area is itself a manufacturing economy and has industries geared to supply the local market, greater ease of transport between it and another major industrial region may lead to the eclipse of local manufactures. This will occur because transport costs will absorb a smaller part of any savings in manufacturing costs arising from internal and external economies of scale. As the protection afforded by distance is reduced, small units supplying the local market will be replaced either by large factories serving an extended area or by works that are located in large centres to obtain external economies. (The two phenomena are in practice closely linked.) Bread baking in rural areas is declining as large urban bakeries achieve scale economies: Indian hand weaving was largely destroyed by the influx of Lancashire wares in the nineteenth century. Hence, one commentator has remarked of intranational improvements in communications that 'the real problem of [remote] areas is that not only does road transport favour centralization, but the better the road system the greater are the forces of centralization.'[15] This is therefore another important reason for the worldwide phenomenon that *within* countries economic growth tends to be concentrated in a few areas of large population, such as south-east England, the Rhineland area of Europe, New England and South Honshu (Japan).

The two differential effects of cheaper transport that have been discussed above, namely the differing incidence according to type of material and location, are clearly self-limiting. The smaller the cost of transport in relation to the value of commodities, the smaller the differential effect that will attend any further cheapening. It has been argued elsewhere[16] that in the United Kingdom the measurable costs of transport are now probably so small for a wide range of manufactures that, in terms of transport cost alone, location is for them immaterial within the greater part of lowland England excepting only the remote south-west. Furthermore, the range of manufactures for which this is true and the extent of the area within transport cost differences are small are both increasing, probably quite rapidly.

*Some Final Remarks on Demand*

If the demand for some goods can be deferred, for several years in the case of ships, in other cases demand is ephemeral and, if it is not satisfied immediately, may cease to be expressed. The *raison d'etre* of daily newspapers is to provide news and, however accurate and skillful the reporting, there will be no market if the paper is consistently twenty-four hours behind its competitors. It is, therefore, essential for newspaper offices to be located where ready access to news and readers can be had—usually centrally in the larger urban centres. Similarly, the number of hours in each week during which many people are simultaneously free to patronize cinemas, theatres, clubs, etc., is limited and such places of entertainment must therefore be located within easy reach of residential areas or where workers on their way home can conveniently tarry.

The demand for a particular commodity or service may be very fickle, as in the bespoke dressmaking and tailoring trades, and dependent upon personal contacts. In such cases, the location of dressmaking and similar trades is conditioned by easy access to the appropriate clientèle and this factor has dominated the location of these trades within London. Thus:

> For the printing industry the essential factor of location is that summed up by a writer on printing trades in the city of New York: 'the importance of the elements of time and personal contact.' These elements have already been found to be of the greatest importance to other old-established London trades, in particular clothing. In all these trades, however, the importance of the factor has been somewhat eroded away in the present century by improved communications and by the growth of factory production. It continues to tie to central locations those branches of industry dependent upon novelty as a basic principle of sale: women's outerwear and daily-newspaper printing. Where the response to the demands of the market is more predictable or less immediate, then the industry has deserted its traditional sites, particularly where the development of factory production has increased demands on space and weakened the hold of traditional labour pools.[17]

Demand may fluctuate within quite wide limits although in a reasonably predictable manner. The electricity supply industry is a case in point, demand being minimal at night, rising to a double maximum in the early morning and early evening, and also varying with the time of year. To meet these peak demands, capital equipment must be installed that is under-used for a great part of the time. Idle capital equipment is expensive and four remedies may be sought, all of which are employed in the United Kingdom.[18] A conventional coal or oil-fired power station requires a great deal of capital in relation to the current cost of operating it, whereas the newly developed gas turbine generator displays the opposite characteristics. The base load may therefore be supplied through the grid by conventional stations, many of which are located on or near the coalfields or tidewater, while peak demand is met by gas-turbine plants located in or near the centres of consumption. Likewise, obsolete plants whose running costs are too high for regular use but whose capital has been partly or fully depreciated are kept in being as peak and emergency suppliers.

The second device is the construction of a grid system whereby differences in the timing of peak demands in various places reduce the magnitude of variation in total demand. The United Kingdom grid serves this purpose, among others, and it has been linked to the French grid for the daily exchange of power across the channel. A grid is a special case of the general one mentioned on p. 192 of the possible advantages to be derived from a geographically extended market and the relationship of this to geographic pricing policies.

A third stratagem is provided by storage. Electricity itself cannot be stored but it is possible to use surplus electricity generated by base-load stations at night and the middle of the day to pump water into high reservoirs. This water can then be used to generate hydro-electric power during the periods of peak demand. The Trawsfynydd nuclear power station in North Wales will supply base-load electricity into the national grid and hard by is an important pump storage scheme which is already operating.

Finally, pricing policies may be designed to even out the daily or seasonal fluctuation in demand. The area boards that retail electricity in Great Britain operate schemes for the off-peak supply of power at favourable rates, coupling the concession with the development of domestic heating systems based on the principle of storing heat during limited periods of time for steady emission. (For a fuller discussion of prices, see Chapter 7.)

To conclude this section on demand, there is a final set of factors which in the long run affects the structure of demand within a given community. The various age-groups of a population differ in the contribution they make to society and the goods and services that they require or are able to command. If the proportion of the population in these age-groups changes over time, then irrespective of any alteration in total population, income level and techniques there will be consequential effects upon the structure of the economy, which in turn implies some shift in location patterns. A country like Nigeria, Ceylon or Malaya which has a large proportion of children must devote considerable resources to the construction of schools, the provision of equipment therefor and for the training and maintenance of teachers. Since the majority of children will be day-pupils (Northern Nigeria is an exception), the schools will be distributed roughly in accordance with the existing population. On the other hand, the location of teacher-training establishments, which commonly are residential, and also of the manufacture of school requisites, may be conditioned by very different considerations—much of the equipment may even be imported. In contrast, elderly people may require less food and clothing than children but use more fuel (in temperate and cool climates) and require the services of a domiciliary medical service. But residential 'homes' for the elderly need not necessarily be near existing centres of population in the way that most schools must: in England, there is a large number of nursing homes of all kinds in Surrey, Sussex and along the south coast generally, taking old folk from all parts of the kingdom. Such establishments can be located for reasons of climate, beauty of surroundings or cheapness of property rather than for proximity to population centres.

The demographic situation then effects details of the economy and of location patterns as well as having the fundamental effect through the relationship of the number of productive workers, mouths to be fed and resources that forms one of the central concerns of those interested in economic development.

*Substitution*

Underlying a great part of the arguments so far presented in this book is a common idea that now can be made explicit. If one motor vehicle manufacturer adopts a policy of vertical integration, its own production of pig iron and forgings, for example, replaces the purchase of these items from specialist producers. When metal manufacture replaced cotton textiles in Scotland, one kind of industry was substituted for another. Similarly, in advanced countries bread often ousts potatoes as the major starch food—the one is substituted for another. It is the fact that substitution can take place in all kinds of direct and indirect ways that confers upon economic phenomena the complex inter-relatedness that has already been remarked.

As we have seen, in the manufacture of any particular commodity or the provision of a service, one productive resource may be substituted for another. This may, for example, be the replacement of labour by capital or land, or of one kind of labour for another (or kind of capital or raw material). Or it may occur by changing the location of the production or the source of particular materials, or again through changes in the markets served. Conversely, any one resource—a body of metallic ore, a particular site or a group of workers for example—may be employed in different types of productive enterprise, which may be regarded as potential substitutes.

From the viewpoint of consumption, one finished or part-finished product may be substituted for another, or for some kind of service, or vice versa. Such substitution may occur the better to satisfy a given end, as with the demise of hand tinplate mills in favour of modern mechanized plants. Or substitution may occur as the structure of wants changes: pre-packed fruits and vegetables are tending to replace less attractively presented produce in America and Europe.

Relationships of actual or potential substitution ramify throughout the whole economic system and are contingent upon detailed and changing technical considerations as well as the minutiae of personal attitudes. In some cases, substitution is easy because few technical or other problems are involved: for example, vegetable oils derived from the oil palm, ground-nuts, cotton seed, olive and maize are competitive over a wide

range of uses because modern methods of refining and reforming mean that one oil can readily be used in place of
another. On the other hand, no direct competition exists
between electricity produced in Europe and in North America
since problems of transmission rule out any trans-Atlantic
transfers: substitution between generating stations on either
side of the Atlantic is impossible at present.

To thread our way through this maze of relationships,
recourse must constantly be had to the concept of opportunity
costs. Every decision to use or not to use some resource, commodity or service, involves questions of opportunities that will
be foregone.

*Conclusion*

Most commodities and services may be substituted for at least
a few others; in many cases, the range of potential substitution
is very wide. It follows that the factors influencing the demand
for any one commodity are extremely complex and furthermore that the strength of demand varies from place to place
and over time. Changes in demand occur both in the short
run and over long periods of time. The former are largely due
to changes in relative prices and also to the whims of public
fashion; advertisers seek to exploit human frailty and on occa-
sions they are very successful. Long-term changes in demand
also occur in response to variations in relative prices, which
may be the consequence of technical advances which affect
supply costs; but demand also responds to changes in *per
caput* income. The mutability of demand is thus an important
dynamic factor that leads to change of all kinds, including the
substitution of one means of production or one product for
another. In this way, the structure of the economy alters and
hence the relative importance of the factors of location. In
particular, the growth of tertiary occupations encourages the
growth of great urban agglomerations.

Since the prices of goods vary over time, it is important to
enquire about the terms of trade. These may be conceived on
a sectoral or a geographic basis. Movements in the terms of
trade have an important effect in redistributing incomes
between kinds of industry and between regions of the world
and hence affect the rate and nature of economic growth in

different places. The terms of trade between basic raw materials and manufactures is being changed by the improvement of transport allied to other developments. Basic materials can be transported further relative to the distance manufactures can be moved than used to be the case and this tendency encourages industrial agglomerations. A similar terms of trade effect from transport improvements operates for regions that have been isolated but where external communications are markedly improved in relation to general betterments.

If these are the more important aspects of demand that have been dealt with in this chapter, another significant matter remains to be discussed. The geographic pattern of demand is in part affected by the pricing policies that are adopted by firms, especially as this affects the geographic pattern of prices. The whole question of geographic price policies is discussed in the next chapter.

### REFERENCES

1 P. L. Yates, *Forty Years of Foreign Trade*, 1959, pp. 39–40. J. D. Coppock, *International Economic Instability: The Experience After World War II*, 1962, pp. 33–39.

2 J. D. Coppock, 1962, *op. cit.*, pp. 102–03.

3 C. G. Clark, *The Conditions of Economic Progress*, 3rd edition, 1960, Chapter 8.

4 British Iron and Steel Federation, *Annual Statistics*.

5 W. Isard, 'Some locational factors in the iron and steel industry since the early nineteenth century', *Journal of Political Economy*, 1948, pp. 203–17. See also N. J. G. Pounds and W. N. Parker, 1957, *op. cit.*, (Chap. 4), and N. J. G. Pounds, *The Geography of Iron and Steel*, 1959.

6 The President's Materials Policy Commission (Paley Report), Vol. 2, *Resources for Freedom*, 1952.

7 G.A.T.T., *Trends in International Trade*, 1958, p. 43.

8 The example used gives the barter (or merchandise) terms of trade, *i.e.*, the terms of trade for the exchange of *goods*. If non-commodity transactions are included, then the terms of trade are described as the terms of trade on current account.

9 J. D. Coppock, 1962, *op. cit.*, Appendix A–2.

10 S. E. Harris, *The Economics of New England*, 1952, p. 95.

11 E. O. Heady, *Economics of Agricultural Production and Resource Use*, 1960, p. 461.

12  *The Economist*, 24th October 1964, p. 411.

13  C. P. Kindleberger, *The Terms of Trade. A European Case Study*, 1956, p. 293.

14  M. Chisholm, 1962, *op. cit.*, (Chap. 2), pp. 183–88. The following discussion is based on the assumption that the user of transport is charged on the basis of the cost of providing the transport service. Some transport operators, notably railways, set charges on the basis of what the 'traffic will bear'. The argument is not affected except where the degree of such discrimination changes over time, in which case some modification may be necessary.

15  A. A. L. Caesar, 'Planning and the geography of Great Britain', *Advancement of Science*, 1964, p. 234.

16  M. Chisholm, 1964, *op. cit.*, (Chap. 4).

17  P. G. Hall, 1962, *op. cit.*, (Chap. 4), p. 110.

18  G. Manners, 1964, *op. cit.*, (Chap. 2), pp. 126–37.

# CHAPTER 7

# Pricing Policies

In a recent study of the ways in which competitive processes do and do not operate, J. M. Clark observed that if the space he devoted to questions of spatial price competition between buyers and sellers 'appears disproportionate, the justification is that this is perhaps the largest area of unfortunate immaturity in competitive pricing theory'.[1] Although some attention is now being given by economists to questions of prices in space, the problems of collecting data, the interpretation thereof and the fitting of observed facts to deductive theories are formidable and far from resolution.

The geographic pattern of prices is one aspect of the general problem of 'discrimination'. If a seller charges a different price to two customers for an identical article, and the discrepancy is not related to differences in the cost of supplying the article, discrimination is said to occur. If, however, factors like the size of the consignment, the regularity of the order, distance of shipment, etc., do result in variable costs to the supplier, he is not said to discriminate between buyers if his price varies from one to another in accordance with these cost considerations. In the geographic context, an absence of discrimination implies that there is a single price at the point of origin, for an order of a given size and regularity, and that the purchaser pays the cost of transport thence. In this way, prices will increase away from the point of origin by the amount of transport and related costs of movement. For most agricultural products, the situation would be reversed, the price at any one point of production being determined by the price ruling in the relevant market minus the cost of transferring the produce thither.

Formal location theory seems universally to assume that this form of non-discriminatory pricing is usual, if not universal.

For example, although Hoover devoted a good deal of space to other pricing policies (basing-point pricing, zoned prices and uniform delivered prices), the tenor of his remarks shows clearly that these were regarded as exceptions to the general rule and of small moment:

> Freight absorption by sellers is quite common but is confined largely to finished goods and a few others in which transportation costs are a very small part of the price.[2]

A more extreme view of the matter was taken by Lösch, when he declared that, 'To set uniform delivered prices is to eliminate the most important regulator of a rational spatial arrangement,'[3] which is non-discriminatory—or free-on-board (f.o.b.) works—pricing.

There are four basic types of geographic pricing policy:

1. Prices varying according to the cost of transfer:
   (a) F.o.b. works.
   (b) Basing-point pricing.

2. Delivered prices uniform within:
   (a) Zones.
   (b) The national territory (single zone).

In this chapter, an attempt is made to examine the geographic implications of the different pricing policies and furthermore to show that non-discriminatory (or f.o.b. works) pricing is, at least in some countries, a good deal less common in practice than it 'ought' to be according to orthodox location theory.

*Prices f.o.b. Works*

In most of the literature on location, it is assumed that the price of any manufactured commodity is set at the point of origin thereof, the factory, and that the purchaser pays all the transfer costs of removing it thence. The price to the purchaser will vary according to his location relative to the supplier. The nearer he is the cheaper the commodity. In the simplest case, transport costs are assumed to be proportional to distance; more sophisticated analyses may be based upon tapering freight rates and the use of alternative means of transport. It is important to note that the purchaser pays for the transport *in fact* even though *nominally* the consignor may pay the transporter, adding the transport cost to the bill he renders.[4]

In these circumstances, the traditional analysis of market areas may be developed as shown in Figure 4. Imagine three producers at A, B and C, with unit production costs for an industrial commodity represented by the vertical lines AN, BP and CR. The unit costs of transport are represented by the solid line NM, NO, PO, etc. The market area of B is the extent of territory over which the delivered cost is less than that at which A and C can quote, in this case extending to points X and Y along the section shown—the actual market areas are obtained by rotating the transport cones about the vertical axes AN, BP and CR. In these circumstances, B can undersell A and C within its own territory and will capture all the sales; likewise, A and C will gain an exclusive interest in their respective territories.

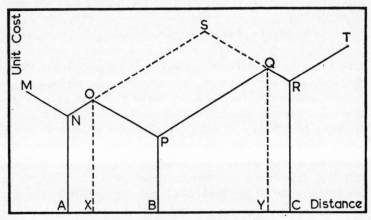

Figure 4.   Pricing f.o.b. works

Under this form of non-discriminatory f.o.b. pricing, there is a mutual advantage in consumers being near the suppliers and vice versa. The purchaser gets his supplies more cheaply the nearer he is to the consignor. The seller's interest in proximity derives from:

1. His fear of being undercut by potential rivals.

2. The possibility that if consumption is markedly price-elastic, proximity to the purchaser, with the consequence of

lower delivered price, will result in an increase in the volume of sales.

The 'pull' is not of equal strength in both directions and will vary according to:

1. The cost of transport of the goods in question in relation to its value.

2. The importance of the commodity to the purchaser.

3. The costs involved in alternative locations for producers and consumers.

4. The price-elasticity of consumption.

5. The magnitude of scale economies in production.

The manufacture of pig iron traditionally has shown a close association with the sources of iron ore and fuel largely owing to the high cost of transporting the necessary materials, the large share that these represent of total costs and the considerable loss of weight in manufacture. Conversely, bread baking is located as near to the final consumer as is possible for essentially the reverse reasons. In both cases, technical advances in the respective industries and in transport have modified and are modifying these traditional relationships.

Within the form of analysis developed above, there is clearly scope for various discriminatory practices. Consider again producer B in Figure 4, whose market area is bounded by X and Y. With a non-discriminatory f.o.b. system of pricing, the price to the purchaser at any point is given by the lines PO and PQ. However, the *potential* price to a purchaser if he bought from the cheapest alternative source is given by OS and QS; the vertical distance between these lines and PO and PQ represents the potential *extra* charge that B could make at each point without losing custom to his competitors A and C. Whether he will in fact realize this monopoly element in part or in full will depend upon his assessment of the price elasticities of demand, the possibility of rivals setting up in a location neighbouring his own and the further possibility that his rivals A and C may engage in a retaliatory form of discrimination.

This last possibility takes the following form. Producer A, in seeking to capture markets in the territory of B, may choose to absorb freight on shipments beyond the point X where NO and PO intersect. In this way, he can match the price to the purchaser offered by B, preventing the latter from realizing any monopoly component in his revenue. Freight absorption by A may be justified if there are substantial unrealized economies of scale in manufacture, such that the cost of producing the marginal units is less than the marginal revenue despite freight absorption. A sophisticated literature has developed which elaborates this train of thought and the reader is referred in particular to the work of Lösch and Greenhut.[5]

## Basing-point Pricing

If f.o.b. works pricing is regarded as the normal system of setting prices, the basing-point method has for long been regarded as the major exception and, especially in the American literature, a good deal of attention has been devoted to the effects of this aberrant arrangement.[6] In its simplest form, the basing-point system regards all of the production of the commodity in question as originating from a single point, the basing point. Thus, a uniform ex-works price is set for all producers, irrespective of their actual costs of production, and the price that will be quoted to any customer is calculated by adding to this 'base' price the cost of transport *as if* the consignment originated from the basing point. The Pittsburgh Plus arrangements for the marketing of steel in the United States is a renowned, though now defunct, example, in which steel consignments were charged as if originating from Pittsburgh. We will first examine single basing-point pricing and then, more briefly, discuss the multiple basing-point.

Figure 5 illustrates the single basing-point system, with P representing, for the sake of argument, Pittsburgh as the basing point. Q is another producer of steel at some other location, such as Chicago or Birmingham. PB represents the 'base' price, set at a level designed to ensure 'normal' profits, and QE represents the actual costs of production (including 'normal' profits) at Q. With freight rates calculated from P, the actual price paid by a purchaser at any point is shown by ABC: this price will be paid whether or not the steel is actually shipped from P or Q. This means, then, that any shipment made by Q in the area to the right of X will yield an *extra* profit to the extent that ABC is above DEG. However, if Q sells to points to the left of X, then Q suffers a *reduction* in profits, measured by the extent to which the realized price ABC is below the actual costs of production and transport, DEG.

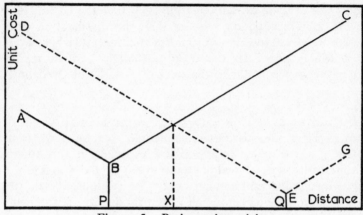

Figure 5.   Basing-point pricing

The effects of the basing-point system on the location of steel manufactories has been much discussed. *If* the basing point is central in the market area involved, and *if* all manufacturers sell to the whole of the market, then agglomeration of producers at the basing point will be encouraged to the extent that the resulting advantages are not offset by increased raw material and/or processing costs at the point of agglomeration— *e.g.*, water, important in processing, might become very costly. However, if the basing point is eccentric in the market area and if some or many manufacturers can achieve scale economies without selling on the national market, then manufacturers can increase their profits by locating outside the basing point and directing the greater part of their sales away from the basing point.

It appears that in the case of steel production in the United States, the second set of circumstances has been more important than the former for, as A. R. Burns observed, steel production rose more rapidly outside than in the Pittsburgh area between 1916 and 1931.[7]

Although it is impossible to generalize about the direct effects of basing-point pricing on the location of the producers employing this system, two indirect effects may be adduced with confidence. Reference to Figure 5 will show that in the 'natural' market area of Q, lying to the right of X, the price that consumers have to pay under a basing-point system is higher than it need be were supplies obtained from Q on a non-discriminatory f.o.b. basis. It follows:

1. That if the demand for the product is at all price elastic, the total quantity demanded from Q will be less than it might otherwise be. Since Q cannot lower its price to exploit the situation, the scale of its output will be curtailed in some degree. In this sense, therefore, agglomeration at P is encouraged, since expansion elsewhere is somewhat retarded.

2. If his other costs of production are little affected by location at P or Q or elsewhere, a purchaser will choose to locate at P since his purchase price is there the least.

There is little doubt that a basing-point system will tend to encourage fabricators, such as users of steel, to locate near the basing point and this is probably the most important single effect of the system. If fabricators congregate in this vicinity, then it follows that the steel manufacturers will find it profitable to locate at the basing point, for this tends to remain centrally placed in their market.

This distinction between the direct and indirect effects of the basing-point system on location patterns is crucial to the understanding of the conflict of opinion that has raged about it. It is also the essential basis of the conclusion arrived at by G. W. Stocking[8] that:

> in practice basing point pricing is apt to handicap the mills of the younger, smaller producing areas and favour the mills of the larger, older producing areas.

Some of the effects of the basing-point system in the United States are shown by Stocking's analysis of the economy of the South. In 1922, fabricators of steel located at or near Birmingham, Alabama, had to pay $5.7 for a hundred kilogrammes of certain classes of steel whereas Pittsburgh industries paid only $5.2. This cost differential in material supplies represented a substantial proportion of the selling price of goods such as rivets, ships, springs and boilers manufactured by southern firms:

| price disadvantage on steel supplies as a percentage of selling price | number of cases |
|---|---|
| 1·0–2·9 | 3 |
| 3·0–5·9 | 3 |
| 6·0–8·9 | 2 |
| 9·0–9·9 | 3 |
|  | 11 |

But the disadvantage shown by these calculations was based on the freight differential applied to nationally uniform mill prices and Birmingham, whence the southern fabricators in question obtained most of their steel, was in fact a low-cost producer. Stocking quoted the 1939 census of industry to show that the cost of materials and labour per metric ton of pig iron in the State of Alabama was $11.4 compared with $14.1 in New York State, the cheapest of the major producers: the cost was $16.8 in Pennsylvania. As a result, the cost of finished steel was substantially lower at Birmingham than elsewhere, though this advantage has since been much reduced. Therefore, the real handicap imposed upon southern fabricators was greater than is suggested by the above tabulation. The whole economic development of the South was probably retarded to a considerable extent.

Under a multiple basing-point arrangement, several centres are used as basing points. The ex-works price may be uniform among these bases, or each factory may set its own basic price. In either case, a firm making a quotation to any particular customer will calculate the delivered price from the basing point that can give the lowest quotation; all bids to supply any particular customer will therefore be identical. If the number of basing points is limited, then the effects on location patterns will be similar to those described for the single basing point except that there will be two, three or more centres of concentration. For example, there were only two basing points in 1934 for southern pine lumber mills, situated in Florida and North Carolina, though numerous mills were scattered from Texas to Virginia.[9] When, as was formerly the case with the United States cement industry, very large numbers of basing points exist, the locational significance of the system becomes negligible as compared with pricing f.o.b. works.

Although the basing-point system is an interesting example of geographic pricing policy, its importance must not be over-rated. It appears to have been more common in the United States than elsewhere, having been introduced in 1880 by the steel industry, but in 1948 it was finally declared to be illegal—as the result of a test case involving cement. F. Macklup lists eighteen products or groups of products for which single or multiple basing-point pricing has prevailed at some time or other in the United States: apart from steel and cement, goods as diverse as wood pulp, corn oil and oak flooring have been sold in this manner.[10] Though now illegal in the United States, the effects of basing-point pricing probably still persist. Basing-point pricing has, however, been traditional in the international marketing of crude petroleum. The Gulf coast of the United States was once the world base for petroleum prices but during the Second World War and its aftermath additional basing-points were recognized—Venezuela and the Persian Gulf, for example. In the late 1950s, a general weakening of the petrol-eum market occurred which persisted in the early 1960s and unofficial discounts from the posted prices obscure the real situation and diminish the significance of the basing points.[11] The only other important current example of basing-point pricing of which the author is aware is that of steel within the European Economic Community.[12] Figure 6 shows the distri-bution of all the E.E.C. steel basing-points that can be shown separately at the scale allowed by the page size of this book. The geographic effects of basing-point pricing for steel in Europe are probably not great, since in the years 1957–58, 85 per cent. of all steel output in the Netherlands, Belgium, Luxembourg, the Saar and Italy was within twenty kilometres of the relevant basing-point. In France, 50 per cent. of output was within twenty kilometres of the basing point, the mean dist-ance being 34 kilometres. In Western Germany, only 40 per cent. of output was as close to the basing point and the mean distance was as much as 67 kilometres. On average, therefore, distortions of location patterns arising from the E.E.C. basing-point system of steel pricing cannot be great, though in extreme cases, as with Lorraine tinplate marketed on a basing point 700 kilometres away at Bordeaux, the effects may be significant.[13]

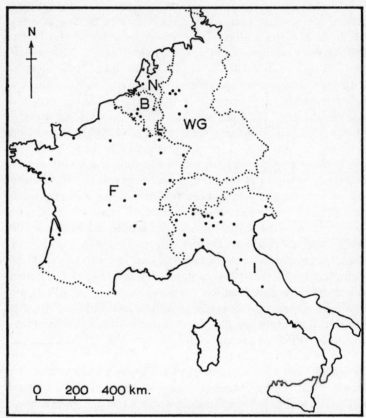

Figure 6.   Basing point for steel sales in the European Economic Community

*Uniform Delivered Prices*

Delivered prices that are uniform throughout zones or whole national territories have been recognized to occur but have been discounted in previous work on location as being an unimportant aberration. The first purpose of this section is to present evidence which the author has been able to collect showing that, at least in the United States and the United Kingdom, uniform delivered prices are much more significant than has been commonly supposed. The geographic effects of this pricing policy are then examined and after that the question whether uniform delivered prices are a rational method of pricing is discussed.

Virtually all goods entering international trade are priced f.o.b. the works or port of export. For this important class of trade, prices do generally vary between locations according to the cost of transport, insurance, etc., in the manner of orthodox theory. For the world as a whole, trade in manufactures is increasing at about the same pace as total industrial production (Table 28), which implies that if any change in the relative importance of f.o.b. works (or port) pricing is occurring it is due to changes within national territories.

TABLE 28

INDICES OF QUANTA OF WORLD PRODUCTION AND TRADE
1958 = 100

| Year | Total trade | Exports of manufactures | Production (mining and manufacturing) |
|---|---|---|---|
| 1961 | 124 | 126 | 122 |
| 1960 | 119 | 122 | 118 |
| 1959 | 108 | 108 | 110 |
| 1958 | 100 | 100 | 100 |
| 1957 | 102 | 101 | 103 |
| 1956 | 97 | 95 | 100 |
| 1955 | 89 | 86 | 95 |
| 1954 | 82 | 79 | 86 |
| 1953 | 78 | 75 | 86 |
| 1952 | 73 | 69 | |
| 1951 | 74 | 69 | |
| 1950 | 67 | 57 | |

Source: Monthly Bulletin of Statistics, U.N., January, February and March 1963.

At the other extreme, the price of goods sold retail in the national market is in many countries uniform throughout the country. This practice was nearly universal in the United Kingdom and Western Germany, for example, until the early 1960s. But resale price maintenance is now being abandoned,

N

in face of the aggressive selling tactics of supermarket stores and discount houses and, in the United Kingdom, of an Act prohibiting it. However, manufacturers still set uniform prices to the wholesale outlets and these in turn normally do not distinguish between retail outlets on account of the locations of the retailers. There are discounts for large orders and a retail outlet may now pass on some or all of these discounts to the consumer and even reduce its profit margin. Geographic variations in retail prices are therefore related to the volume of turnover of the outlets and not to the location of the outlet in relation to the point of production. A principle effect of abolishing resale price maintenance may therefore be to establish a geographic pattern of price related to the size of outlets, which will be determined very largely by the density of population and the ease of access to shops. Prices are already noticeably higher in the small village stores than in the big urban supermarkets.

There is a third class of goods for which data on pricing policies are scanty in the extreme. These are goods which are neither exported nor used for final consumption but are components or part-manufactures. Such products include steel, raw fuels, textile fibres, electric parts and vehicle engines; they are of considerable economic importance and affect many of the basic patterns of location. The succeeding paragraphs piece together the available evidence for the United States and the United Kingdom.

The United States Federal Trade Commission conducted an enquiry among 3,561 firms in 1928[14] and discovered that 44 per cent. of the sample sold their wares exclusively on an f.o.b. works basis. Eighty-one per cent. of firms supplying transport equipment used exclusively f.o.b. pricing, compared with 39 per cent. for iron and steel products (excluding machinery) and 2 per cent. for rubber products. However, of those firms, amounting to 82 per cent. of the sample, which sold either all or some of their goods on an f.o.b. works basis, 15 per cent. gave their customers a partial freight allowance and in these cases the prices paid by customers were made somewhat uniform geographically. Thirty-six per cent. of the whole sample reported selling at least some goods at a nationally uniform price while 27 per cent. said that they used some zone prices.

Nationally uniform prices were more common with rubber products (86 per cent. of reporting firms), leather and printing and publishing, and less common with petroleum and coal products, iron and steel (excluding machinery) and transport equipment (5 per cent.). Only 8 per cent. of the firms reported using basing-point pricing on any sales.[15]

The above figures do not enable one to assess the importance of the various pricing systems in relation to the quantities of goods involved but they do indicate that geographically uniform prices were more common than is often admitted, even in a country so big as the United States. The point is confirmed by the more recent study made by G. Ackley[16] who quoted seventeen commodities for which nationally uniform prices prevailed in the early 1940s, ranging from aluminium to rayon yarn, sheet brass to electric turbine generators. Since it is probable that more rather than fewer goods are now sold on geographically uniform prices than in the late 1920s, it is evident that in the United States at least this system of pricing must be accepted as important.

For intermediate products in the United Kingdom, one of the more accessible sources of information is the reports of the Monopolies Commission, evidence from which is summarized in Table 29. The Commission, while reporting adversely on price collusion between manufacturers, has built up no consistent view on the question of geographically uniform prices maintained by individual firms. For example, Imperial Chemical Industries, Ltd., and Fisons, Ltd., still maintain uniform delivered prices for fertilizers in England and Wales.[17] The same is true of other commodities where geographically uniform prices prevailed at the time of investigation.

It is clear that uniform delivered prices are not found only where transport is a negligible factor. British Oxygen supply about 95 per cent. of the domestic market for certain industrial gases, notably oxygen and dissolved acetylene, and make a geographically uniform charge despite the fact that *on average* transport costs are as much as 23·5 per cent. of total costs for compressed air and 25·6 per cent. for medical oxygen.[18] For sand and gravel in central Scotland, the cost of transport over twenty-two kilometres was equivalent to the quarry costs of production and yet uniform delivered prices prevailed within

TABLE 29

UNITED KINGDOM MONOPOLIES COMMISSION: industries not primarily manufacturing for final consumption with a geographically uniform price at the time of investigation*

| Industry | Area within which uniform prices were found to prevail for part or all sales | Year of report |
|---|---|---|
| Car electric equipment | Great Britain and U.K. | 1963 |
| Chemical fertilizers | Mainly England and Wales U.K. in some cases | 1959 |
| †Electrical and allied machinery and plant | U.K. | 1957 |
| †Electronic valves and cathode ray tubes | U.K. | 1956 |
| Industrial and medical gases (mainly oxygen, acetylene, propane) | U.K. | 1956 |
| Standard metal windows and doors | England and Wales, with 6¼ per cent. surcharge for N. Ireland, Channel Isles, Isle of Man, Scotland | 1956 |
| Sand and gravel in Central Scotland | Central area of Central Lowlands | 1956 |
| †Hard fibre cordage | U.K. | 1956 |
| Semi-manufactures of copper and copper-based alloys | British Isles, except N. Ireland, Eire and in some cases Scotland | 1955 |
| Pneumatic tyres | U.K. | 1955 |
| Imported timber | Three small regions of England | 1953 |
| †Insulated electric wires and cables | U.K. | 1952 |
| Cast iron rainwater goods | U.K. | 1951 |

* Other industries on which the Monopolies Commission has reported which are excluded from this table are ones manufacturing solely or predominantly for final consumption by the public.

† Indicates that the existence of geographically uniform prices is inferred from the existence of agreed prices and the methods described for arriving at a quotation in a particular case. In other cases, the geographically uniform prices were specifically remarked by the Commission.

two zones of the lowlands, one zone extending approximately forty by twenty-four and the other fifty-one by thirty-five kilometres.[19]

The evidence reported for chemical fertilizers is particularly interesting, since it reveals a divergence of practice between suppliers, products and areas. The two main companies, Imperial Chemical Industries, Ltd., and Fisons, Ltd., employed a uniform price c.i.f. (*i.e.*, delivered to) the nearest railway station for most of their products but some small producers of superphosphate in England and Wales charged on an f.o.b. works basis. But in Northern Ireland and Scotland, where sales by other companies were important, an f.o.b. works system prevailed for most kinds of fertilizer sold by the two principal companies.

In the course of his investigations into the establishment of ninety-eight branch factories in Great Britain in the post-war period, F. W. Luttrell found that materials and components were 'usually' supplied to the works at nationally uniform prices.[20] In a recent sample survey in Scotland, 'about 70 per cent. of firms had 50 per cent. to 100 per cent. of their purchases delivered at standard national prices'.[21] Another sample survey, of 121 manufacturing establishments in Northern Ireland, has given similar results. The proportion of raw materials bought at nationally uniform delivered prices was less than 30 per cent. in only two classes of industry, was between 30 and 50 per cent. in seven industries, and in four of the remaining six industrial classes was over 70 per cent.[22] The British steel industry has been operating since the 1930s a pricing system which in practice nearly gives nationally uniform delivered prices for many products. Courtaulds, Ltd., set a uniform delivered price for their synthetic textile fibres[23] and Polymer (U.K.), Ltd., do the same for synthetic rubber.[24] Most of the products of Imperial Chemical Industries, Ltd., are sold at a uniform delivered price, the exceptions being a few bulky chemicals of low unit value, such as sulphuric acid.[25] Finally, zone prices prevail for coal, petroleum products, gas and electricity.

It seems probable that in Britain, a country of small extent, uniform delivered prices are more usual than f.o.b. works prices, except for a very limited range of basic commodities like iron ore, coking coal and stone. Even in a country of continental proportions, nationally uniform and zone prices are sufficiently common, even ignoring retail sales, for it to be perilous to assume the *de facto* advantages of geographic proximity for both parties to a transaction without investigating the actual circumstances of each case. This is a much-neglected field of geographic and economic research that would amply repay cultivation, particularly with a view to discovering whether, as seems probable, uniform delivered pricing is becoming relatively more important than formerly.

## Consequences of Geographically Uniform Prices

To examine the effects of geographically uniform prices, prices f.o.b. works will be taken as the norm for comparative purposes. Thus, when we write of a 'tendency' in location patterns, this should be taken to mean the direction in which a geographically uniform price causes location patterns to diverge from what they would be under the f.o.b. works system. The account attempts to establish only the *direction* of the effects of uniform delivered prices and makes no pretence to discuss the *magnitude* of the economic forces involved, since this will vary according to the cost of transport, the importance of each particular product to the purchasers and vendors and the relative magnitude and regional variability of all the other costs involved.

There is one conclusion on the general effects of uniform delivered prices that cannot be accepted:

> Its [geographic price discrimination] importance, however, is easily overestimated. Regardless of the pricing tactics used, it is still advantageous for a seller of a commodity to be located at or near the centre of a large market with as few near competitors as possible. .. the principal systems of geographically discriminatory pricing—flat delivered prices and basing-point systems—grow out of conditions that would lead to market-area overlap even in the absence of any formal arrangement. The seller under a flat delivered price system chooses to extend his market area even in the face of lower net yields on more distant sales, because freight costs are a small item anyhow. . . . The basing-point system grows out of situations in which the plants remote from main centres of the industry have not enough capacity to meet the whole demand in their vicinity, which continues to be supplied partly by plants in the main centres. Under these

circumstances prices naturally grade upwards from the 'surplus' to the 'deficit' areas.[26]

The reader will note that Hoover's conclusion depends upon certain assumptions which are in fact unrealistic. The more important are:[27]

1. He considered the locational effect on sellers only, ignoring the possible locational response of buyers.

2. He considered only the short-run, leaving aside any long-term adjustments.

As in the previous discussion on the basing-point systems, it is essential to make these distinctions.

Under a uniform delivered price system, the whole cost advantage of proximity between buyer and seller is in the first instance reaped by the seller, since any saving in transport costs accrues entirely to the latter. For the buyer, proximity is immaterial, except that in the long run his location relative to the seller may affect the price which he, in common with all other buyers, has to pay.[28] Thus, if buyer A chooses to locate at a great remove, the *average* costs of distribution will be raised but if these are passed on to all buyers, A will only have to meet the *average* extra cost instead of the greater *marginal* costs were prices f.o.b. works. The United Kingdom motor car industry illustrates this point, for electric equipment typically represents 7–9 per cent. of the total costs of manufacture[29] and as we have seen, this kind of equipment is supplied on a uniform delivered price basis; the same is true of tyres, which may represent 2–3 per cent. of costs. Thus, at least 9–12 per cent. of costs, represented by these items alone, is invariable with the location of the car manufacturer within the United Kingdom. Therefore, uniform delivered prices will facilitate a more dispersed pattern of buyers than under an f.o.b. system of pricing, if other location factors so permit. In the long run, the greater dispersal of consumption will raise average costs and cause an extension of the market areas of the suppliers, leading to an increasing degree of overlap. This situation can be avoided only if factories refuse to deliver beyond the point at which all profit is absorbed by the cost of transport, a proposition which requires that a number of complicated and unlikely conditions be fulfilled.[30]

If demand for a particular product is rising, the time will come for the installation of new production capacity. Should this be built by one of the firms already in the business and setting geographically uniform prices, the new capacity will normally be located in one of two ways:

1. By increasing the size of an existing plant to obtain scale economies greater than the increasing costs of marketing in areas remote from the works.

2. By erecting a new plant at some other location which will enable the marketing territory to be divided between the two works, savings on selling costs being greater than the possible scale economies of production.

The addition of capacity to existing steel works is an example of the first case but in the limiting situation a new works may become essential.

When pricing is f.o.b. works, a rather more complicated choice has to be made. If there is a considerable price elasticity of demand, it will be worthwhile for the firm to pass on some or all of the economies which arise from either 1. an increase in the size of the original plant, or 2. the saving in transport costs that could be obtained by erecting a second plant and so dividing the market. Which solution is adopted will then depend upon the relative magnitude of the savings. But if demand is inelastic with respect to price, the producer may be indifferent in his choice.

If the new capacity is installed by another firm which uses the same pricing system as the original firm, the pricing policy has an important effect. With a uniform delivered price, the competitor will seek that location which, other things being equal, minimizes marketing expenses and both works are likely to be established in the same general area (assuming that there had been little shift in the geographic pattern or demand in the meantime). Under f.o.b. works pricing, the new plant is more likely to be located to serve a regional market protected by distance from the original supplier. Thus, we have the apparent paradox that uniform delivered prices tend to encourage the dispersal of consumers and the agglomeration of producers, taking the long-term view. In this way, uniform delivered prices tend to encourage competition between firms which compete in the same national or regional market, so reducing the monopoly element in local markets conferred by the protection of distance, but this may lead to monopolistic conditions in the national market if scale economies of production are great.

In the same way that multiple basing points modify, and in the extreme case eliminate, the location influence of the single basing point, so the use of multiple price zones modifies the effects of a single zone, or nationally uniform delivered price. In the extreme case, if zones are numerous and the price in each is closely related to the costs of transport, the end-result approximates to the f.o.b. works system.

### Are Uniform Delivered Prices Rational?

For many goods, the cost of transport is not important in intranational movements. Hence, any geographic price variations arising from f.o.b. works pricing would be negligible, whereas the cost of calculation might be relatively great. The administrative saving obtained by quoting a single delivered price may more than offset any additional costs incurred by the marginal increase of long-haul consignments. This point was made by Lösch, who estimated the cost of a 500 kilometre rail haul in Germany in 1938 as a percentage of the factory cost of a number of items, of which the following are a few examples:

| | |
|---|---|
| Building stone | 213% |
| Portland cement | 53% |
| Pig iron | 27% |
| Electrolytic copper | 5% |
| Cotton yarn | 2% |
| Tin | 1% |

Uniform delivered prices are also rational when the commodity in question moves in small quantities to (and perhaps from) a large number of places. When this situation obtains, the costs of invoicing are much greater than when there is the regular movement of large quantities to few destinations. In this respect, the supply of retailers may be contrasted with the movement of coal to electricity generating stations.

If uniform delivered prices may be justified on grounds of administrative cost savings, they may also contribute to the promotion of sales. This view is held by many firms with national or large regional markets, on the ground that advertising campaigns are facilitated and the customer can know exactly what the cost will be to him without recourse to elaborate calculations or time-consuming enquiries. It must remain largely a matter of opinion whether this is important, though the logic of the argument as it affects location matters may be stated quite simply. If a uniform delivered price encourages additional purchases in distant areas, where the unit cost to the producer, on the basis of immediately past average manufacturing costs plus transport, is greater than the realised price, this apparent 'loss' will be justified if there are unrealised economies of scale in production. So long as the marginal saving in production cost (calculated for the total output) is greater than the marginal cost of supply to the distant customer, the operation will be justified. Clearly, this requires a calculation of marginal elasticities of demand in the various parts of the market area and of marginal production costs, without which a conclusive solution is impossible.

If delivered prices encourage the extension of the market area, particularly in conjunction with advertising and other promotion activities, then several firms may obtain a small share of the national market instead of having a large share in a local market area. For industries where demand is seasonal or irregular, benefits may arise from selling nationally rather than locally, for substantial local variations in demand are likely to average out over the nation. The steadier pattern of demand for the firm's goods that will result from selling nationally should make it possible to use plant and equipment nearer to capacity than would otherwise be the case: it may even make possible a reduction in the number of production units. The economies achieved in this way may more than compensate for the additional selling costs involved.

This situation is likely to prevail only in industries where:

1. There are significant scale economies.

2. The month by month pattern of demand varies from region to region.

Private cars, refrigerators and domestic air-conditioning plant are cases which fit these conditions. Furthermore, this problem of regional variability in demand applies with greater force in the larger nations: there is far greater regional seasonal variation in demand in a country such as the U.S.S.R. than in Belgium, or even the whole of north-west Europe. So this factor tends to operate in favour of uniform delivered prices over large areas.

Thus, uniform delivered prices are not intrinsically irrational or economically wasteful, though they may so be in particular cases.[31] Furthermore, with the changes that are taking place in manufacturing techniques and types of products and the increased relative efficiency of transport, it seems probable that in future the range of goods sold on a uniform delivered price will increase and that the sizes of such market areas will expand, making this method of pricing progressively more important in relative terms.

## The Rôle of Transport in Geographic Price Patterns

Transport rightly occupies a central position in the literature on location and has long been recognized as a key factor in determining geographic patterns. Furthermore, the importance of transport has attracted the attention of economists to such good effect that there is a copious literature on the economics of the industry. Since the subject is already well-documented, with sources of information and analyses of principles easily available, it is unnecessary to discuss the whole field in the present work.[32] Discussion may most aptly concentrate on flat-rate charges, since this system of pricing transport services has been discussed very little and has a strong bearing upon geographically uniform prices for goods.

Under an Act of 1933, the then privately owned British railway companies were given the power to make 'agreed charges' with customers, instead of charging all consignments according to the published schedules of freight rates. Under these 'agreed charges', known since 1953 as 'agreed flat rates', the shipper may be charged on the weight or number of items consigned, irrespective of the distance which each shipment travels. The charge for each item or unit weight is fixed by conducting a survey of the actual pattern of traffic of the firm in question for a specified period of time. In this way, the actual charge for each consignment, based on a distance scale, is obtained, from which the average per ton or item can readily be determined. This average actual charge is then normally the charge that will be adopted under the flat rate agreement, subject to renegotiation at periodic intervals on the basis of repeated sample surveys of the traffic. This basic form of agreement has many variations, such as clauses concerning the quantity of goods to be handled in this way and terms for the return of empty containers.

In 1962, this form of agreement applied to more than one-tenth of the tonnage of general merchandise handled by British Railways' freight trains and over one-fifth of the revenue from this class of traffic. About one-fifth of the revenue from goods consigned by passenger trains was obtained from similar agreements. It is true that general merchandise accounts form a fairly small part of the freight traffic of British Railways (see Table 30) but of this sector the proportion moving under flat rate agreements has been rising rapidly since 1957.[33] Indeed, British Railways regard this method of charging freight as one of the weapons which will be of value to them in trying to win back traffic from the roads.

TABLE 30

GREAT BRITAIN: freight traffic of British Railways

|  | million metric tons of freight | | million net ton-kilometres | | average length of haul, kilometres | |
|---|---|---|---|---|---|---|
|  | 1951 | 1961 | 1951 | 1961 | 1951 | 1961 |
| Merchandise and livestock | 54·8 | 38·6 | 11·5 | 9·1 | 211 | 233 |
| Minerals, etc. | 61·9 | 54·9 | 8·4 | 7·0 | 136 | 127 |
| Coal and coke | 171·4 | 147·4 | 17·4 | 12·6 | 101 | 85 |
| TOTAL | 288·2 | 241·1 | 37·3 | 28·7 | 129 | 119 |

Source: Annual Abstract of Statistics, 1962, p. 191 and 1959, p. 197.

The prime advantage of flat-rate agreements to both parties is the great reduction in clerical work that results from the simplified documentation. An extreme example of the kind of saving that may be obtained by the shipper is that of a horticultural co-operative, Littleton and Badsey near Evesham; they do most of their sales business by telephone and now that they operate a flat-rate agreement with British Railways it is easy to compare price quotations in, say, London and Newcastle, whereas previously complicated mental arithmetic was necessary to adjust for differing freight rates.

Flat rates are likely to occur only where large quantities of goods are involved, as with mail order houses and the dispatch of spare parts by Vauxhall, Ltd., of Luton. They are also more frequent when the traffic consists of individually small consignments destined to a large number of places than when the reverse is true, since these are the conditions which yield the bigger clerical savings. Finally, the traffic pattern must be reasonably stable, otherwise sampling becomes hazardous from the viewpoint of both parties.

It appears that the greater part of traffic moving by British Railways under flat rates is goods for final consumption, not intermediate articles. The same is probably true of goods moved by road contract hauliers: British Road Services, the largest single road haulier, consider that flat rates apply to distribution rather than to trunk haul services. But owing to the fragmentation of the road haulage industry and since contract patterns are usually less stable in road than in railway traffic, flat rates are less common with road haulage than with rail.[34]

The geographic averaging of transport costs occurs in another form. With the growth of road haulage, large numbers of firms run their own fleet of lorries exclusively for the movement of their own wares. In Britain, such activities are carried on mainly by 'C' licence hauliers, the great and growing importance of whose activities is shown in Table 31. In the case of small firms, it is common for the accounts of the transport department to be merged with those of the section concerned with marketing or production, and in this way the true costs of transport cannot be obtained. Even where a separate transport account is kept, many firms make no attempt to allocate costs to particular consignments and do not, therefore, readily concern themselves with the marginal variation in costs between different hauls. The result is that over a very wide range of road operations, transport costs are in fact averaged.

Retail shops often provide a free delivery service within a specified radius or make a fixed additional charge for the service irrespective of the distance involved. Guiness the brewers from their Park Royal brewery in London absorb freight on deliveries to bottlers, who are charged a uniform price. The same

TABLE 31

GREAT BRITAIN: road freight traffic

| | Thousand million ton-kilometres | | | Licensed goods vehicles, thousand | |
|---|---|---|---|---|---|
| | 1952 | | 1961[2] | 1952[3] | 1961[3] |
| | a[1] | b[2] | | | |
| Total road | 30·6 | 29·8 | 45·3 | 1,006 | 1,439 |
| 'C' licence | 16·9 | | | 834 | 1,254 |

*Sources:*
1  *Annual Abstract of Statistics*, 1962, p. 186.
2  *The Transport Needs of Great Britain in the Next Twenty Years*, Ministry of Transport, 1963, p. 20.
3  *Annual Abstract of Statistics*; 1962, p. 186 and 1959, p. 192.

kind of thing is also true of a wide range of intermediate goods shipped under 'C' licence (and also 'contract A' licence) in Britain, largely because a proper calculation of the costs incurred on each consignment is not considered sufficiently rewarding to be undertaken.  This is likely also to be true in any economically advanced country with a good road system where the distances are comparable to those in Britain, though less relevant to countries the size of Canada or Australia. Wherever it does occur, it clearly provides an important reason for setting geographically uniform prices and avoiding the difficulties of f.o.b. pricing.

## Conclusion on Uniform Delivered Prices

Enough evidence has been adduced to show that uniform delivered prices do occur over extensive territories for a range of goods that is wider than has commonly been allowed.  Furthermore, it is clear that the system is logical and economical in at least some circumstances, largely on account of savings on clerical work and the habit of transport operators to offer flat rates.  The latter habit turns up in unexpected quarters; for example, the railway corporation in Nigeria charges on a mileage basis for most goods, but groundnuts from the Kano area are moved to Lagos, the port of export, at a standard tariff irrespective of the station of origin.  As a general conclusion, therefore, it is evident that no analysis of location patterns, whether particular or general, is complete in the absence of data on the geographic patterns of prices.

*Some Other Aspects of Pricing*

The greater part of this chapter has been devoted to the geographic pricing policies of industrial firms selling within a national territory. The list of problems has not been exhausted and in this concluding section an attempt will be made to indicate some of the other aspects of the general problem of prices in space.

Theories concerning the location of agricultural production usually proceed from the premise that prices for agricultural products are determined in the major urban areas, these being the places where demand is expressed even if consumption does not physically occur there. The numerous producers individually have no control over the prices they realize, these being determined by the price at the main market centres minus the costs of conveyance thereto from the farm. This situation, or approximations to it, is common and the effect may be seen in the geographic regularity of farm price differentials for several crops in the United States.[35]

A significant exception to this rule is provided by the pricing policy of the Milk Marketing Board, a statutory monopsony that handles virtually all liquid milk movements from farms in England and Wales. For equivalent grades of milk, the net price at the farm gate is virtually uniform throughout England and Wales, irrespective of the location of the producer with respect to the point of use and of the manner of utilization. The producers of cotton and coffee in Uganda receive a standard price that does not vary with their location[36] and in the Ivory Coast a similar situation prevails for coffee and cocoa.[37] Another example appears to have been in Japan and the Philippines before the last war for the marketing of rice. In the former country, a maximum and minimum price was set at the beginning of each season: in the Philippines, a minimum price only. The relevant agencies intervened if the limits were exceeded.[38]

Geographic differences in prices may occur because national frontiers create discrete market areas. In the United Kingdom, the import of coal requires ministerial sanction, which in recent years has not been forthcoming. It has therefore been possible for the National Coal Board to export coal at prices significantly lower than those ruling in the home market, in the knowledge that re-import is impracticable. The export prices are determined by prices ruling on the Continent, which reflect lower production costs there, a more liberal attitude to imports of cheap American coal and, in some countries, freer competition from oil.

Finally, as already noted in the case of electricity supply (p. 167), the relationship between supply and demand may vary on a daily or seasonal basis and this may occasion geographic differences in prices. This is clearly seen in the holiday industry, where the relative cost of accommodation in, say, the Riviera and Switzerland depends upon the season of the year and its effects upon sea-bathing and skiing. Similarly, transport companies such as British Railways seek to maintain a constant use of passenger facilities by offering concession fares, such as those which are available on Sundays and in the middle of the week to selected destinations. Quite apart from effects upon prices in space, the march of the seasons is reflected in seasonal price changes that are designed to even out the flow of production: domestic coal in the United Kingdom may be had at a discount in the summer months when demand is normally slack, and agricultural fertilizers are similarly cheapest in July and dearest from February onwards.

In addition to price variations of the above kind, which are reasonably systematic and intelligible, the geographic patterns of prices are in some cases remarkably complex and based on criteria that are different from those that have been assumed to operate in the discussion so far. An outstanding example is provided by the price of coal in Great Britain, coal being mined and marketed by a single authority, the National Coal Board. Coal sold for non-domestic use is priced f.o.b. the pit but the system of arriving at the pithead price is highly complicated and is not directly based on either the price users would be willing to pay in the open market or costs of production. For domestic coal, representing about 15 per cent. of output, the country is divided into sixty zones, within each of which a uniform price is established for each grade of coal at the points of rail delivery. The zone prices vary widely, on account of transport costs and variation in the pithead price, but the differentials between particular grades of coal are maintained in all the zones, irrespective of variations in the relative distances to the sources

of the different coals. The determination of pithead prices
pays no regard to local differences in production costs. The
general price level is determined on the basis of average
production costs for the whole industry, the price of each grade
being ascertained on a points system designed to measure the
value of the grade to the consumer. Once these national prices
have been obtained, an adjustment is made for each coalfield,
the nature and purpose of which can be illustrated by reference
to Lancashire:

> The demands of industrial consumers in that county
> cannot be satisfied entirely from local production, and they
> have to be supplied from the East Midlands and the North
> Eastern coalfields as well as from those in Lancashire.
> The transport of East Midlands and North Eastern coal
> to markets in Lancashire costs more than that of the local
> coal. Under competitive conditions such as those which
> prevailed between the wars, there is a tendency for only
> one price to rule for all consumers at the same place for
> coals of equal utility. Lancashire coal, quality for quality,
> therefore commanded a higher price at the pit than did
> coal from the two other coalfields. In devising their price
> structure the Board followed this precedent by applying a
> coalfield adjustment to the Lancashire coal and pursued
> a similar policy in other areas where they thought this
> to be appropriate.[39]

The over-all result is a complicated system of pricing the logic
of which is not entirely evident.

Finally, the growth of large companies with numerous plants
in scattered locations raises the vexed question of intra-company pricing for those goods that are supplied by one unit to
another within the organization. One might assume that each
plant or division would be expected to operate on a fully
commercial basis, charging a market price for all that it supplies to other sections of the same organization. This solution
may not be feasible if there is no proper 'market' for the commodities, as happens with highly specialized components and
semi-manufactures. Even where it is possible, firms have been
so loth to pursue the policy that the *Harvard Business Review*
has published at least one article urging the advantages of
adopting competitive pricing policies for intra-company

O

transactions.[40] In the absence of sound pricing policies, the locations of the constituent parts of large companies cannot be properly assessed and the results may be illogical, or non-optimal.

## Conclusion

The general question of how firms set prices for their products is a difficult one and remains only partially resolved. It is a field of economic investigation in which there have been some fierce controversies. Therefore, we must be somewhat diffident in embarking upon an investigation of the geographic aspects of pricing.

However, sufficient empirical evidence has been adduced in this chapter to show that the common assumption that prices are set f.o.b. works cannot be sustained as the general case. Instead of prices varying with location relative to the point of supply, in direct relation to the costs of transfer, we have seen that many prices are uniform over large areas. It follows that the orthodox reasoning about the mutual advantages of proximity for both buyers and sellers is not valid as the general rule, though it does of course apply where prices are f.o.b. works. The effects of uniform delivered prices upon location patterns are complicated and depend in part upon the nature of competition in the industry in question. Nevertheless, it does seem warranted to conclude that a uniform delivered price will encourage the dispersal of buyers if other considerations so permit. But each case ought to be examined separately in the light of the particular pricing policies employed and the general conditions affecting the location of the seller and of the buyers.

Despite the opinions of Hoover, Lösch and others, that geographically uniform prices are logically indefensible, it is evident that a firm may gain from this form of pricing. Administrative and selling costs may be reduced and customers know exactly where they stand. Furthermore, if flat-rate agreements operate for transport, or if inadequate transport accounts are kept by the firm, there may be no basis on which to operate any pricing policy other than that of uniform delivered prices. Where economies of scale in manufacture are significant, nationally uniform prices may enable substantial manufacturing economies to be obtained through the increase in volume of sales that uniform delivered prices may make possible. Geographically uniform prices are therefore not necessarily irrational and there is some reason to suppose that they will become more rather than less common in the future.

## REFERENCES

1 J. M. Clark, *Competition as a Dynamic Process*, 1961, p. 303.

2 E. M. Hoover, 1948, *op. cit.*, (Chap. 2), p. 29.

3 A. Lösch, 1954, *op. cit.*, (Chap. 2), p. 165.

4 There are numerous business practices but the form is largely immaterial so long as the effect is that the purchaser pays for the transport. Small discrepancies may arise from the fact that under some contractual arrangements ownership of the goods changes at the point of origin whereas in other cases the ownership changes at the destination or even at some intermediate point. Even if the buyer pays the full freight, his insurance bill may vary according to the proportion of the journey for which he owns the goods in question.

5 A. Lösch, 1954, *op. cit.*, pp. 139–67. M. L. Greenhut, 1956, *op. cit.*, (Chap. 2), pp. 141–62. See also E. H. Chamberlin, 1933, *op. cit.*, (Chap. 2), who argued in his appendix 'Pure Spatial Competition' that any monopoly profit arising out of locational advantages will be transferred from the entrepreneur to the landowner in the form of higher rental payments, since potential competitors will bid up the rent. This will not occur if the site in question is owned by the entrepreneur.

6 In the literature devoted to location theory, references may be found in: E. M. Hoover, 1948, *op. cit.*, pp. 56–57; A. Lösch, 1954, *op. cit.*, pp. 164–65; M. L. Greenhut, 1956, *op. cit.*, p. 308–16.

7 A. R. Burns, *The Decline of Competition*, 2nd impression, 1936, p. 341. The single basing point formally ended in 1924 but multiple basing points existed until 1948.

8 G. W. Stocking, *Basing Point Pricing and Regional Development*, 1954, p. 200. See also F. Macklup, *The Basing-Point System*, 1949, p. 237.

9 A. R. Burns, 1936, *op. cit.*, p. 298.

10 F. Macklup, 1949, *op. cit.*

11 J. M. Clark, 1961, *op. cit.*, pp. 316–19. C. Issawi and M. Yeganeh, 1962, *op. cit.*, (Chap. 3), pp. 64–70. See also A. Melamid, 'Geography of the world petroleum price structure', *Economic Geography*, 1962, pp. 283–98.

12 In addition, cement in the United Kingdom is marketed on a basing-point system.

13 J. E. Meade (ed.), *Case Studies in European Economic Union*, 1962, pp. 260–62.

14  Federal Trade Commission, *Report of the Federal Trade Commission on Price Bases Inquiry*, 1932. The sample contained firms manufacturing for final consumption but it is not possible to determine how many: the fourteen categories listed suggest that the bias was toward firms supplying intermediate goods. Some of the details are quoted by A. R. Burns, 1936, *op. cit.*

15  The categories are not all exclusive, with the result that the same firm may be counted two or more times.

16  G. Ackley, 'Price policies', in *Industrial Location and National Resources*, National Resources Planning Board, 1943, pp. 302–17. The *Price Bases Inquiry* noted that 39 per cent. of firms manufacturing paper and paper products sold at least some goods on a uniform delivered price basis and this situation still obtains for Kraft and corrugated papers (see H. A. Stafford, Jr., 'Factors in the location of the paperboard container industry', *Economic Geography*, 1960, p. 262).

17  Personal communication from Fisons, Ltd., 7th March, 1963.

18  'Report on the supply of certain industrial and medical gases', *Parliamentary Papers*, 20th December, 1956, p. 66.

19  'Report on the supply of sand and gravel in central Scotland,' *idem.*, 22nd March 1956, p. 12 and Appendix a.

20  F. W. Luttrell, 1962, *op. cit.*, (Chap. 2), vol. 1, p. 319. The industries studied were: shoe, hosiery, clothing, textile, metalworking (engineering, electrical goods and metal goods) and woodworking.

21  Scottish Council, undated, *op. cit.*, (Chap. 2), p. 75.

22  Northern Ireland Development Council, *Fifth Report 1960–1961*, Appendix.

23  Personal communication.

24  *The Times*, 29th January 1963.

25  Personal communication, 12th June 1963.

26  E. M. Hoover, 1948, *op. cit.*, pp. 57–58.

27  Note also that geographically uniform prices are not confined to products where transport costs are relatively unimportant (p. 185).

28  The buyer may have an interest in proximity which is based upon quality of service, speed of delivery, ease of personal contact, etc.

29  G. Maxcy and A. Silberston, 1959, *op. cit.*, (Chap. 3), pp. 27 and 31.

30  A. Lösch, 1954, *op. cit.*, pp. 159–60, concluded that pricing f.o.b. works or on a uniform delivered basis 'makes no difference to the seller (in the average case of linear demand) . . . so long as his sales area is determined by competition and not, say, by governmental authority. The size of his sales area and thus the number of independent enterprises as well, no less than the size of their profits, will be the same in either case.' M. L. Greenhut (1956, *op. cit.* Chap. 2 pp. 160–61) arrives at the same conclusion. This proposition is untenable in a dynamic situation. In Figure 7, an entrepreneur at A has unit costs of manufacture AB and obtains a 'normal' profit BC. Under an f.o.b. works price, his market area is limited at X and Y by competitors. The only way in which the situation can remain unchanged on

converting to a uniform delivered price (GJKH) is if the volume of rotation of DGJ + EKH = JCK. (Sales are assumed to be proportional to area.) Where this condition is satisfied, the transport loss on sales beyond J and K is balanced by the gain on the transport account for nearer sales. In other words, the entrepreneur is expected to behave in a highly sophisticated manner, *as if* using f.o.b. works pricing: 'the elimination of too distant buyers is caused . . . by the refusal of the entrepreneur to deliver'. (Lösch, p. 160, fn.) But the moment there are any shifts in the geographic pattern of demand, for whatever reason, the marginal effects upon the producer are different under the two systems of pricing. Under an f.o.b. works system, an increase in sales beyond J and K makes no difference to his profits: with uniform delivered prices, such an increase will either be reflected in lower profits or a rise in the average (delivered) price. The long-term effect of uniform delivered prices must be to encourage an expansion of the market area and an increase in prices, unless the greater sales produce scale economies sufficient to offset the increased delivery costs. Incidentally, Lösch's conclusion quoted above apparently contradicts his dislike of delivered prices (Lösch, p. 165), though the discrepancy is explained by the shift from a short- to long-term view of the matter and from the seller's to the buyer's stance.

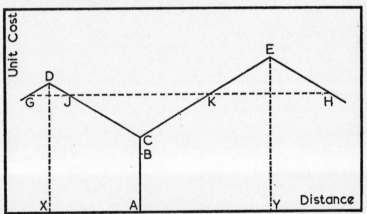

Figure 7. Comparison of pricing f.o.b. works and uniform delivered pricing

31 The Monopolies Commission found it hard to understand the logic of uniform delivered prices for industrial gases, where transport costs average some 25 per cent. of costs (p. 185).

32 S. Daggett's *Principles of Inland Transportation*, 4th edition, 1955, has a strong geographic emphasis.

33 Interview with representatives of the British Railways Board, 2nd April 1963.

34 Personal communication, 21st March 1963.

35 For some easily accessible examples, see: W. Warntz, 1959, *op. cit.*, (Chap. 2).

36  A. M. O'Connor, 'New railway construction and the pattern of economic development in East Africa', *Transactions and Papers*, Institute of British Geographers, June 1965, pp. 27–28.

37  *West Africa*, 5th June, 1965, p. 615.

38  V. D. Wickizer and M. K. Bennett, *The Rice Economy of Monsoon Asia*, 1941, esp. p. 183.

39  *Report of the Committee of Inquiry into 'Coal Distribution Costs in Great Britain'*, Cmnd. 446, 1958, p. 28.  See also R. C. Estall, 'The London coal trade', *Geography*, 1958, pp. 75–85.

40  J. Dean, 'Decentralization and intracompany pricing', *Harvard Business Review*, July–August 1955, pp. 65–74.

# CHAPTER 8

# The Rôle of Government

'It is important to remember that the subordination of economic affairs to political direction was an established European tradition supported by centuries of practice before Europe began to experience that rapid industrialization which ultimately affected the greater part of the world.'[1] With rapid industrialization during the last century, many of the traditional forms of regulation become anachronisms, hindrances to change that were swept away in the name of free trade and competition. However, the retreat of government from economic regulation went much further in the United Kingdom than in France, for example: this is illustrated by the piecemeal building of competitive private railways in the former country whereas in the latter construction was delayed to permit a national survey to be undertaken and the government participated in much of the railway development. Furthermore, in almost all parts of the world, governments have recently been reasserting control over the economy of their respective countries, playing an ever bigger part in the lives of their citizens and consequently the geography of their domains.

Government influence is exercised in two main ways. First, by control over the expenditure of part of the national income. In many countries, one-quarter to one-third of the national income is spent by government and in some the proportion is even higher. The share spent by government has tended to rise during this century in almost all countries, as is illustrated by data for the United Kingdom (Table 32). Control of expenditure implies two important effects upon the geography of a country, through the disposition of resources between various uses, so affecting the structure of the economy, and between places. The second major kind of government effect lies in the enactment of laws that specify the limits of individual and corporate freedoms, ranging from laws governing the location of new industrial plants to those that insist upon the education of children. Such laws again affect the structure of the economy and the geographic distribution of resources.

TABLE 32

UNITED KINGDOM: proportion of Gross National Product spent by government (central and local)

| Year | Percentage | Year | Percentage |
|------|------------|------|------------|
| 1955 | 37·3 | 1880 | 10 |
| 1952 | 41·9 | 1870 | 9 |
| 1950 | 39·5 | 1860 | 11 |
| 1938 | 30·1 | 1850 | 12 |
| 1933 | 25·9 | 1841 | 11 |
| 1928 | 24·2 | 1831 | 16 |
| 1920 | 26·1 | 1822 | 19 |
| 1910 | 12·8 | 1814 | 29 |
| 1900 | 15 14·4 | 1800 | 24 |
| 1890 | 9 8·8 | 1792 | 11 |

Source: A. T. Peacock and J. Wiseman, *The Growth of Public Expenditure in the United Kingdom*, 1961, pp. 37 and 42.

N.B. The figures for 1900 and earlier are not quite comparable to those for 1890 and later. High levels of government expenditure occurred during the Napoleonic Wars and the South African War in 1900.

Governments have therefore traditionally played an important part in moulding the geography of the world and though this activity slackened in the nineteenth century it is being reasserted in the present one. In addition, international agreements of all kinds are becoming increasingly important in the lives of us all and in some areas supra-national organs of government are being evolved, as in the European Economic Community.

In terms of geographic and economic analysis, government activity is characterized by some notable peculiarities. In most situations, there are many individuals or firms making decisions about what to produce (or buy) and where so to do, but each country has only one central government. Therefore, in most economic analysis the problems of monopoly and oligopoly are special cases at one end of a spectrum: with governments, a monopolistic or monopsonistic situation is usual. The power of government may or may not be curbed by checks and balances within the political system but whether it is or is not is immaterial to one central fact. When there are many individuals, a sufficiency of observations will usually enable some reasonable predictions to be made about patterns of behaviour in given situations, since irrational or mistaken decisions may appear as quantifiable deviations from the norm. This is the tacit assumption underlying most studies in location patterns and also provides the rationale for the newer kind of study that has the curious name 'social physics'.[2] With only one government ruling a given area, each decision may be unique and therefore general rules of behaviour are far harder, if not impossible, to ascertain. Indeed, it is an evident fact that many government decisions are taken for a variety of reasons that may have little to do with economics or geography—electoral expediency, the predilections of ministers and the balance of their personalities and questions of administrative ease, to name only a few. Governments come and go and with them ideas on how society should be organized.

Government is therefore a potentially dynamic element in the geography of most countries and is apt to have an important influence owing, first, to the large proportion of expenditure which is directly controlled and, secondly, to the ramifications of legislation. However, the behaviour of governments is not amenable to strict analysis and prediction. Thus, it is not possible to set out systematically all the ways in which government activities affect the geography of the world and the most that can be attempted in the space which is available is to indicate the kinds of effect that must be looked for and some of the complications that often render it a hard task to identify these effects.

*Kinds of Government Activity*

Government influence can be exercised directly at any or all points in the economy: production, exchange and consumption and the factors of production, land, labour and capital. Since all these parts of the economy are intimately inter-related and inter-dependent, the curiosity of the geographer must explore all forms of government action to seek the effects which indirectly, as well as those which directly, affect spatial patterns of economic activity.

In terms directly of production, governments often own or at least control productive enterprises. Wartime ordnance factories

in the United Kingdom, which were often located with a
view first to the availability of labour and second to safety
from enemy attack, have become the nucleus of peace-time
industrial estates: Newton Aycliffe is a case in point, now
become a thriving town. The Italian parliament has decreed
that two-fifths of the investment by State-owned industries—
which include petroleum, petro-chemicals, electricity and
steel—must be located in the poorer, more backward south of
the country. Even where enterprise remains private, government may sanction new development only in specified places.
Such is the case in France, where a virtually absolute pro-
hibition on new industrial development in the Paris area is
in force. Or again, government, acting through its own
administration or through agents, may initiate and enforce
agricultural development projects, such as the Gezira scheme
in the Sudan and land reform in Egypt. The total direct
subsidy to agriculture in the United Kingdom amounts to
£350 million a year.

In the field of trade, there is a long tradition of official
control. At one time, only a limited number of 'staple' towns
were permitted to export the wool of England and Wales, while
Lancashire currently shelters behind 'agreements' that limit
the import of cotton cloth from abroad. The United States
has chosen to protect its domestic watch industry by imposing
heavy duties on imports from Switzerland while India completely bans the import of a wide range of consumer goods.
Other countries operate complicated currency controls, one
effect of which is to discriminate between classes of imports
and exports either by assigning different exchange rates or by
crediting (debiting) certain items with foreign exchange rights
while other goods are accounted for exclusively in the local
currency. Argentina used to do this. The Navigation Acts
that Britain repealed in the nineteenth century have reappeared
as the 'Buy American' legislation, which requires that American
'aid' goods be shipped in American vessels, whose freight rates
are substantially higher than those of other flags.[3]

Consumption may be affected in several ways, even excluding physical rationing, which is an expedient only for short-
term emergencies such as war or famine. Where taxation on,
or subsidy of, consumption differentiates between classes of

goods, or between goods and services, the relative prices to consumers are affected and in some degree the pattern of demand will be altered. The varying levels of purchase tax in the United Kingdom discriminate against 'luxury' goods in particular, whereas a tax on business turnover is neutral in its effects in this context.[4] The taxation of personal income may also have an important effect. In most countries, income taxes are 'progressive', in that the rate of tax is higher on higher incomes, and in this way income is redistributed from the rich to the poor. The effect of progressive taxation may be reinforced by the provision of social welfare benefits that are used most by the poorer sector of the community. Since the income elasticity of demand varies at different income levels (p. 154), redistribution of incomes will affect the over-all pattern of consumption. Finally, the manner in which government chooses to spend that part of the national income which passes through its hands is exceedingly important: more rockets means fewer schools, more roads means fewer hospitals. And schools will not necessarily occupy the same sites or regions where otherwise weapons would be made.

Government also has an important rôle in helping or hindering the mobility of land, labour and capital. Until recently, the migration of Italian workers from the countryside to the towns, and from the south to the north, was deliberately hindered by regulations concerning the acquisition of residence permits and limiting the opportunities for finding work.[5] On the other hand, the European Economic Community is reducing and will ultimately abolish the administrative obstacles to intra-Community migration. Whereas the European Coal and Steel Community has actively sought to help the migration of coal miners from declining fields,[6] in the United Kingdom the government has taken little part in helping internal migration (the National Coal Board has, however, been active and successful in effecting transfers of coal miners). The availability of land for various purposes is closely conditioned by legislation, as under the Town and Country Planning Acts of the United Kingdom and zoning ordinances promulgated by American cities. Finally, since the 1920s, international movements of capital, hitherto largely unregulated, became generally subject to government scrutiny and control and currently the greater part of international capital transfers take place directly between governments or through international agencies such as the International Monetary Fund.

All the government activities that have been mentioned so far constitute single acts that in principle can be viewed in isolation from all other changes, on the *ceteris paribus* principle. In addition, there are concerted programmes of regional development in which a series of measures will be implemented simultaneously or in planned sequence. One of the better known is the Tennessee Valley Authority project, begun in the 1930s;[7] another is the post-war programme for improving the lot of the southern Italians.[8]

The reader will appreciate that under each of the main headings mentioned the number of examples that could be quoted is legion. Suffice it to note that the effects of government upon the location of activities must be sought in all parts of the economic system and not merely in terms of direct intervention in the location of production.

*Identifying the Effect*

In many cases, the effectiveness or otherwise of government activities in influencing location patterns and the prosperity of regions can be gauged with reasonable precision. The decision to subsidize the erection of a paper pulp mill at Fort William, Scotland, had an immediate effect in enabling British Railways to agree to keep open the line to Fort William and beyond, whereas without the new project they would certainly have sought to close it. The direct effect of creating additional employment will also be measurable, though the indirect, or multiplier, effects are harder to assess, and in particular, how much of the multiplier effect 'leaks' to other parts of the United Kingdom or even abroad. But in many cases, it is not even certain *where* the initial effect is felt, at least without careful consideration, and it is to this general question that we will advert.

An example will illustrate the nature of the problem. Under the European Free Trade Association, tariffs between the member countries are being reduced. In Norway, an investigation was made of sixty-three imported items, which in 1960 were subject to heavy duties, to discover who was benefiting from tariff reductions. Although in 1963 retail prices had fallen to some extent in thirty-three cases, foreign suppliers had taken the opportunity to raise their prices on twenty-four goods and middlemen had increased their percentage markup in thirty-eight cases. Over-all, the middlemen had 'gained the most'.[9] The initial expectation that a tariff reduction would benefit the consumers in full is not entirely correct and in the case cited some of the advantage was transferred abroad. Why should this happen?

A partial answer is given by the contrasting behaviour of the petroleum companies in Western Germany and the United Kingdom. In the former country, a fuel oil tax was imposed in 1960 to protect the indigenous coal industry but 'was largely ineffective as, in general, the tax was absorbed by the suppliers and the prices to consumers were not raised'.[10] The reason was partly that the market for petroleum products was intensely competitive and partly that the price of coal was influenced by the import of cheap American supplies. Had any oil companies passed on the duty to consumers, they risked losing sales to coal and/or to other petroleum companies that refrained from so doing. In contrast, the petroleum market in the United Kingdom was at that time less competitive, being dominated by Shell–BP and Esso, the import of American coal was prohibited and the British coal industry was less efficient than the Ruhr mines. The duty on fuel oil could be, and was, passed on to the consumer in full.[11]

The true incidence of a tax or subsidy therefore depends largely upon the strength of the bargaining positions of the buyers and sellers involved. This is related not only to the degree of monopoly or competition (between buyers and sellers and among themselves) but also to the price-elasticities of supply and demand (p. 56). The consumption of liquor, tobacco and, in some countries salt, is very little affected by the price (consumption is inelastic) whereas the production thereof is: therefore, these are excellent subjects for raising revenue and the taxes are paid by the consumer. The excise duty on a bottle of whisky bought in London is *paid* by the Londoner and is not transferred to the distiller, even though the duty was *collected* when the bottle left bond in Scotland. In contrast, the export taxes that Nigeria levies on oil palm products, cocoa and groundnuts, all of which compete in the international market with similar or alternative products from elsewhere, are probably passed back to the peasant producers. They serve, therefore, not to increase foreign exchange earnings but to redistribute the proceeds between the federal government and private citizens.

The assessment of secondary and more remote adjustments to any policy decision can provide some very knotty problems. During the negotiations for the entry of Britain into the European Economic Community that came to an abortive end in 1963, a great deal of work was done to analyze the probable impact on the economy of the United Kingdom. The prospect of completely unfettered agricultural imports from Europe alarmed some sections of opinion, for the rapid increase in Community agricultural output was remarked. In the event, the United Kingdom did not join the Community and still exercises some control over farm imports, even from Commonwealth countries and the European Free Trade Association (the terms of which agreement exclude agriculture). By not opening our doors to the Community, British agriculture appears to retain its comfortable, subsidized and protected status. But if agricultural output in the Community continues to increase as rapidly as it has done in the past, the scope for exports to Europe by New Zealand and Argentina, for example, will decrease and there may even be increasing competition for outlets in Asia and elsewhere. The pressure from New Zealand, Australia, Denmark and others for a more liberal attitude toward imports into Britain could become embarrassing: though the front door was safely bolted, the back door may be battered in.

At a smaller scale, the history of the green belt around London is instructive. Properly implemented only after the last war, the policy has been to designate a swathe of territory between about nineteen and fifty kilometres from the centre of London as a zone within which urban development of all kinds would be severely restricted. The purpose was to limit the spread of London, thought to be already too big, and to provide open space for recreation. In the event, the continued increase in population, the demand for more physical space per family, combined with excellent transport facilities, has resulted in development leap-frogging the green belt. In a functional sense, London has continued to grow and thousands of workers daily traverse the green belt. The policy, though superficially successful, has not produced quite the expected result.[12]

*Unintentional Effects*

The examples that have been mentioned above are ones in which policies have been undertaken with deliberate intent to affect the geography of the country or countries concerned, even though the ultimate results may not be quite what was intended. In practice, a very wide range of legislation and administrative action may have a purpose far removed from considerations of geography and yet have an important bearing thereon. For example, the universal provision of old-age pensions in advanced countries, to meet a real social need, confers upon the elderly an independence of action that could not be entertained when the old had to rely upon the younger members of the family for succour. Thus is created a potential for mobility among elderly people that previously did not exist on a significant scale and many people choose to retire in places removed from the scene of their labours. Sun, sea, seclusion or other factors may be the dominant consideration in these removals and entirely new or much expanded centres of purchasing power appear on the map, which may in turn attract market oriented industries. The island of Majorca has benefited enormously from the influx of retired persons, many of whom seek to stretch a meagre pension further than it would go in their native land where living costs are (or were) higher.

Another example is provided by the regulation of the maximum speeds of heavy commercial road vehicles, the hours of driving per day, the number of men manning a vehicle and related matters, as embodied in the Road Traffic Acts of the United Kingdom. These regulations have been introduced to protect drivers against exploitation and thereby to ensure that fatigue does not endanger safety. One consequence, however, is that for distances up to about one hundred and thirty kilo-metres a vehicle can make a round trip in one day, whereas after that distance and at each multiple of one hundred and thirty kilometres, costs rise sharply on account of overnight subsistence allowances and overtime payments or because more vehicles are required to move a given volume of freight. Under United Kingdom conditions, therefore, a firm supplying the national domestic market would want to find a location that gave it access to as large a share of the market as possible within a radius of one hundred and thirty kilometres: the area of Nottingham–Coventry is the one that meets this requirement.[13] Should the critical distance be less or more, the most desirable location, from this one point of view, would differ.

Subsidized council housing has become very important in the United Kingdom since the First World War. The original intention was to provide decent accommodation, adequate for health and reasonable comfort, for those who otherwise were condemned to live in squalid and insanitary conditions, a social aim that was both just and humane. With increasing standards of living and the natural evolution of families, many occupants no longer need a subsidy, while poorer folk may have to wait years for a council house. One effect is to make housing artificially cheap for a large sector of the population, who then desire (and are able) to use more space than otherwise would be the case: the pressure for urban sprawl is thereby increased. In Scotland, there is a special effect of importance. An unusually large proportion of council property in Scottish cities is old and the rents charged have been related to historic costs rather than to replacement costs: twelve or fifteen shillings a week has been a common level of rent. A new and much better house will cost at least twice that sum but, accustomed to low rents, people are unwilling to pay the economic price even when they can well afford to. One consequence is that the development corporation of East Kilbride new town cannot charge an economic rent for the houses it is building and, for this reason among others, the finances of the corporation have been in a sorry state and the success of the enterprise jeopardized.

One last example of the unintentional effects of legislation is provided by the history of water control in Italy. When the country was unified under Piedmont in the middle of the last century, Piedmontese law was applied to the whole domain. The laws regarding the control of water had been framed for the physical environment of northern Italy, where a great need was for the drainage of land in the vicinity of towns to control the breeding of mosquitoes and hence to limit the incidence of malaria. In the Po valley, such drainage provided excellent agricultural land, and municipal activity in drainage therefore greatly helped the growth of farm production and the increase of prosperity. However, in the southern part of the peninsula, many settlements had been for long established on the hillsides above the malarial lowlands and therefore the public health reason for water control by the municipalities did not apply. Furthermore, the Piedmontese laws were framed in terms of drainage, whereas in the south the more important requirement for agriculture was the construction of dams to store water for irrigation. Thus, until comparatively recently little change in the agriculture of the south occurred while in the north much progress was being registered, one reason being that laws suitable for one environment were not appropriate in another.

## Measurement of Effects: Regional Income Accounting

As we have seen, almost every activity of government discriminates in one way or another between classes of person and regions of the country. The distribution of income and wealth between classes of person has exercised economists for many years.[14] The parallel problem of regional inequalities in wealth and income and the effect of government intervention thereon has received comparatively little attention, though interest in the question appears to be growing.

One reason for this lack of interest has been the difficulty of devising techniques of analysis. The single most useful method is the compilation of regional income estimates in which transfers to and from government are recognized, but regional income accounting has had to wait upon the development of national income accounting, which itself only began after the First World War. Thus, much of the work in regional income accounting has been conceptual in nature in an attempt to provide a framework of analysis[15] and the few attempts to apply theory to particular countries must be treated with great reserve, as for example the set published for the United Kingdom for the year 1948.[16]

It has been estimated that the over-all error in figures of

P

national income is liable to be of the order of 10 per cent.[17] Such an error may not be serious for temporal comparisons of the performance of a particular economy if the bias is a constant one but comparisons of the income of two countries in the same year may be grossly misleading if one estimate errors by 10 per cent. positively and the other by an equal but negative amount. The probable errors are greater for the individual components of the total and for the regions that constitute a part of the national territory. In compiling national income figures, more data are directly recorded than is the case with regional accounts and this is an important reason for the lesser accuracy of regional than of national accounts. For example, the foreign trade of a nation is usually carefully recorded whereas the transactions of any one region with the others in the same country is not. Therefore, in regional income accounting much more estimation is required than is the case with national accounts. Furthermore, with national income accounting, it is usually possible to check calculations by a form of double-entry book-keeping, but this is often not possible with regional accounts. For example, at the national level the inland revenue department may collect data on personal income for tax purposes and the types of income—wages, profits, etc.—may be distinguished. The element of wages and salaries can be checked against figures obtained from censuses of industry for the cost of labour and against estimates obtained from multiplying wage rates by the number of employed persons in each wage category. At the national level, the circular flow of income can be measured as value of production, value of income or value of spending and the three totals, suitably adjusted for saving, foreign exchange transactions, etc., should be equal. At the regional level, a single estimate may have to suffice and errors will go undetected.

The essence of the problem is that a regional economy is 'open', i.e., that 'foreign' (or external) transactions of all kinds are important and that, whereas records of these 'external' transactions are available for a national economy, they do not usually exist for a region. This is the same problem that arose from our examination of the concept of the multiplier as it applies in geographic terms (p. 99) and to the related question of urban economic base studies (p. 44).

Nevertheless, some estimates have been made of the net impact of government expenditure and revenue collection on regional economies. In the period following the last world war, the outflow of funds from New England to the federal treasury (calculated on the basis of taxable incomes) exceeded the inflow of monies therefrom:

> This broad generalization applies to grants of the federal government, to federal assistance generally, to outlays on public works, to defence expenditures, to disbursements of lending agencies, to civilian pay rolls, and even to benefit payments of the Veterans Administration. Perhaps the only important exceptions are the federal payments for Old Age and Survivor's Insurance and (the) administration of unemployment compensation.[18]

The disproportion between federal receipts and disbursements appeared to be an important factor retarding development in the region relative to the rest of the country.

If New England has tended to suffer from a net drain of federal resources out of the region, Florida in particular has gained through the operation of the Cape Kennedy rocket launching site and the industrial development that is associated therewith. In 1954, even before rocketry became a boom industry, the South Atlantic region of the United States derived 13 per cent. of all personal income from federal wages and salaries, compared with a national average of 6 per cent.[19] The regional distribution of United States federal expenditure (but not revenue) has been carefully investigated[20] and one aspect thereof, military contracts, subjected to very thorough study.[21]

The most comprehensive data on the regional patterns of government revenue sources and expenditure of which the author is aware are available for Japan. These are not published as part of regional accounts and therefore it is not possible to identify the net effects of government activities upon regional incomes. However, it is possible to show the pattern of net transfer between regions on account of government activities in collecting and disbursing funds. The transactions recorded are equivalent to over one-third of the national income and therefore potentially may effect a very big geographic redistribution of prosperity. The relevant data, averaged for three years in order to eliminate any freak circumstances, are displayed in Table 33. The data are collected through the Bank of Japan and relate to the region in which the transactions are *recorded*, which may differ from the

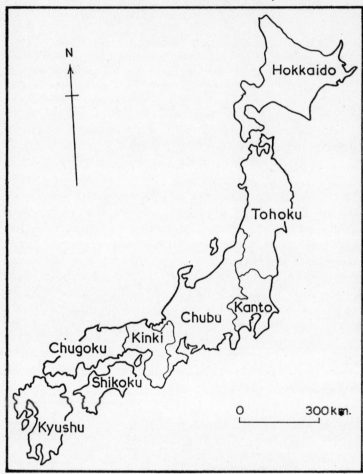

Figure 8.   Bank of Japan regions (See Table 33)

region in which the payment is really made or received. However, there is no *prima facie* reason why the apparent geographic distribution of revenue should be biassed more or less than the apparent distribution of expenditure. Furthermore, the individual items of revenue and expenditure tend to

## TABLE 33

JAPAN, 1959–61: Treasury revenue and expenditure by regions

AVERAGE OF YEARS 1959–61 INCLUSIVE

| Region | Population, 1960 million | Revenue thousand million yen | Expenditure | Revenue thousand yen per caput | Expenditure thousand yen per caput | Excess (+) or deficiency (−) of expenditure over revenue, thousand yen per caput |
|---|---|---|---|---|---|---|
| Kanto | 23·0 | 2,115·2 | 2,694·0 | 92·0 | 117·2 | +25·2 |
| Tohoku | 9·3 | 186·5 | 215·9 | 20·0 | 23·2 | +3·2 |
| Hokkaido | 5·0 | 189·7 | 196·5 | 37·7 | 39·0 | +1·3 |
| Shikoku | 4·1 | 74·4 | 70·2 | 18·1 | 17·0 | −1·1 |
| Kyushu | 12·9 | 285·8 | 255·5 | 22·2 | 19·8 | −2·4 |
| Chugoku | 6·9 | 177·3 | 150·9 | 25·5 | 21·7 | −3·8 |
| Chubu | 16·6 | 575·6 | 381·9 | 34·7 | 23·1 | −11·6 |
| Kinki | 15·5 | 788·0 | 305·2 | 50·8 | 19·7 | −31·1 |
| TOTAL | 93·4 | 4,392·4 | 4,270·2 | 47·0 | 45·7 | −1·3 |

*Source*: Data kindly made available by Professor K. Murata, Chuo University, Tokyo. The regions are shown in Figure 8. 1008 yen equals £1 sterling at the official rate of exchange.

show the same pattern as the aggregates. Thus, the big apparent differences between revenue and expenditure are almost certainly real but too much should not be made of the small discrepancies: the distinction between $+1 \cdot 3$ thousand yen *per caput* in Hokkaido and $-1 \cdot 1$ thousand yen in Shikoku is unlikely to be significant whereas the contrast between both these regions and Kanto and Kinki is undoubtedly valid. The net effect of government financial activity in Japan seems to favour the north-east of the country to the detriment of the other areas.

Regional income accounts are few and somewhat unreliable. In time, more will become available and their reliability will undoubtedly be improved. In this case, they will provide invaluable data on the rôle of governments in affecting the net actual flow of income between regions but this can only be a partial measure of the effects of governments upon the geography of their respective territories. Regional income accounting cannot provide a tool for measuring the opportunity costs incurred in decisions about the location of factories or the imposition of import duties, etc. To take a specific example, a considerable sum of money has been used to induce motor car manufacturers to establish new works on Merseyside, in south Wales and in Scotland rather than in the Birmingham–London area. These outlays can in principle be allocated to the regions of the United Kingdom and could thus enter into regional income accounts. What could not readily be shown from such accounts is the location of the multiplier effects: the construction materials may be obtained from outside the regions in which the investment was taking place and likewise components for the vehicles. However, it appears that some manufacture of components is developing in Scotland at least, but this is a long-term matter which again cannot easily be analyzed by means of regional income accounts. Finally, regional income accounts could not compare the actual situation after the investment has occurred with what would have been the situation had the investment been located elsewhere.

However precise the available data, and however plentiful, it seems that an assessment of the rôle of government in shaping the geography of an area must retain an element, probably a large one, of judgment. The same is, of course, true of all economics and all economic geography, but it appears most evident in considering the place of government in the scheme of things.

## Conclusion

Governments can have a great effect upon the geography of a country, not only directly and deliberately but also indirectly and accidentally. The importance of government derives in part from its control over expenditure and in part from legislation that may touch innumerable facets of the economy. The geographer must therefore look critically at all government activity to see whether there are important indirect and unintentional effects upon the spatial patterns of activities in addition to the more obvious intended and direct effects.

In an important respect, the difficulties that arise in identifying the effects of government activity symbolize one of the general features of economics that has already been mentioned. All parts of the economic system are interdependent and consequently a change anywhere in the system is likely to have far-reaching effects. It follows that an analysis which is based on the *ceteris paribus* principle, of allowing only one factor to vary at a time, is not really appropriate. The correct habit of thought is to admit that many forces are operating simultaneously. Furthermore, these forces are simultaneously operating at various scales and allowance must be made for this fact. For example, the location of new steel capacity in Britain is conditioned by the complex circumstances within the country, which include political considerations. But the world market for steel products, particularly the location of any surpluses or deficits, changes in the size of ore carriers and the sources of ore, etc., are all important factors. Both the internal and the external factors should be thought of as operating simultaneously, not seriatim.

It has been the purpose of this book to set out some aspects of economic thought that are important for the analysis of geographic patterns of activity. If it has succeeded in conveying the inter-related nature of economic mechanisms and some notion of the way in which forces operate simultaneously, the author will be satisfied. But it would be better still if readers now turn to some of the works of economists for a fuller and more rigorous treatment of the concepts that have been discussed and for guidance on those topics that have been omitted from the present work.

## REFERENCES

1 W. Ashworth, *A Short History of the International Economy Since 1850*, 2nd edition, 1962, p. 125.

2 J. Q. Stewart and W. Warntz, 'Macrogeography and social science', *Geographical Review*, 1958, pp. 167–84.

3 For a discussion of governments and trade, see W. S. Woytinsky and E. S. Woytinsky, *World Commerce and Governments. Trends and Outlook*, 1955.

4 European Productivity Agency of the Organization for European Economic Co-operation, *The influence of Sales Taxes on Productivity*, 1958. Contains details of taxation arrangements in various countries.

5 V. Lutz, 1962, *op. cit.*, (Chap. 3), pp. 36–37, and Chap. 10.

6 H. Bourguinat, *Espace économique et intégration européenne*, 1961, p. 36.

7 G. R. Clapp, *The TVA. An Approach to the Development of a Region*, 1955.

8 V. Lutz, 1962, *op. cit.*

9 European Free Trade Association, *The European Free Trade Association Today and Tomorrow*, 1964, pp. 32–33. *The Economist* of 31st October 1964, contains interesting details of the differing responses to the temporary import duty of 15 per cent. which had just been imposed by the United Kingdom government. Not only were there great differences between products but also for the same class of commodity, particularly cars, responses ranged from partial or complete absorption by suppliers or by dealers to the full passing on of the surcharge to the consumer.

10 P. R. Odell, *An Economic Geography of Oil*, 1963, p. 88.

11 *Ibid.*, pp. 87–89.

12 D. Thomas, 'London's green belt: the evolution of an idea', *Geographical Journal*, 1963, pp. 14–24.

13 A. A. L. Caesar, 1964, *op. cit.*, (Chap. 6).

14 For example, R. M. Titmuss, *Income Distribution and Social Change. A Study in Criticism*, 1962.

15 National Bureau of Economic Research, *Regional Income*, Studies in Income and Wealth, Vol. 21, 1957. W. Isard, *et al.*, 1960, *op. cit.*, (Chap. 5), Chap. 4. W. Z. Hirsch (ed.), *Elements of Regional Accounts*, 1964.

16 R. Stone, 'Social accounts at the regional level: a survey,' in *Regional Economic Planning: Techniques of Analysis*, 1961, proceedings of Conference on Regional Economic Development, Bellagio, 1960. Reprinted as Reprint Series No. 177, Department of Applied Economics, Cambridge, 1961.

17   W. Isard, *et. al.*, 1960, *op. cit.*, p. 87 fn.

18   S. E. Harris, 1952, *op. cit.*, (Chap. 6), pp. 109–10.

19   V. R. Fuchs, *Changes in the Location of Manufacturing in the United States since 1929*, 1962, pp. 149–50.

20   S. J. Mushkin, 'Distribution of federal expenditures among the states', *Review of Economics and Statistics*, 1957, pp. 435–50.

21   W. Isard and I. Ganschow, *Awards of Prime Military Contracts by County, State, and Metropolitan Area of the United States*, 1962.

# Index